Freight Broker and Trucking Business Startup

The most complete Guide to Start, Grow and successfully run your own Freight Brokerage Business and Trucking Company with a Practical Step-by-Step System

TERENCE HARGRAVES

ISBN: 979-8-89965-321-6

Imprint: Staten House

Staten House

TABLE OF CONTENT
Freight Broker and Trucking Business
Startup
BOOK 1: FREIGHT BROKER BUSINESS STARTUP

BOOK 2: TRUCKING COMPANY BUSINESS STARTUP

BOOK 1: FREIGHT BROKER BUSINESS STARTUP

The most complete guide to start and run your own Freight brokerage business successfully with a practical Step-by-Step System

INTRODUCTION

Freight Brokers are used by the industry to arrange for the shipping company's transportation needs.

They serve as a link between shippers and carriers or individual drivers. The majority of newcomers to the freight brokerage industry believe that brokering is the same as trucking. This is the most frequent blunder made by most novice freight brokers. For their matching abilities, a commission is paid to a freight broker. "Truck" brokers, "transportation" brokers, and "property" brokers are all terms used to describe freight brokers. In addition to vehicles, the brokerage business includes air, rail (train), and ocean ships. This course will solely cover the trucking sector in the 48 contiguous states that use trucks for ground transportation.

Freight brokers then go out on the hunt for new clients, searching for wholesalers, manufacturers, farmers, and shippers that utilise freight broker services to transport their goods and products via reputable motor carriers. The duty of a freight broker is to contact them and attempt to figure out their budget and delivery requirements. As a freight broker, all you have to sell yourself to your customers is your integrity, thus proving yourself as a trustworthy freight broker will result in continuing business. A freight broker must have strong bargaining abilities in order to execute a "competitive" deal in which the shipper, carrier, and broker are all pleased. This course includes a database with over +150,000 transportation profiles that you can use to find new customers.

The freight broker should have a good connection with the motor carriers to make this procedure easier. A shipper's credit is typically approved by the broker, who then gets his credit accepted by the carrier. In other words, he collects from the shipper and reimburses the carrier after deducting his commission. Motor carriers may be a carrier firm that hires truck drivers to operate a large number of vehicles or an individual truck driver known as an owner-operator who runs his own trucking business.

A freight broker is paid a commission for successfully connecting a shipper's cargo with the appropriate carrier who will deliver it at a reasonable cost. The majority of brokers believe they are working for the shipper and aim to reduce the carrier's freight costs. In collecting money from the Shipper on behalf of the Motor Carrier (Owner Operator), the Broker must safeguard the interests of the Motor Carrier (Owner Operator).

The Federal Motor Carrier Safety Administration (FMCSA), a Department of Transportation department, is the sole regulating authority for freight brokers. There are certain criteria to meet before you can start working as a freight broker, but no pre-qualifying examinations or exams are required to get started. As a freight broker, it's important to understand the goals of both the shipper and the carrier and to attempt to establish a middle ground that will satisfy both sides.

The transportation sector has its own set of brokers. They don't drive trucks or hire drivers, but they do play a part in the transportation of a range of goods. Brokers involved in interstate commerce are governed by the FMCSA and are subject to a number of federal laws and regulations, including 49 CFR 371. Brokers must register with the FMCSA, retain process agents to receive legal service, and create and maintain adequate financial liability coverage. Brokers also have administrative and financial responsibilities.

Standards for financial recordkeeping Brokers are not allowed to portray themselves as motor carriers or as anything else than suppliers of FMCSA-registered brokerage services. The FMCSA modified 371 and other rules in response to the Safe, Accountable, Flexible, Efficient Transportation Equity Act: A Legacy for Users (SAFETEA-LU) and a petition by the American Moving and Storage Association (AMSA). Consumer protection, financial liability coverage, and business practices are all addressed in these changes for brokers of home products. In the future, the FMCSA will issue U.S. Department of Transportation (USDOT) numbers to all brokers in addition to Motor Carrier (MC) numbers to help them be more easily identified.

As a transportation broker, you'll be tasked with connecting shippers with carriers who can deliver their goods. Transportation is arranged by connecting shippers and carriers. Brokering is defined as providing a service for a fee. If you arrange for the interstate transportation of a product for a shipper by a carrier motor, you are subject to FMCSA regulations and must register with the USDOT under 49 U.S.C. 13904. To be registered, the FMCSA must give you permission to work as a broker. Registration is sometimes known as "authority," "operating authority," or "authorization." All brokers who are regulated by the FMCSA must utilise the services of licenced motor carriers. An approved motor carrier is one that has been given interstate operating authorization and is properly registered with the FMCSA.

Property or freight brokers and home goods brokers are the two types of regulated brokers. Each categorization necessitates the acquisition of a unique registration or authorization. Other than home items, a property broker may arrange shipping of a number of regulated commodities. Automobiles, electronics, and equipment, for example, maybe transported by property brokers.

Only shipments of home items may be transported by a household goods broker. The FMCSA regulates household products, which are defined as follows in 49 CFR 375.103:

- Personal effects, items used, or to be utilised, in a home, as part of the dwelling's equipment, are referred to as "household goods" in the context of transportation. The individual shipper or another person on behalf of the shipper must organise and pay for home goods transportation. Household goods are items that are moved from a factory or shop if they were bought with the intention of being used in a home and are transported at the request of the homeowner, who is also responsible for the transportation costs. The FMCSA regulates household goods dealers, who are defined as follows in 49 CFR 371.103:

- A person who, other than a motor carrier or an employee or a bona fide agent of a motor carrier, sells, offers to sell, negotiates for, or holds itself out as a principal or agent by the solicitation, advertisement, or otherwise sells, provides, or arranges for the transportation of household goods by a motor carrier for compensation is referred to as a Household Goods Broker.

- As a broker, you have the authority to organise the transportation of any regulated commodities (property and household items) as long as you acquire the necessary permissions. If you are an FMCSA-registered broker that arranges freight transportation and wishes to extend your company to include arranging transportation for shipments of household goods, you must apply to FMCSA for additional authorization as a household goods broker. The same is true if you are a licenced home goods broker who wants to extend your company to include regulated freight transportation. As a property broker, you must apply to the FMCSA for extra authorization.

CHAPTER 1: WHAT IS THE FREIGHT BROKERAGE BUSINESS?

The trucking sector, in particular, is essential to the economic and social survival of local towns, the nation, and, yes, the whole globe. Consider the instances when major transportation networks have failed due to natural catastrophes, labour disputes, or technical issues. When cargo is unable to move, the consequences are severe and far-reaching.

The list goes on and on: store shelves are empty, perishable products deteriorate, companies are shut down, people are left unemployed. Although the United States is transitioning from a manufacturing to an information-based economy, and technology is affecting every industry, products will always need to travel.

According to Robert Voltmann, president of the Transportation Intermediates Association (TIA) in Alexandria, Virginia, "logistics professionals in the United States—shippers, intermediaries, and carriers —have changed the way we conduct business." "Our national economy has also been changed as a result of this process. Transportation has evolved into a valuable strategic asset. We've been able to shift to just-in-time delivery, so inventory is now stored in motion. More products are transported than ever before, with more efficiency and reliability."

Take a look around your house or workplace to see what you can find. It's very improbable that you have anything, if anything, that didn't arrive by truck in some form or another. The automotive freight business is massive in size and scope. The good news is that there is plenty of space for you to establish and develop a successful freight brokerage company in this sector.

What is a freight broker, exactly? Simply stated, it's a person or a business that connects a shipper who needs goods transported with a licensed motor carrier who wants to offer the service. The definitions of broker and brokerage service may be found in 49CFR371.3 of the Code of Federal Regulations:

- A broker is a person who, for a fee, organises or promises to arrange property transportation by a licenced motor carrier. When motor carriers, or persons who are employees or bona fide agents of carriers, arrange or offer to arrange the transportation of shipments that they are authorised to transport and that they have accepted and legally bound themselves to transport, they are not brokers within the meaning of this section.

- The arrangement of transportation or the actual transfer of a motor vehicle or property is known as brokerage or brokerage service. It may be done for a motor carrier, a consignor, or a consignee. All additional services provided by a broker on behalf of a motor carrier, consignor, or consignee are classified as non-brokerage services.

A freight broker is a kind of transportation middleman, which is a business that is neither a shipper nor an asset-owning carrier but is involved in cargo transfer. "Transportation intermediates use their expertise, technological investments, and human resources to assist both shippers and carriers in succeeding," adds Voltmann.

Both motor carriers and shippers benefit from the services provided by brokers. They assist transporters in filling their vehicles in exchange for a commission. They assist shippers in locating dependable motor carriers that they may not be aware of in the business; they have been there since the industry's inception in the early twentieth century.

1.1 The players

This industry is broad and large, requiring a diverse group of players. In fact, several businesses utilise brokers as their traffic department, enabling them to manage all of their shipping requirements via the broker.

Brokers who aren't new to the trucking industry may cross paths. But, in order to make things as straightforward and straightforward as possible, let's have a look at who the main actors are and what they do.

- Freight broker: A freight broker acts as a go-between for shippers and carriers. "Truck brokers," "transportation brokers," and "property brokers" are all terms used to describe freight brokers. Though we'll use the word "freight broker" throughout this book, you may hear or see these alternative terms.

- Shipper: A shipper is a company that transports items or commodities. Shippers may be individuals or corporations, but as a broker, you'll most often work with companies in the industrial or agricultural sectors.

- Motor carrier: A motor carrier is a business that transports trucks. There are two kinds of motor carriers: private (a business that transports its own goods by truck) and for hire (a company that is paid to carry merchandise belonging to others by truck). For-hire carriers are divided into two categories: common and contract. A common carrier is obligated to serve the public under two strict conditions: mandatory service and responsibility for products loss or damage. A contract carrier delivers freight under the terms of a contract with one or a few shippers.

- Freight forwarder: Freight forwarders are not the same as freight brokers and should not be mistaken with them. Typically, freight forwarders take custody of the items, combine several smaller shipments into one big cargo, and then arrange for transportation of that larger consignment. Surface freight forwarders utilise motor freight and rail carriage to carry products, air freight forwarders employ cargo and passenger airlines, and ocean freight forwarders use water carriers to transport commodities.

- Import-export broker: These individuals act as intermediaries between importers and exporters (import brokers are also referred to as customhouse brokers). Import-export brokers work with the United States Customs Service, other government agencies, international carriers, and other businesses and organisations engaged in international freight transportation.

- Agricultural truck broker: Agricultural truck brokers, who are usually tiny and only operate in one region of the nation, arrange motor carrier service for exempt agricultural goods.

- Shippers associations: Shippers associations are tax-exempt, non-profit cooperative organizations established by shippers to pool cargo and decrease transportation expenses. Shippers organizations work similarly to freight forwarders, but their services are only accessible to their members and not to the general public. The number of shippers organizations has decreased considerably since the liberalization of transportation in the 1970s.

Of course, in an ideal world, each entity in the business would perform its customary function, and that would be the end of it. The transportation sector, on the other hand, is evolving at a breakneck pace.

1.2 How The Pioneers Started?

When you ask a class of first-graders what they want to be when they grow up, you'll probably hear things like doctor, fireman, police officer, and lawyer; freight broker is unlikely to come up. So, how did the successful freight brokers we spoke about to get started in the industry?

Three generations of Bill Tucker's family have worked at his Cherry Hill, New Jersey brokerage. In 1961, his father established the business by acquiring one of the few remaining broker's licences. Tucker was working in the computer business when his father died suddenly a few years later. He and his mother first chose to sell the company rather than shut it down, so he assisted in its operation while they looked for a buyer. Tucker, however, decided that he wanted the business for himself after months of waiting for a reasonable offer. He worked out a deal with his mother to purchase the business, and now he employs his own sons. Cathy Davis founded MCD Transportation Inc. as a consulting and commissioned sales firm in 1986 and gained brokerage authorization in 1991, after working in the transportation business for a number of years. Her daughters took over the Smyrna, Tennessee business when she died in 2002.

Chuck Andrews founded his company in 1993 in Indianapolis. He was drawn to the brokerage industry after spending his whole professional life working for transportation firms and railways.

If a man blows a tyre, he will contact someone at one or two a.m. to get money to replace it. It's our worry as brokers—we want the freight to arrive on time—but it's not our issue since the driver will contact his dispatcher or company."

Ron Williamson worked for many large companies for 18 years as a corporate traffic manager and director of distribution. He'd previously worked for a railroad and a transportation consultancy company. He could no longer resist the entrepreneurial drive, and in 1981, he established his brokerage company in Bloomingdale, Illinois, as well as two trucking firms.

Specialist or Generalist?

As a broker, you'll be able to handle a wide range of freight. You may handle basic commodity freight, which consists of items that are generally simple to handle and do not need particular care. Alternatively, you may wish to get experience with large machinery, big loads, perishable goods, or even dangerous items.

Don't restrict your speciality to well-known topics; instead, carve up your own niche. Tucker, for example, works with merchants on some intriguing projects. His business is hired by a large national retailer to manage the delivery of point-of-sale advertising displays that must be distributed to hundreds of locations on the same day. It's an essential step, but it doesn't happen often enough for the store to keep the necessary knowledge inhouse. Other large corporations use Tucker's firm to handle shipments associated with store openings and closings.

1.3 Who Is Minding The Store?

Even after deregulation, the transportation sector is still governed by a number of authorities. Intrastate freight, or shipments travelling inside a single state's boundaries, is the least regulated. That freight is governed by state laws and is usually controlled by the state's transportation agency, department of business and professional regulation, and/or department of revenue and taxes.

Prior to 1995, the Interstate Commerce Commission (ICC), an independent body established by Congress in 1887 to oversee commercial activity across state borders, was the primary regulatory agency for interstate shipments (those travelling between states). The ICC was established in reaction to instability in the railroad business, after a Supreme Court decision in 1886 that said that states could not control interstate railways, thereby shifting the regulatory responsibility to the federal government.

The commission's regulatory powers were originally restricted, but by the early 1950s, it had expanded to include all kinds of surface transportation vehicles and channels. The agency was chastised for regulatory overreach and for artificially inflating transportation and shipping costs. Deregulation of the transportation sectors had robbed the ICC of much of its rate-setting power by the early 1980s. The ICC was dissolved by Congress in 1995, and a Surface Transportation Board (STB) under the Department of Transportation (DOT) was established to handle the ICC's remaining regulatory responsibilities. The STB, the DOT, and the Federal Highway Administration are the main authorities in charge of motor freight transportation today.

1.4 Do You Have What It Takes?

This isn't for the faint of heart or the timid individual who prefers shuffling papers behind a closed office door. Courage and an outgoing attitude, on the other hand, aren't enough to ensure a successful freight brokerage.

"Anyone engaged in operations must be able to manage stress, make fast choices, handle numerous duties, have a strong phone voice and communication skills, and possess some basic business knowledge," according to the late Cathy Davis. You must comprehend not only the freight sector but also the business needs that your clients confront.

Communication skills and strong industry background are essential for brokers, according to Chuck Andrews. To show your expertise, you must be able to speak industry jargon. "The worst thing you can do is contact a shipper and start messing about on the phone," he warns. "He'll never give you any freight because he'll see straight away that you're unfamiliar with the industry, and he won't trust his products being transported with you."

You must be "a good all-around guy," according to Ron Williamson. This necessitates familiarity with the financial, sales, and operational aspects of the business.

"The future for intermediaries is extremely bright," says TIA's Voltmann, as asset-owning carriers focus on what they do best and shippers focus on their core skills. Intermediaries offer the creativity and experience that shippers and carriers need. As a consequence, advancements will continue, providing customers with more options and cheaper costs."

So, where should you begin? In Chapter 2, you'll learn all you need to know about laying the groundwork for your freight agency.

CHAPTER 2: WHAT DOES THE BUSINESS REQUIRE?

Many industry participants are unsure what is regulated and what isn't after the collapse of the Interstate Commerce Commission and other elements of transportation deregulation. This chapter will explain the legal and practical criteria for establishing and operating a freight brokerage firm.

Financial responsibility is shown through a surety bond or trust fund. This implies you must show that you have the necessary liquid assets to fulfil your commitments and pay any possible claims. You have the option of using your own resources or hiring a bonding firm. Form BMC 84 is used to submit proof of a surety bond, whereas form BMC 85 is used to file evidence of a trust fund with a financial institution.

Designation of process agents implies you must submit a designation of a person on whom judicial process may be served in each state where you maintain offices or create contracts. When your application is accepted, the FHWA will provide you with a permit with an MC number, which will allow you to work as a broker in the United States. You must also follow the rules or regulations that apply to that individual when acting on behalf of a person obligated by law or FHWA regulations as to the transmittal of invoices or payments.

In addition to federal requirements, you'll need whatever municipal and state governments to need in terms of business licences and/or operating permissions. Find out what you need and what it takes to get these licences and/or permits from your local planning and zoning agency or city or county business licencing department. You may require a municipal or county-issued occupational licence or permission; a fire department permits if you're in a commercial site and/or open to the public.

2.1 Education and experience

Before establishing your own brokerage, the brokers we spoke with suggested working in the business as a shipper, carrier, or both. Not only will you acquire technical knowledge, but you'll also establish connections that are crucial to your success in this industry.

Cathy Davis began her career as an inventory control clerk at a river port before moving on to sales for motor and air freight carriers. "I was lucky to be mentored by the owner of one of the LTL carriers I worked for, and I assisted in the design of a new terminal and sat on an employee advisory board," she said. Her consulting company allowed her to learn even more about being a broker; she worked as an agent for brokers before becoming one herself, giving her both hands-on experience and the chance to establish her reputation. "With complete disclosure of purpose and a formal agreement, I strongly endorse this starting method," she added. She and her children each obtained the Certified Transportation Broker certification from the Transportation Intermediaries Association before taking over the business in Smyrna, Tennessee.

Chuck Andrews, based in Indianapolis, has worked for a large LTL carrier, was the president of a truckload (TL) carrier, and has worked in railroad operations.

New brokers, according to Davis, need "a solid sales experience, excellent business advisers, and a willingness for further education."

2.2 Building carrier relationships

How do you establish strong, good bonds with carriers? Davis said, "Pay on time and at fair rates." Of course, having "driver-friendly" freight is a plus, and communication is essential, she said. "We utilise a load-matching tool to assist in the search for carriers, but we also network with members of different organisations. We consider the carrier to be a client, and we treat them with the same level of professionalism that we do with shippers."

The most difficult aspect of starting a business may be establishing and maintaining connections with carriers. Brokers that owe carriers money are not unusual to go out of business. As a result, truckers are very picky about who they do business with. Even if you have a surety bond and all of your documentation in order, carriers may be wary until you demonstrate that you can and will pay.

It's an issue that can only be solved with time. Expect it will take a long time to develop your company. When you add a trucker, provide a package that contains business information, a list of key employees, bank information, and carrier references to establish yourself as a dependable, professional broker. Remember that getting that initial load moved and then expanding on that for your credit references is the most difficult aspect.

When negotiating payment arrangements with your carriers, it's critical to understand the economics of the transportation industry. ICC rules formerly required freight bills to be paid within seven days; however, with deregulation, this is no longer the case. Carriers, on the other hand, operate on razor-thin margins and pay the majority of their costs on a particular cargo before ever picking it up, so cash flow is just as important to them as it is to the broker.

Some brokers prefer not to pay the carrier until they are paid themselves, and although this is a safe strategy for the broker, carriers are unlikely to be happy about it. "Carriers argue that they use a broker, so they don't have to conduct credit checks on clients or offer the sales and service that we provide," says Bill Tucker, a freight broker in Cherry Hill, New Jersey. "One of the reasons the carriers would sell to you at a cheaper price than they would charge the shipper directly is because of this. 'You manage the credit for your client base, and you pay me whether you get paid or not,' the carriers say. It simply makes things easier and cleaner."

Tucker points out that there are instances when invoicing may quickly increase, such as with high-volume shippers or a unique seasonal scenario, and the broker and carrier agree to share the financial risk. Those contract provisions, however, are the exception.

2.3 Banking on your banker

For brokers, strong banking connections are essential. It's very uncommon for a new broker to need a line of credit of $250,000 to $300,000 in order to pay carriers before receiving payment from shippers. The trucks will not carry your freight if you do not pay them on time. You have no business if you don't have someone to transport your cargo.

Of course, you don't want to go into a bank with nothing in your pocket and ask for a large line of credit. Create a professional document that contains a comprehensive business strategy and clearly shows to the bank that you are not a credit risk and that extending you a line of credit would benefit them. Because you don't have any assets to give a lender as security as a broker, your credit rating and presentation are crucial. Take your package to a business loan officer rather than a personal loan officer. Get a recommendation from a satisfied client, and schedule your initial meeting with the banker—this demonstrates that you respect both the banker's and your own time.

It's a good idea to have connections with more than one bank in these days of banking mergers and acquisitions, as well as staff churn. If you have a single line of credit with one bank and that bank is sold, your line of credit may be terminated without your knowledge. If you have a good connection with a loan officer and he or she is promoted, moves, or changes positions, the new loan officer may not be as responsive to your requirements. Protect yourself by ensuring you have a financial backup plan in place.

Those crucial clients

Sure, you need good connections with your carriers and lenders, but your client base is the most important external aspect of your company. While you'll conduct some cold calling to promote your company, the majority of your clients will come through recommendations, connections, and networking. You may utilise your connections to get in the door, but keep in mind that this is a commercial deal, not a relationship. If your price isn't competitive, just though you know someone doesn't imply they'll offer you their business.

Of course, there's more to it than just the price. It is critical to communicate. Inform consumers about the status of their shipments; this requires nearly daily communication, although it may frequently be accomplished through email. Shippers need the assurance of knowing when their freight is moving according to plan, as well as the ability to respond properly if it isn't. Most shippers are capable of dealing with technical, weather, or traffic delays if they are aware of them. Allow them to discover out from their customers that shipments were not delivered on time; inform them ahead of time that the truck isn't going to make it for whatever reason, and when they may anticipate delivery.

2.4 Record keeping requirements

What kinds of records you must keep are specified in the Code of Federal Regulations? You may maintain a master list of shippers and carriers to prevent having to repeat information, but you must keep a record of every transaction. This record must include the following information:

- The consignor's (shipper's) name and address;
- The number on the bill of lading or freight bill
- The amount of money received by the broker for brokerage services rendered, as well as the payer's name
- A description of any non-brokerage services provided in conjunction with each shipment or other activity, as well as the amount of remuneration received and the payer's name.
- The amount of any freight costs collected by the broker, as well as the date on which the carrier was paid.

These documents must be kept for three years, and each party to a transaction has the right to see the records related to that transaction.

Be careful of what you say.

There may be times when you're with other brokers—or even shippers and carriers—and the topic of discussion is about clients you both have. Protect your clients' privacy as well as the secrecy of their companies. Not only is this good business sense, but you're also forbidden by law from providing information to a third party that might be used against the shipper or consignee.

CHAPTER 3: OPERATIONS

Freight brokering is a straightforward idea. The cargo is delivered to you by a shipper. You fill out your own paperwork and call your carriers to see if they have a vehicle available. If you already have a connection with a carrier, send an amendment to your basic contract describing this specific load and pricing. If the carrier approves, the company's representative will sign the paper and return it by fax or email. (If you don't already have a connection with the carrier, you'll need to establish one before finalizing the transaction on the first shipment.) The driver is then sent by the carrier. It's a good idea to have the driver contact you to check that the cargo was picked up and delivered.

The carrier will give you an invoice and the original bill of lading once the cargo has been delivered. Invoice your client (the shipper), pay the driver, and repeat the process with another cargo, ideally.

3.1 Facts on file

You'll need information from both the shipper and the carrier when planning a shipment. You should keep a lot of this information on file at your office.

Shipper information

Maintaining information on shippers helps you provide better customer service and saves you from having to take the time to ask the same questions with each shipment. Keep the following information:

- Company name
- Physical address
- Billing address, if different from the physical one
- All telephone numbers (cell phones, voice, fax, pagers), including toll-free numbers
- Contact people (including traffic and shipping managers, freight payable per-son, and anyone else you may deal with)
- E-mail addresses of all contacts
- Type of freight shipped (machinery, produce, chemicals, etc.)
- Pallet exchange requirements
- Special requirements
- Pickup information you require (such as warehouse locations or distribution points)

Although this information is unlikely to change often, you should always double-check that you have the most up-to-date information. Anything you learn about over the course of processing a cargo, such as a change in staff or a new phone number, should be updated right away. You should contact each client once a year to review their information. Explain to the client that you have a policy of reviewing your files on a regular basis to ensure their completeness and correctness and that you'd want to go over what you have on file to ensure it's accurate.

This information is important not just for your carriers (how else would they know where to transport the freight if you don't tell them?), but it also provides you with another possible shipper. If the consignee (shipper's receiver) is a factory, they may have items available for your carrier to pick up after dropping off your first cargo. The carrier has a profitable round trip if the consignee has freight to send back to the original shipper—or perhaps someone else in the same area—and your carrier can handle this load as well. The trucker doesn't have to return empty (which means he won't make any money) or go out of his way to locate a load on his own.

Find out ahead of time whether the shipper needs a pallet exchange, which eliminates the need for carriers to return pallets to shippers and for shippers to replace pallets on a regular basis. This is how it works: Pallets are filled with a variety of products, which are subsequently loaded into vehicles. Many truck drivers transport empty pallets in their vehicles. They swap their empty pallets for those utilised by the shipper for the items recently picked up when they get a shipment on pallets. The filled pallets are exchanged for empty pallets when the driver arrives at the destination, refilling the driver's supply.

Include the identifying numbers of the tractor and trailer that transported the cargo when filling out a load sheet for each shipment. It is normal to practise for the carriers to give you their equipment numbers.

Carrier information

Keep track of carriers, even if you don't have any loads for them right now. By keeping track of carriers, you'll be able to see the routes they take and what kind of vehicles they drive. When a shipper calls, you'll be able to swiftly choose a carrier using this information. Keep the following details in mind:

- Carrier's name
- Type of carrier (contract, common, etc.)
- Physical address
- Billing address, if different from physical address

- All telephone numbers (cell phones, voice, fax, pagers), including tollfree numbers
- Contact person (in most cases, the dispatcher)
- E-mail addresses of all contacts
- Other terminals, phone numbers, and contacts
- Type and size of the equipment available
- Motor carrier's license number
- Federal tax identification number
- Whether or not the carrier offers pallet exchanges
- Carrier's traffic lanes and backhaul requirements

In addition to the fundamental information about a carrier that aids in your decision-making, you should acquire the following extra facts before entrusting that carrier with a load:

- Copy of current insurance certificates and updates
- Certificate of authority
- Copy of current general commodity tariff and updates (if applicable)

These important papers demonstrate that the carrier is permitted to carry freight and is covered by insurance in the event that cargo is lost or damaged. Not only should you check that the carrier is insured, but you should also keep track of when the insurance will expire. When that day comes, make sure the coverage has been renewed by contacting the provider. A clause in most insurance certificates states that if coverage is cancelled, the holder will be informed by the firm.

In addition to these things, get a statement from your carriers stating that they are fully responsible for all fuel taxes, including ton-mile taxes (taxes based on weight and distance) in all states they pass through. They shall also pay penalties for any breaches committed while on lease or contract. Though most carriers make paying penalties a regular part of their business, you should acquire a formal agreement to that effect and keep it in your files.

You should also save copies of any contracts, bills of lading, and invoices you send or receive, as well as all communications, agreements, rate quotes, policy changes, memoranda, and so on.

3.2 Finding carriers

In the United States, there are more than 600,000 interstate motor carriers. As a broker, your duty is to find those who can offer the services your clients need and to verify their trustworthiness before recommending them.

Carriers may be found in a variety of directories and trade publications. Word-of-mouth is another excellent method to discover carriers; while you're networking, take attention to what others are saying about certain trucking firms and follow up on positive feedback.

Trucks may be seen at truck stops and on the highway. Speak to the driver and learn about the business if you notice clean and well-maintained vehicles. If speaking with the driver isn't possible, write down the business name and headquarters address (which should be on the truck or cab) and contact the company. Of course, don't forget about the internet as a carrier source. Shippers and carriers may publish their freight and equipment requirements on a variety of internet databases. After you've chosen a carrier that seems promising, you'll need additional information before entrusting a cargo to it. Request a copy of the carrier's authorization certificate, current insurance certificates, and current rate. You should also get recommendations from happy clients and thoroughly investigate them. Finally, verify the carrier's financial status with a credit reporting agency or a financial rating service. You want to be certain that the carriers you deal with are dependable and financially stable.

Use big airlines with terminals all across the nation sparingly. These carriers don't transport goods from the point of origin to the point of destination; instead, they relay a load from one terminal to another. This procedure takes longer and requires more handling, which raises the chance of loss or damage. It's preferable if the same driver picks up and delivers the cargo.

Some carriers use a practice known as pooling, in which cargo is dropped off and left until a driver with the appropriate equipment and destination is available to pick them up. Though this may seem to be a cost-effective technique, it results in delays in travel time, and you should avoid carriers that utilise it. By allowing your shippers to fulfil tight delivery deadlines, such a policy will offer you a competitive advantage.

3.3 Rates and commissions

It's a good idea to start with FTL shipments since they're simpler to manage than LTL shipments. Many carriers won't accept a partial load, so you'll have to arrange for the driver to pick up two or more LTL shipments bound for the same location. When you're just starting out, this may sound daunting, but as you acquire expertise, you'll be able to manage both FTL and LTL shipments with ease.

The weight of the cargo and the distance it must travel are the two most important considerations in determining freight costs. The kind of truck required, whether the driver must make one or more trips to pick up the freight and if the driver must make more than one stop to deliver the products, all influence rates. Each cargo is entitled to one free pickup and delivery; you may typically negotiate a fee with the carrier for subsequent stops.

Get a sense of the current "going rates" for the kinds of shipments you're likely to handle before you start searching for rates for particular shipments. You may accomplish this by obtaining and reviewing copies of tariffs from various carriers.

Many shippers, particularly big businesses with skilled traffic departments, will tell you how much they're prepared to pay rather than leaving it up to you to estimate a fee. If this sum is too high, you'll have to either bargain with the shipper or reject the cargo.

It's not easy to figure out the freight price. Carriers negotiate prices depending on a variety of variables, including commodities, value, equipment availability, volume, customer service characteristics, and payment history. As a broker, you must be aware of market problems as well as factors that may lead to per-mile rate hikes or reductions, such as driver shortages, fuel surcharges, seasonal fluctuations, toll highways, and so on.

The commissions you get on each load are the source of your revenue. You may charge the shipper for the amount you'll pay the carrier plus your commission, or the carrier can bill the shipper directly and give you a commission from the proceeds.

Billing and commissions are usually handled by having the carrier charge you first, and then you bill your consumers. Bill Tucker, a freight broker in Cherry Hill, New Jersey, says this is simpler and less complicated for clients than being invoiced directly by the carrier. Your clients will get several types of invoices on various billing cycles if the carrier bills them directly, and they will have to perform the additional effort of matching the bill to the cargo. "It gets a little complicated when their computer produces a bill of lading for the broker and the carrier bills them," says the broker.

Your commission is adjustable, and you may earn as much as the traffic will allow. The average broker commission is between 5% and 11% of the shipping costs, with some brokers earning even more, while a new broker may anticipate making between 8% and 10%. Knowing your market is crucial in this situation. If you work in a highly competitive market, such as Atlanta, where there is a lot of freight but few vehicles, your commission will be much lower than the industry average.

Remember that your commission is your gross income, and you must pay your overhead out of it: rent, taxes, payroll, sales commissions, utilities, loans, and so on. Most brokers, according to Ron Williamson, are fortunate to make a net profit of 1–2% after costs.

Although the overall freight charges for shipments must be agreed upon by you, your carriers and your shippers, the costs of carrying freight may be broken down into smaller components. These figures are used by shippers to establish pricing for their products and calculate profit margins, as well as by carriers to evaluate their own profitability. Carriers, for example, are interested in the overall cost for any particular journey as well as their fee per mile. Shippers are often interested in the cost per hundredweight (abbreviated "cwt"), which is usually measured in 100-pound units. Simple arithmetic may be used to compute these figures.

Quoting Rates

To quote a rate for a customer, follow these 10 steps:

1. Find out the point of origin.
2. Find out the destination.
3. Determine the gross weight of the load.
4. Ask if the carrier will need to make stop-offs or split pickups.
5. Check whether pallets are required.
6. Find out when the load(s) will be ready for pickup.
7. Find out when the load(s) can or must be delivered.
8. Ask if appointments are necessary at origin or destination.
9. Find out who gets billed for the freight charges.
10. Obtain the frequency and number of similar shipments.

You'll be able to contact carriers for accurate quotations with this information. Few things in our industry are more aggravating than quoting a cost based on inadequate information, only to discover later that the client needs more services for which you must charge, which means you must notify them that their final price will be greater than your initial estimate. (This, needless to say, irritates consumers.)

3.4 Documents

After you've matched a cargo with a carrier, you'll need to fill out a few pieces of paperwork. First, you and the carrier must agree on a contract that covers both current and future transactions. The Transportation Intermediaries Association includes sample agreements in its New Broker Kit (contact information can be found in the Appendix under "Publications, Books, and Training Resources"). However, the freight brokers we spoke with advised that you create your own contracts, agreements, and forms, tailoring them to your specific operation.

You must submit the carrier a load confirmation and pricing agreement form for each particular cargo after you have a carrier agreement on file. When the carrier picks up the cargo from the shipper, the shipper will provide the carrier with a bill of lading that details the items being carried as well as any special arrangements the driver will need to make. When the driver arrives at the consignee (shipment destination), he must have someone sign for the cargo. If the freight is unloaded at the consignee's site by an independent contractor, the driver must acquire a contract labour receipt from this worker.

The driver or trucking business will bill you, the shipper, or the consignee for transportation services, depending on your agreement with the carrier.

Carrier/Broker Agreement

The carrier/broker agreement spells out the conditions under which you'll operate with a certain carrier. It should include all of your interactions with a certain carrier and should also account for any future changes.

Make careful to include all of the following in the carrier/broker agreement:

- Write down the carrier's motor carrier (MC) or licence number, as well as the company's complete name and address.
- If you'll be dealing with this carrier on a contract basis, make it clear that the freight and rates for each cargo will be negotiated.
- Declare that the carrier is responsible for any damage or loss to the freight while it is being transported.
- Keep in mind that while the freight is in the carrier's custody, the carrier is liable for any bodily harm or damage to cars or equipment.
- Specify when the courier will be paid and what they must deliver before you pay (such as bills of lading).

Bill of Lading

The shipper will give a bill of lading to the driver at the time of pickup. This form will contain information about the load's type and size, as well as its destination and any special handling requirements. The driver acknowledges receiving the cargo specified by the shipper by signing the bill of lading.

The shipper and the carrier develop and manage the bill of lading. Although you will not be actively involved as the broker, you must maintain a signed copy in your files. This is typically sent to you together with an invoice for transportation services by the carrier.

Contract Labor Receipt

Contract workers may sometimes assist drivers in unloading trucks after they arrive at the consignee. If they do, the worker will hand over a contract labour receipt to the driver, which the carrier will forward to you. The worker is paid by the driver or carrier, who then reimburses you. If your shipper is willing to cover this expense, take advantage of it. Even if your shipper refuses to pay for contract labour, you may wish to absorb the cost in order to have good ties with the driver and carrier.

Invoices

The carrier sends you an invoice together with the bill of lading after making the delivery and receiving proof of delivery. You may create your own invoice to send to the shipper using these documents (unless the carrier bills the shipper directly).

The billing date, the pickup and delivery dates, the origin and destination, what was delivered (commodity, pieces, and total weight), and any extra costs should all be included on your invoice (such as fees for exceeding weight limits or charges for contract labour). As soon as you get your carrier's full invoice and bill of lading, charge your shipper.

When a shipper sends a delivery "collect," you charge the consignee instead of the sender. On these shipments, the shipper should give you billing information.

Contract of Carriage

Although a contract of carriage is not a document in and of itself, it is critical that you comprehend the idea and what it entails. A frequent misunderstanding among otherwise well-informed transportation professionals is that the bill of lading constitutes a contract of carriage. "A bill of lading is definitely a receipt used in a contract of carriage," explains Bill Tucker, "but there are numerous components needed by that contract that are not usually mentioned on the bill of lading." "Some examples include the contract price, the services to be delivered, procedures to be followed to manage exceptions, and any relevant accessorial charges."

What is a carriage contract? "A contract of carriage between a common carrier and a shipper (with or without the involvement of a broker) often consists of some kind of bill of lading, whether 'standard' or not, as well as any tariff requirements, pricing, regulations, and service descriptions," Tucker explains. "The parties' purpose; the regulatory requirements that must be obeyed, whether federal, state, or local; and any other 'usage of trade' and precedent within which this transaction has occurred" are all part of the entire contract.

3.5 Are you on a mission?

Most company owners have a clear grasp of their businesses' purpose at any given time. They understand what they're doing, how and where they're doing it, and who their clients are. However, problems may emerge if that goal isn't clearly stated, written down, and conveyed to others.

Even in a small firm, a written mission statement may assist everyone involved to understand the broad picture and stay focused on the company's real objectives. Your mission statement should at the very least explain who your main consumers are, list the services you provide and describe the geographic area in which you operate. A mission statement should be brief—no more than three sentences in most cases. It's a good idea to keep it around 100 words. Anything longer isn't a mission statement and will most likely confuse your workers. It's not necessary for your goal statement to be creative or appealing; it simply has to be true.

Ask yourself the following questions to help you create a successful mission statement:

- What is the purpose of my business? Who are we here to serve? What is the purpose of our existence?

- What are our advantages, disadvantages, possibilities, and threats?

- Given the above, as well as our skills and resources, what kind of company should we be in?

- What are the things that are most essential to us? What do we believe in?

MCD Transportation, located in Smyrna, Tennessee, has the following mission statement:

To offer reliable transportation services to our clients based on fair and competitive pricing schemes with a focus on customer care for all parties involved. To be attentive to the requirements of customers and to respond in a professional and timely way. Customers, carriers, and suppliers must be seen as our sole assets if we are to continue to succeed.

The mission statement is not only utilized as a marketing tool but workers are also encouraged to evaluate it on a regular basis and propose modifications, they believe are necessary.

3.6 Seasonal issues

No industry is more likely to be impacted by seasonal problems than transportation. The amount and kind of freight movement is often influenced by the season. There will be an excess of trucks and drivers ready to carry goods at times, and balancing the government budget will seem to be an easier job than locating a single vehicle and driver at other times. Even if you don't handle produce, produce season may result in a shortage of vehicles, limiting your capacity to service your clients. Another hectic time is the fourth quarter when Christmas goods and year-end orders are in high demand.

There's also the problem of weather, in addition to equipment availability. Snow and ice may make driving hazardous and cause delays in transportation. In certain areas of the nation, fog and rain may be a year-round issue. Road closures may occur in regions prone to wildfires during dry seasons owing to excessive smoke and fire leaping over roads. Tornadoes endure just a few minutes, and storms pass through in less than a day, yet the damage they leave behind may have a significant effect on truckers' capacity to transport goods.

The effect of seasons on your income goes beyond the mechanics of seasonal issues—getting freight on trucks and transported. Build your client base with accounts that aren't too seasonal if at all feasible. Expect certain slowdowns at different times of the year; plan for them and utilize the opportunity to assess your company and address any internal problems that need to be addressed. During sluggish times, you may also boost your sales efforts. It's critical to know your client base so you can properly anticipate and plan for sluggish times, particularly when it comes to cash flow adjustments.

3.7 The impact of 9/11 on brokers

Following the terrorist events of September 11, 2001, all means of transportation have been subjected to enhanced security measures. One problem that has a significant effect on brokers is who is driving the vehicles. "You used to be able to drive straight up to the shipping pier, grab your cargo, and leave," recalls Joe Workman, president of Transportation Resources Inc. in Winter Park, Florida. "Now, many businesses demand drivers present identity before entering the premises, and other organisations need pre-qualification before picking up cargo. Shippers are more cautious than ever before about who is transporting their cargo."

Many shippers, according to Workman, want to be able to communicate with drivers by mobile phone or satellite. "If our drivers don't have good on-the-road communication, we can't utilise them, and that reduces the number of trucks we have available."

If you wish to work with air freight, you should be aware that airlines now demand cargo to originate from reputable shippers. Customers that transport sensitive or dangerous goods have unique needs, which you should learn about as soon as possible.

CHAPTER 4: WHAT CAN GO WRONG?

The ability to deal with issues is critical in the freight industry. What could possibly go wrong? Everything! There are certain factors that are beyond your control, no matter how effectively you manage your side of the business, and your shippers will still turn to you for help with them.

Brokers are usually not responsible for the loss or damage of cargo while it is being carried since they are not carriers. They may be held responsible, though, if they are careless or provide services other than brokerage. Apart from the question of responsibility, part of your service package should involve helping your clients with issues, whether or not you are at fault.

4.1 Transit delays

It's almost difficult to describe all of the potential causes for freight delays in transit. Weather is usually a significant factor to consider. Trucks break down, traffic jams occur, roads are blocked, and drivers get ill—all of which your clients will expect you to handle. MCD Transportation in Smyrna, Tennessee's Cathy Davis recounted a nightmarish scenario with the legendary "driver from hell." "Even though the business had signed a contract agreeing to the conditions, the freight was held hostage [for payment] by an owner/operator," she added. To keep the customer's manufacturing line running, we had to pay air freight costs to send additional material."

The majority of your issues will be minor, but if freight does not move as planned, your clients will turn to you for crisis management and information.

4.2 Cargo loss or damage claims

You are not liable for cargo loss or damage claims as to the broker. Keep in mind that, although common carriers are usually accountable for the loss or damage of the products they transport, they are not liable for losses caused by acts of nature, war, or government; losses caused by the shipper's defaults; or losses caused by the nature of the commodities. Whatever the cause of the loss or damage, you must be familiar with the claims procedure and be ready to help your shippers as needed.

If the driver fails to examine the freight and verify the bill of lading before the shipment is loaded, the carrier is left with no choice but to pay a claim if the cargo is damaged or short when it reaches the destination. There will be instances when the loading crew makes a mistake but discovers it after the fact and initiates a bill of lading modification, absolving the driver and carrier of any possible claim liability.

If a specific driver or carrier can't depend on them to do so, and drivers keep filing damage claims, they should inspect each load to make sure the papers match the cargo and sign shippers and figure out why. The person who is in charge of precisely what is received. It may be providing shoddy security. There will be instances when it is impractical, illegal, or impossible for the driver to discard part of the transported items. You must examine cargo in a rough manner. For example, if the carrier drops a trailer at the shipper's source to identify and fix the issue or stops utilising that site to be loaded by the shipper's driver or carrier. Workers and then picked up for transportation later, the driver will have no idea what happened.

Inside the trailer, the driver may not be able to accurately count the number of boxes on each pallet if the shipper assembles and shrink-wraps pallets of boxes. In such situations, the driver should put on the bill of lading "shipper's load and count" and/or "contents and condition unknown," which transfers responsibility for shortages, overages, and hidden damage back to the shipper.

The consignee's receiving person should examine and count the cargo after it arrives at its destination, noting any inconsistencies or apparent damage on the delivery receipt.

Notify the carrier and dispatcher as soon as you hear of a possible claim —possibly from the shipper, consignee, or driver. They will notify you if they learn of a potential issue from the delivery driver. Alternatively, you may not learn about a claim until you get the proof of delivery and bill of lading, which includes damage notations.

Damage notations may not always result in a claim. For example, even if the outside of a box has been damaged, the inside may be OK.

The amount in issue, as well as the shipper's history and reputation, influence how the claim is handled. The carrier would most likely pay without a thorough inquiry for a minor claim when damage was plainly recorded on the delivery receipt. In the case of a bigger claim, the carrier may dispatch an inspector to examine the damaged items. If a carrier decides that insufficient packaging caused the damage, the claim may be denied. Therefore, consignees should retain the damaged goods and packing materials until the claim is settled.

Shippers often use standard forms to submit their claims. All you have to do is provide the shipper with the carrier's name and address, and if required, help them in achieving a fair and timely settlement.

Explain to your shipper that he or she must provide the following information to the carrier on a signed form if he or she is unfamiliar with the procedures for making a claim:

- Name and address of the carrier
- The total amount of the claim
- Pick-up date
- The delivery dates
- Previous claim history
- Full name and address of the shipper
- Full name and address of the consignee
- Defects or scarcities

The shipper must also provide any necessary or acceptable supporting documents, such as:

- The cost of transportation
- A bill of lading is a document that describes the contents of a shipment
- Invoice
- Inspection report (if applicable)
- Loss statement itemized

The carrier has 30 days to either settle the claim or recognize it and inform the shipper of any further information needed to complete it. Carriers are required by federal law to investigate disputes quickly and either settle the claim within 120 days or notify the claimant of any delays, with the claimant being notified of the claim's progress every 60 days.

4.3 Responding to problems

It's possible that you'll lose a client because of a service issue that wasn't strictly your responsibility. However, you'll find that most shippers understand when things go wrong—when drivers don't show up, when equipment breaks down, when highway accidents happen, and so forth.

What's important is that you don't overlook or conceal issues from your shippers or carriers. Be proactive in your approach. When you discover a problem, quickly notify everyone who needs to know, and then do all you can to get the freight back on the road.

CHAPTER 5: GETTING YOUR LICENSE

The rules governing applications for operating authority are stated in regulations, 49 CFR §§365 and 366. The process to obtain operating authority as a broker begins with FMCSA's application for Motor Property Carrier and Broker Authority Form (OP-1).

Becoming a freight broker requires the applicant to submit three forms to the FMCSA.

5.1 Form #1: OP-1 Form

The first is Form OP-1, which is a broker authorization application. The OP-1 form may be found on FMCSA's website at http://www.fmcsa.dot.gov/forms/print/r-l-forms.htm as a Portable Document Format (PDF) file.

You may also submit your OP-1 application through the internet. Online registration is available at http://www.fmcsa.dot.gov/online-registration. This technique is strongly suggested. Step-by-step instructions for completing the online OP-1 form for the relevant broker authorities are available. The application form for the Motor Carrier Authority is four pages long.

The Federal Motor Carrier Safety Administration issues a broker authority licence, which is needed to operate as a freight broker in the United States. If the applicant intends to run his brokerage under a business name rather than his legal name

(DBA), he must provide his name, business contact information, and the legal name of his company as specified in his home state when applying for broker authorization. When filling out the OP1 form, choose "broker of property" as the filing option. The OP-1 form may be printed once you've downloaded it and filled in the necessary information straight on the form from your computer. You may also print a blank form and manually fill it out if you like. If you don't have access to the FMCSA's website, you may request that an OP-1 form packet be sent to you by calling 800-832-5660. You may mail the form after it's been completed. Instructions are included with the OP-1 form to help you in filling out and submitting the form.

The OP-1 form has a non-refundable filing cost of $300. Once OP-1 has been approved (4-6 weeks), first, FMCSA will send you a letter with your FMCSA number on it. After a few weeks, you will get a final authorization letter.

Operating Authority

The FMCSA operating authorization is also known as an "MC," "FF," or "MX" number, depending on the kind of permission issued. Unlike the application procedure for a USDOT Number, a corporation may need several operating permissions to support its intended commercial activities. The kind of operation a business may conduct, the cargo it can transport,

and the geographical region in which it can lawfully operate are all determined by the Operating Authority.

Costs for obtaining an Operating Authority?

For each Operating Authority, separate filing fees must be provided. The fee for each Authority requested is $300.00, which must be paid at the time of processing.

Definitions of Common, Contract, and Broker Authorities

- For-hire truck transportation is provided by common carriers to the general population.

- Common carriers must get cargo insurance as well as both liability (BI and PD) insurances.

- On the basis of contracts, contract carriers offer for-hire truck transportation to particular individual shippers. Only liability (BI & PD) insurance is required for contract carriers.

- Brokers are paid to arrange the transportation of other people's goods, and they use for-hire carriers to perform the actual truck transportation. A surety bond or a trust fund agreement must be filed by the Broker.

5.2 Form #2: BMC-84 OR BMC-85 Form

The BMC-84 or BMC-85, on the other hand, is used to provide evidence of a $10,000 surety bond (BMC-84) or trust fund (BMC-85). Proof of Financial Responsibility is a critical component of your application. You must be adequately protected as a broker. Financial responsibility refers to your company's liability protection. As financial responsibility, everyone must have either a Surety Bond or a Trust Fund. Obtaining and retaining operating authorization requires proof of financial responsibility. You will not be given power as a broker until you have it. As a requirement of your operating authorization, you must keep your bond current. If you decide to change bonding firms or the financial institution that maintains your trust fund while doing business as a broker, you must submit a new BMC84 or BMC-85 Form with FMCSA demonstrating that your company still has sufficient financial responsibility.

Keep in mind that financial accountability is a requirement of your power. Your broker authorization will be withdrawn if FMCSA receives notification that you no longer have financial responsibility. As a broker, you must provide a Property Brokers Surety Bond (Form BMC-84) or a Property Brokers Trust Fund Agreement (Form BMC-85) as evidence of a trust fund or a surety bond protecting your company. The BMC-84 and BMC-85 forms have no filing fees since they are just legal

requirements to show evidence of coverage. The bond price you pay will be determined by the kind of bond and the financial institution that will supply your business with the Surety Bond. If the broker fails to follow out their contracts, agreements, or arrangements for the provision of transportation by approved motor carriers, the surety bond or trust fund guarantees the broker's financial obligation by making payments to shippers or motor carriers.

The rule, 49 CFR 387.5, defines financial responsibility as follows:

Financial Responsibility—the financial reserves (such as insurance policies or surety bonds) necessary to meet the liability levels specified in this subpart (49 CFR Part 387, Subpart A) for public liability.

To comply with FMCSA's financial security standards, brokers must acquire and submit a $75,000 surety bond or trust fund agreement with the agency beginning October 1, 2013.

Replacement of Broker Surety Bonds or Trust Fund Agreements -Broker surety bonds or trust fund agreements approved by the FMCSA under these regulations may be replaced by other surety bonds or trust fund agreements. As of the effective date of the replacement surety bond or trust fund agreement, the retiring surety or trustee's obligation under such surety bond or trust fund agreements is deemed to have ended.

However, such termination shall not impact the surety's or trustee's obligation under this agreement to pay any damages resulting from contracts, agreements, or arrangements made by the broker for the provision of transportation prior to the effective date of such termination.

Cancellation Notice - Only 30 days written notice to the FMCSA is required to cancel the surety bond and trust fund arrangement. For the surety bond, this must be signed on required Form BMC 36 by the principal or surety, and for the trust fund agreement, this must be done on specified Form BMC 85 by the trust or/broker or trustee. The notice period begins when the notification is received at the FMCSA's Washington, DC headquarters.

5.3 Form #3: BOC-3 Form

The Form BOC-3, Designation of Agent for Service of Process, is an essential component of your broker authorization application (often referred to as a process agent). A process agent is a person who accepts legal documents on your behalf and forwards them to you for action. According to 49 CFR 366.4, brokers must designate a process agent for each state in which they maintain offices or issue contracts (b). The BOC-3 is the final form, which is used to register process agents. There is room on the form to provide the contact information for all

process agents from each state if necessary. The BOC-3 form has a filing cost of $50. A list of Processing Agents is available in Appendix B at the conclusion of the course.

If you do not satisfy all of the broker criteria within 20 days of submitting your OP-1 application, the FMCSA will send you a notice stating that you have 60 days to complete all of the requirements, or your application will be rejected. To be an active broker, you must fill out both the BOC-3 and the BMC-84 forms.

When you've completed the OP-1 Form, BMC-84 or 85 Form, and BOC-3 Form, you're ready to apply for broker authorization. Before submitting the forms, double-check their correctness. Errors and omissions may cause your application to be delayed in processing, delaying the granting of your authorization.

5 STEPS TO GET A FREIGHT BROKER LICENSE

1. ESTABLISH YOUR BUSINESS STRUCTURE
2. SUBMIT AN OP-1 FORM
3. OBTAIN YOUR SURETY BOND (BMC-84)
4. SELECT A PROCESS AGENT
5. REGISTER THE BROKERAGE

ONCE LICENSED, YOU CAN BEGIN CONDUCTING BUSINESS AS A FREGHT BROKER.

Broker Application Review by the FMCSA

After you submit your application for broker authorization, it will be evaluated by FMCSA personnel. FMCSA personnel must evaluate your application for accuracy, completeness, and sufficiency of proof that you, as a broker, have the necessary financial responsibility and are fit, willing, and able to comply with all relevant laws and regulations, according to 49 CFR 365.109.

Minor mistakes on your application may be rectified throughout the review process; however, applications that are incomplete will be rejected. The granting of your operating authorization will be delayed if your application is rejected. It is critical that you verify the form before submitting it to confirm that all of the information is correct and that the form is complete. Follow the instructions carefully while filling out the OP-1 form or when submitting the OP-1 form online.

Applicants seeking home goods broker authorization must complete a second stage in the evaluation process. Applicants for home goods broker authorization are vetted to further safeguard consumers from misleading business practices in the sector. The application's information is scrutinised and, in many instances, confirmed to verify that the applicant has not used the name of another business to avoid responsibility for non-compliance with Federal rules. It may take up to 10 weeks to complete the vetting process. If you're seeking authorization

as a home goods broker, it's critical to make sure your application is complete and correct, including avoiding any omissions. If omitted information is discovered during vetting, the application may be rejected.

If your application is found to be acceptable by the FMCSA, a notice of the application will be published in the FMCSA Register. You must provide a Form BMC-84, proof that your brokerage is protected by a surety bond of $10,000 or $25,000, depending on the kind of brokerage, property, or household items, if you did not do so during the application procedure. Before permission may be given, a Form BMC-85 is needed as proof that your brokerage is protected by a trust fund of $10,000 or 25,000.

Anyone who opposes the acceptance of your application for authority on the grounds that you are not fit, willing, or able to comply with FMCSA's rules has 10 days after the summary of your application for authority is published in the FMCSA Register to submit a protest. If no one objects, the application will be granted a certificate that makes it effective.

UCR Registration - Unified Carrier Registration system

The UCR Agreement covers passenger and property activities in interstate commerce by motor carriers, private motor carriers, freight forwarders, brokers, and leasing companies. Most interstate carriers and brokers must get a state authorization

known as unified carrier registration. If you have a USDOT, MC, or FF number, you will almost certainly require the UCR to be in state compliance. The UCR 2013 Application may be found in Appendix C. You may also get it from https://www.ucr.in.gov/.

Brokers and freight forwarders pay the lowest fees, which are determined by fleet size. The number of commercial vehicles registered on your USDOT number or the total number of commercial vehicles operated determines the size of your fleet.

Leasing businesses (that are not motor carriers), brokers, and freight forwarders (that do not operate commercial motor vehicles) will be charged the lowest UCR fee for the registration year. Bracket 0-2 = $150 Depending on the state you register in, this cost may differ. All registrants must make an annual file of necessary information under the UCR Agreement.

5.4 Requirement for all freight brokers

All brokers must comply with all the requirements of the regulations in 49 CFR §371. These regulations require records to be kept and apply to how you conduct business. The FMCSA encourages you to familiarize yourself with these regulations; you can access them on the FMCSA Web site at www.fmcsa.dot.gov.

Records, Rules, & Accounting

A broker shall keep a record of each transaction. For purposes of this section, brokers may keep master database lists of consignors and the address and registration number of the carrier, rather than repeating this information for each transaction. The record shall show:

- The name and address of the consignor;

- The name, address, and registration number of the originating motor carrier;

- The bill of lading or freight bill number;

- The amount of compensation received by the broker for the brokerage service performed and the name of the payer;

- A description of any non–brokerage service performed in connection with each shipment or other activity, the amount of compensation received for the service, and the name of the payer; and

- The amount of any freight charges collected by the broker and the date of payment to the carrier.

Brokers shall keep the records required by this section for a period of three years. Each party to a brokered transaction has the right to review the record of the transaction required to be kept by these rules.

Misrepresentation

When working as a broker, you may not do business, including advertising, in any name other than the name stated on your registration or operating authority.

- A broker shall not perform or offer to perform any brokerage service in any name other than that in which its registration is issued.

- A broker shall not, indirectly or directly, represent its operations to be that of a carrier. Any advertising shall show the broker status of the operation.

Rebating &Compensation

A broker shall not charge or receive compensation from a motor carrier for brokerage service where:

- The broker owns or has a material beneficial interest in the shipment.

- The broker is able to exercise control over the shipment because the shipper owns the broker, the broker owns the shipper, or there is common ownership of the two.

- A broker shall not give or offer to give anything of value to any shipper, consignor or consignee except inexpensive advertising items given for promotional purposes.

Accounting Requirements, in Compliance with Regulation, 49 CFR §371.13

If you operate other businesses in addition to your brokerage, especially other transportation businesses such as motor carriers, then you must maintain your financial accounts so that revenues and expenses.

Your brokerage is separate from those of the other businesses. If your brokerage and the other businesses share common expenses, then your records must show which expenses belong to the brokerage.

Doing Business Only with Motor Carriers Having Valid USDOT Numbers and Operating Authority, 49 CFR §371.105

As a household goods broker, you may do business only with a motor carrier that has a valid USDOT number and valid *household goods motor carrier authority.* You may not arrange transportation with motor carriers having only property motor carrier authority or household goods authority that is under suspension or has been revoked. You are encouraged to regularly verify the authority status of motor carriers that you do business with. You can check the status of a motor carrier's operating authority by going to the FMCSA Licensing and Insurance Web site at http://li-public.fmcsa.dot.gov. When you arrive at that Web site, click "Continue" at the bottom. On the next webpage, click "Choose Menu Option" in the upper right corner. When the drop-down menu appears, click "Carrier Search." On the next webpage, enter the motor carrier's USDOT or MC number and click "Search." You will see the results of your search, provided that the motor carrier is registered with FMCSA. If the carrier you are searching for appears, then choose either "HTML" or "PDF" to get a status report.

5.5 Things to know before you start

The first thing to start up the business professionally is to decide the form of business and giving it a name. Incorporation is not mandatory but recommended. Other forms that can be well considered are the sole proprietorship, partnership, Sub Chapter S Corporation and the Limited Liability Company (LLC). Incorporation can be easily processed without hiring an attorney. The Federal Identification Number (FEIN) is needed for incorporation or partnership businesses. You need to apply to get the FEIN. However, for Sole proprietors, Social Security Number is sufficient for completing the paper works.

Forms of business you can consider for your freight brokering business:

1.   Incorporation

2.   Proprietorship

3.   Partnership

4.   Sub Chapter S Corporation

5.   Limited Liability Company

6.   UCR Registration (Page 9)

7.   SCAC Code Registration (Page 74)

Regarding the selection of the business name, it can be your own name or any other name you would like your business to be called as. The name has to be unique, and the broker needs to enquire that the name is available and not being used by someone already. The terminology used is the doing-business-as name or the fictitious name. A country or state level search can be done to confirm its availability.

If the business you are planning is a partnership business, then it is highly recommended to work out the partnership agreement. The partnership will form an outline for the scope of functions and expectations of each partner. The business set-up requirements for a freight broker are very basic and inexpensive. A toll-free number is highly desirable but not essential. We recommend using

RingCentral.com for ALL your telecommunication needs. Using the RingCentral.com service allows you to have a virtual office. You can make UNLIMITED incoming and outgoing calls within the US, and they give you a local fax line that will send PDF fax documents to your email, and you can get this package for around $30.00 a month.

Creating an office is quite simple as a freight broker. Being a freight broker is the perfect business that can be operated within the confines of your home. When you decide to increase the size of your brokerage by adding freight agents, a true office will definitely be needed at that time.

Whether you're telecommuting to your new office or working at home, running your freight, setting up your office requires some diligent thought and planning. Consideration needs to be made with thought to functionality, lighting, and ergonomics. Another important thing to remember is that if you tend to take a home office deduction on your federal income tax return, there are other issues you will be aware of.

Start-up requirements include:

1. A personal computer.
2. High-speed Internet connection: cable or DSL.
3. A telephone with RingCentral.com.
4. A reliable fax machine or RingCentral.com
5. Filing cabinet
6. Load Board membership (FindFreightLoads.com)
7. Microsoft Office (Word & Excel Mainly)
8. Email system (Gmail or Yahoo)
9. Website – (Included with course)

Common Equipment Types

Dry Van – Box Trailer

Freight trailers (also called dry vans or simply "boxes") are designed to carry virtually any kind of boxed, crated, or palletized freight.

Configurations

Standard lengths: 28', 32', 36', 40', 42', 43', 45', 48' and 53'. Standard widths: 96"-102" Maximum weight loaded: 46,000 lbs. Standard heights: 12.5'-13.5' overall. Shorter trailers are typically used for local deliveries or in tandem "truck trains." Standard axle/wheel configuration: 2-axle/8-wheel.

Features and Options

- Roll-up doors, rear swing doors. One or two side doors, roller beds.

- When used for produce, "Produce Vents" are added and insulated with roofs of Wood, Tin, or Fiberglass.

Reefer (Refrigerated Trailer)

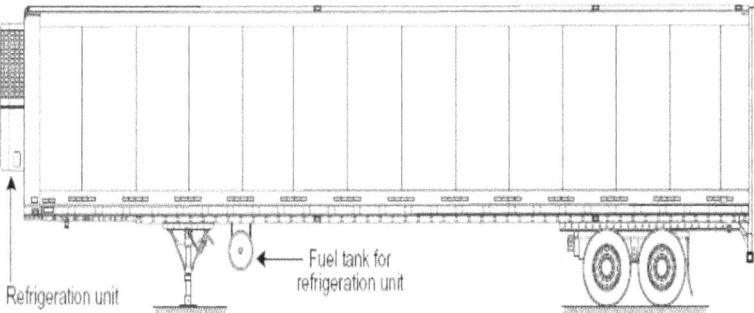

Refrigeration unit

Fuel tank for refrigeration unit

Use

Reefers are insulated and refrigerated trailers designed to transport perishable items.

Commodities transported include vegetables, fruits, milk, juices, meats and poultry

Configurations

- Standard lengths: 28', 32', 36', 40', 48' and 53'.

- Standard widths: 96"-102".

- Standard heights: 12.5'-13.5' overall.

- Shorter trailers are typically used for local deliveries or in tandem "truck trains."

- Standard axle/wheel configuration: 2-axle/8-wheel. For heavier loads: 3 axle/12-wheel or 4-axle/ 1-wheel configurations are also available.

Features and Options

- Rear swing doors or roll-up doors.

- One or two side doors.

- Moveable bulkheads, lift gates, and temperature recording and monitoring systems.
- Single or multi-temperature models.

Flatbeds and Single Drop Decks (Step Decks)

- Platform (flatbed) trailers are designed to transport oversize cargo that normally would not fit into standard freight trailers.
- Platform trailers are used especially for the transport of goods that must be loaded from the side or top of the trailer.
- Standard cargo for platform trailers includes ocean freight containers, machinery, construction equipment, lumber, and plywood, steel, pipe and rebar.

Variations

- Standard lengths: 26', 40', 42', 45', and 48'.
- Extended Lengths: 60', 65' and 70'

Double Drop's and RGN's (Removable Goose Necks)

Use

- Speciality trailers are designed to transport oversize cargo that normally would not fit onto standard freight trailers.
- Speciality trailers are used especially for the transport of goods that must be loaded from the top of the trailer.
- Standard cargo for speciality trailers includes Heavy Equipment, Machinery, Farm Equipment, Windmills, Transformer's etc.

Variations

- Standard lengths: 48' and 53'.
- Extended Lengths: 60', 65' and 70'
- Weight allotted for hauling determined by Axle's included on trailer and configurations.

Equipment Type	Average Legal Weight	Average Legal Dimensions
FLATBED 40' to 50'	40,000 – 48,000	Length: 40' – 53' Width: 8'6" Height: 9'
EXTENDIBLE (STRETCH) FLAT 40' to 75'	40,000 – 44,000	Length: 40' – 75' Width: 8'6" Height: 9'
STEPDECK (DROPDECK) 11' 37'	40,000 – 46,000	Length: 35' – 37' Width: 8'6" Height: 10'
EXTENDIBLE STEPDECK 11' 37' to 60'	37,000 – 40,000 40,000 – 44,000	Length: 37' – 60' Width: 8'6" Height: 10'
DOUBLE EXTENDIBLE DROP 10' 26' to 50' 5'	35,000 – 40,000	Length: 24' – 30' Width: 8'6" Height: 11'8"
DOUBLE DROPDECK 10' 30' 5'	35,000 – 40,000	Length: 26' – 50' Width: 8'6" Height:11'8"
DOUBLE DROP/LOWBOY (R.G.N) 10' 24' to 30' 5'	36,000 – 42,000	Length: 24' – 30' Width: 8'6" Height: 12'

Containers (Skeletal Carrier / Drayage)

- Container carriers are designed to transport standard international cargo   containers of 20'--45'.

- Some models are able to transport non-standard and oversize containers.

Configurations

- Models designed to transport a single specific size container (20', 40', 45', etc.)

- Models designed in adjustable ("zoom") configurations to work with a range of different sized standard and non-standard containers.

- Configuration / wheel standard: 2-axle/8-wheel. For heavy loads: 3 - axle/12-wheel configurations are also available.

- Brackets are specially designed to hold the container carrier.

Tankers (Food Grade / Chemicals / Petroleum)

- Tanker trailers are designed for the carrying of a wide range of goods fluids.

- Standard cargo carriers include refined gasoline, heating oil, natural gas and acids, and industrial chemicals, caustic soda, clay and mud and cooking oils, corn syrup, orange juice, milk and other foodstuffs. Requires some cargo tanker trailers specially designed fluid. For example, carriers designed to transport caustic soda and acids require some aspects and exterior paint and equipment that will withstand the effects of corrosive goods.

Variations

- Standard lengths: 40 '0.42' 0.43 '0.45', 48 'and 53'.

- Configuration / wheel standard: 2-axle/8-wheel. For heavy loads: 3 - axle/12-wheel 4-axle/16-wheel or configurations are also available.

Features and Options

- Multiple Compartments (1-7)

- vacuum pumps

- Measurement equipment

- Insulated Tanks

- Pressure Tanks

- Ladders

- Walkways

- Hose Carriers

- Belly cabinets

Dry Bulk Trailer - Hopper

Use

Dry trailers are mainly used in the transportation of dry commodities such as grain, shelled corn, hulled rice, beans, gravel, limestone (loose and pulverized), and sand. It is a safe transportation method and very useful for long distances.

Variations

- Standard lengths: 26' to 42'.

- Standard widths: 96"-102".

- Hopper configurations: single, double and triple.

- Open and closed-end configurations.

- Steel and Aluminum models.

- There are available singles, doubles, and three-trailer truck "trains".

Notes

- Dry bulk trailers use rolled tarpaulin tops rather than rigid tops.

- Typical dry bulk trailers usually use hoppers to unload or empty conveyor systems.

- The international trailer manufacturers produce a variety of models that are designed for different freight configurations.

Logistics Van &Deep Drop Furniture

Use

- Deep drop vans are designed especially for transporting large, bulky and relatively light cargo (weight to volume).
- Deep drop vans are mainly used in the transportation of specific kinds of goods such as furniture, household and electronics.

Variations

- Standard lengths: 45', 48' and 53' overall.
- Standard heights: 13' 6" overall.
- Standard widths: 96"-102" overall.
- Rear door(s): Standard swing doors.
- Side doors: 1 or 2 side swing doors.

Options & Features

- Using the lower rear surface to facilitate loading.
- Air ride suspension to protect the fragile cargo.
- Compartments belly met and ramps.

Auto Transport Tractor Trailer

Use

Trailers are used to transport auto transport cars, sports cars, small trucks. It is the movement of these goods from the former manufacturing plants to distributors, but the most common ports (Ro-Ro ships) to distributors of the Interior.

Auto variations:

- Auto transporters are produced in two general configurations
- The trucks are produced cars in two models
- Trailers are capable of transporting up to nine vehicles pulled by tractor unit standard.
- The truck tractor is up to three vehicles, while the trailer transports up to six cars.

There is also private covered car trailers that are specially made for use in the transportation of high-value cars.

Notes

Different trailer manufacturers from all over the world produce a wide range of models that have been designed for different shipping configurations.

There is a large market for private party auto transporter in the transfer of families and the transfer of specialized vehicles and high-value locally and internationally as well.

Dimensions, weight and capacity are the data that varies according to the requirements of cargo, manufactured goods Trailers, a national model, and the state, as well as the requirements of the provincial road.

General Guidelines

Maximum Overall Dimensions (Un-Permitted) Width: 96 inches Width: (Designated Highways): 102 inches Height: 13 feet, 6 inches GVW: (Gross Vehicle Weight): 80,000 lbs. Length of Semitrailer: 53 feet Length of Semitrailer: (Non-Designated Highway): 50 Feet Length of Combination Tractor Trailer: (With or Without Load) No Limitation Units Permitted in Train: (2) Semitrailers or Truck and Semitrailer

- Truck-Tractor, Semitrailer and Trailer or Tractor and Length of a Combination of Tractor, Semitrailer, and Trailer or Tractor and (2) Semitrailers or truck and semitrailer of the trailer with or without load or pickup truck, Semitrailers are designed for recreational living purposes, and additional trailer or Semitrailer: 65 feet.

- The Semitrailers that are longer than 50 feet shall have a wheelbase of 37 feet to 41 feet. This is measured from the kingpin coupling to the centre of the axles or to the centre of the tandem axle assembly in case it is equipped with (2) axles.

- Semitrailers longer than 50 feet are limited to 3 axles and shall operate only on designated highways.

- The measurement of Semitrailers and Trailers shall be done from the front vertical plane of the foremost transverse load-supporting structure to the rearmost transverse load-supporting structure. Safety and energy conservation devices are not supposed to be included in the length measurement, but not limited to impact-absorbing bumpers, rear view mirrors, turn signal lamps, marker lamps, steps and handhold for entry and egress, flexible fender extensions, mud flaps or splash and suppressant devices, load-induced tire bulge, refrigeration or heating units, or air compressors. However, any device that is not designed or intended to be used in cargo-carrying shall be excluded from the length determination.

Projection Beyond Front of Vehicles: 3 feet

Overhang beyond the rear of vehicles: Any amount is permissible as long as it doesn't exceed the legal length. However, if this overhang is 4 feet or more, then a 12 -Inch red square flag in the daytime and a red light or lantern at night shall be displayed on the extreme rear.

5.6 Finding and soliciting shippers

Developing Shipper Relationships

Searching for Shippers is among the initial stages of the freight brokering business. However, before you begin the marketing operations, you'll need to have at least a good website, which is considered to be a good place to start your marketing campaign. Your broker's course includes free website templates. Even if you are operating a small freight brokerage, a professional website will be helpful in giving your clients and shippers the impression that you are an established freight brokerage company. When you market your services to shippers, they will want to see your website and more than likely; your website will be one of the key factors affecting their decision of making business with you or not. Your website will be the main source that describes all your services, testimonials, and contact information.

Within your broker's course, you will be provided with a shipper and carrier database of over 250,000 profiles in excel format. Upon using this list of data, you will be able to market your business by sending out emails, brochures to their business address and make phone calls to set up appointments. Pay your attention to plan a marketing strategy rather than just making indecisive searches or phone calls. Define your target area, set goals and work from there. It is good to start with e-mail marketing as you will reach a lot of clients with little effort, but making calls and setting up appointments is where most of your leads will start to convert into reality.

The Approach

One of the best approaches is to target a specific market segment. By developing certain markets, you will be referred to other customers; in addition, through this method, other carriers are much easier to find as well. As a search criterion, try targeting your business based on the following criteria;

- The shippers' location and the freight's destination.

- Type of cargo (agricultural, perishable, oversized, bulk commodities, etc.)
- Loads' size, specific industries, or some other special shipping segment

Upon choosing a particular demographic, you shall consider what type of cargo would be most comfortable brokering. You may choose to broker general commodity freight, which is more stable and less volatile, or you focus your expertise in areas such as heavy haul, temperature-controlled, hazmat loads, or oversized loads.

Once you find a shipper, you shall approach the right person. In this industry, you'll need to talk to the appropriate person in charge. Generally, the "Traffic Manager" is the person that you'll need to contact. Thankfully, in this industry, the "Go to People" is not that evasive, and there are very few loops to jump through to get to the right person.

Key Contacts:

- Transportation Manager
- Sales Agents & Brokers
- Logistics Department
- Traffic Manager

As mentioned previously, your first goal is to look for shippers who need shipping services. As a service industry, you have no physical storefront that customer can visit it or a product to hand them for examination. Therefore, your website acts as a "virtual" storefront for you. Marketing Campaign Should Include:

1. Telephone calls
2. Brochure distribution
3. Promotional Emails with cover letters

Also, you need to pay attention to marketing over the internet through social networks like Facebook, Twitter, Craigslist Ads and Transportation ads.

Shipper Requirements

The shippers are always concerned about the limited budget to which they want their shipment to be constrained. However, the budget varies according to the fluctuation in the supply and demand of any load type. Shippers want their cargo to be transported by the carriers with safety, efficiency and within their estimated costs. They do not usually have industry knowledge or time to spend on finding reliable carriers themselves. Therefore, your clients (shippers) are constantly looking towards finding reliable and honest freight brokers to build strong business relationships.

There are two types of brokers. Truck Brokers (the motor carrier with Authority and a Broker's License) and Property Brokers (Only having a broker's License, CAN NOT move freight). A Property Broker has NO LIABILITY and only makes a commission for facilitating the move of the load, while the truck broker HAS LIABILITY and may hire other carriers/owner operators to move the freight creating liability.

(Please Note this is due to be changed 10/01/2012 – Carriers will have to have Broker Authority)

The reason for this embodies the difference between having an "Authority" and "License" A carrier has "Authority", which means having the shipper's permission to take ownership of the cargo to deliver the load by interstate or intrastate transportation. When taking over the cargo, the carrier must show proof of cargo & liability insurance as upon the receipt of the cargo for transportation; they have become responsible for it.

A Broker obtains a "License" and can only arrange the transportation of the shipper's cargo with carriers (owner-operators with Authority). A broker's license is NOT a "mode" of transportation, and a property broker cannot take ownership of the bill of lading. Property brokers are in a fiduciary (trust) relationship with the motor carrier actually hauling the brokered freight. The broker collects the money from the shipper and then pays the motor carrier their rate, less his commission.

In the case of a carrier (brokers) loads their excess to another motor carrier (sub-haulier), there will be no ''Broker's license'' required. However, both parties need to share 100% labiality for the cargo. So many truck brokers think that they are not responsible for freight that they subcontract from one motor carrier to another.

Carrier Requirements

Carriers are certainly looking for the best price that they can get for shipping the cargo. The motor carriers and shippers also have to face cost constraints. The carrier company shall take care of many different costs such as truck maintenance, employee salaries, fuel costs etc. If they learn how to manage such costs efficiently, they can achieve good profit.

To facilitate a smooth process, a freight broker is required to make a win-win situation for all. This can be achieved by the excellent negotiation skills to devise a transaction in which all parties (broker, carrier and shipper) are satisfied.

Broker Requirements:

The broker looks for shippers who are in need to ship cargo, and then they look for reliable carriers who are able to cover the loads. It's the freight broker's responsibility to do perfect load, carrier matching and keeping the shipper's cost as low as possible or at least within their budget.

When a broker starts his new business, he may need to make a lot of research on the phone and the Internet to gather a useful database of carriers and shippers. This course will give you a database of 350,000 shippers and carriers to help you to overcome this process.

The broker's activity key role is to achieve reliable relationships between the shippers and carriers and provide the shipper with

a list of different options that can meet their needs of delivering their cargo. This is an art that will greatly determine broker performance and start bringing in recurring business. The next important step to success in the business is to do a credit check in order to be on the safe side deals with new shippers. Try to avoid problems before they occur. Don't be trapped even if a shipper has good credit; it may take from 45, 60, to even 90 days before receiving a check from them, so you either need to have GREAT cash flow management, or you can factor your invoices with freight factoring companies that will pay faster just less their processing fees.

With new carriers, you'll need to do a similar credit/background check. The broker needs to pre-qualify carriers, which mean they should have all their operational and insurance documents ready. No too many traffic citations or Highway Patrol Inspections. Also, there is some web service that can be used to check the carrier's authority status; SAFER is one of those useful services. http://www.safersys.org/CompanySnapshot.aspx

Use the carrier's USDOT# to search the SAFER Web service. Cargo insurance is not required to be obtained by freight brokers as they use the cargo insurance of the carrier. But the "Contingent" cargo insurance should be purchased as a plan B insurance in case the carrier's insurance does not pay or pays for only part of the insurance claim. This is always a great

backup to protect both you and the shipper, and ignore this drove many new brokers into financial troubles, so never think that you can abandon insurance coverage.

In order to start your business relationship with the shipper, you'll need to first get "set up" with the shipper. The "set-up" process involves faxing the shipper an information packet, including all important documents such as their motor carrier number, proof of surety bond, insurance certificate in case the contingent cargo coverage is purchased, W-9 form and all other crucial information the broker want to include or the shipper may have specified. As soon as the shipper accepts and verifies your information, you can now start a business with him. This packet IS NOT like your marketing packet that you will send out to potential clients. This "Set-Up" packet is specifically to provide more information about your brokerage to the shipper who intends and agrees to start a business with you.

Some professional freight brokers can send a "broker-shipper" agreement that is rarely done in the case of new brokers as they still do not have enough experience to do such agreements. This agreement ensures the shipper that their loads will be covered by the broker. This course included a sample of broker-shipper agreement contracts. If you are a creditable broker, you will make demands in your contract that you can fulfil.

The shipper might ask the broker to give his quote to deliver one or a large number of loads before deciding to start the business relationship with you. In the previous chapter, we have reviewed how to do rate calculation; this will be helpful to prepare your rate sheet previously, to be always ready to send your "Set-Up" package in case the shippers request to include your rate sheet.

What Do You Say?

If you contact your customer, whether, via phone or e-mail, you will want to speak in terms that they understand, so you shall not appear uneducated in the industry. Shippers have the desire to deal with reputable and established companies that can handle the movement of their freight with the smallest number of problems. The only thing they may need is consistency and reliability for the shipment of their various products.

It is preferred to have a previous good working knowledge of the transportation vernacular prior to contact a shipper for the first time. It's been said by Human Resource experts that we only have "15 Seconds" to make a first impression. Do not worry if you have never had any previous experience in "Direct Sales" as most of the work in this profession is completed using a telephone or email. It would be beneficial to spend a little time on the phone or in practice sessions with a partner "role-playing" prior to set up a perspective sales meeting with a client

personally. This is also called the "Elevator Pitch". You have the time to go from one floor to another in an elevator to get your pitch in. Can you do it?

Prospecting For Customers

Find Your Customer Base

In order to be a successful freight broker, you will need to have a good database of customers. Shippers are always looking for the safest, efficient and cost-effective methods to transport their products. The information mentioned below will provide you with a general knowledge base that will grant you the required skills to manage and find appropriate freight and customers.

Gather the Information

There are several useful methods to find your customer database. It can be as easy as picking your phone to do a call. Products manufactured in the U.S.A. have to be shipped to the retail or wholesale distributor.

Targeted markets:

- Distributors
- Warehouses
- Cold Storage Facilities
- Growers & Packers

- Membership Associations

- Trucking Companies

- Manufacturers

- Wholesalers

5.7 Databases

The information databases are provided by third party resources. However, you have to be aware of what kind of information is included in the database you are purchasing and whether it is useful and up-to-date or not before paying your money. You may try one of the following resources:

- Contact DB (Website Link -http://www.contactdb.com)

- Info USA (Website Link -http://www.infousa.com)

- Selectory D&B (Website Link -http://www.selectory.com)

How to Search?

You can reach a huge variety of sales and contacts information by performing searches of various membership databases. You can perform the search process for membership directories and get the membership directories and their buyer's guide for free and easily via various trade organizations.

Using Truck Load Boards

Load boards are websites that are widely used by freight brokers to post the shipper loads available with them in order to find available ready trucks to cover them.

On the other hand, the load boards are used by the carrier companies to post the availability of their trucks. So simply, the carrier companies are searching for brokers and loads matching their post requests. The usage of loading boards can come up with the desired solution within few minutes.

Load boards operate differently. Some may allow the broker to post load and to perform searches for trucks as well, while other load boards operators automatically notify other load boards with the broker loads post as soon as it is posted, achieving a quick matching.

Nowadays, load boards provide many customized services, but the primary one for the freight brokers off course being posting loads and searching for available trucks to cover these loads.

Qualifying Prospects

Sales Strategy

You need to gain and maintain very strong negotiation skills so you can market your freight brokerage successfully. Almost everyone isn't good at negotiating. Many are intimidated by the person on the other end of the line. If you are not feeling comfortable with negotiations, then keep in mind that this job

requires frequent situations and negotiation skills are highly involved in the daily procedures of your business. However, you can enhance your negotiation skills, and you may need a few ideas and thoughts to overcome your fears and become a successful negotiator.

Before quoting freight rates, it is very important for you to remember your service value. You should know and understand your product and its value, which you introduce to your customers. Your previous customers will give you a bit of information so that you can keep your competitors' products and services on the top as those customers will tell you about your weaknesses and strengths points according to their experience and needs. By that time, you shall be open-minded and accept their criticism in order to develop yourself. If you do that, you will gain your customers and grow your business.

Study your competition:

As it is essential to know which rates are being quoted on lanes and how your competitors are meeting them. You should understand other's pricing and how they are getting them in order to improve your predictive abilities. You should study and research your competitors. Customers are always looking for a better deal, so they are going to hang around to get the best possible prices. If you understand your competitors, that will make you develop your services and will grant you the lead during negotiations.

Understand Your Sales Strategy

Firstly, you should define your strategy before beginning negotiations. Then do as many plans as possible that you may propose as further opportunities to your client's in case your first suggestion wasn't accepted. Your strategy should be flexible enough to work efficiently with all of you provided opportunities when negotiating a rate. If you succeed in developing such a strategy for marketing your service, then you will definitely acquire the forefront in negotiations with your clients.

Rates Quoting

Define spot quote?

A spot quote is a group of rates for a month. It is calculated based on the current market, and it is done without a contract. So the spot quote is a rate quote for an individual Line Haul. So you should start talking to carriers who run this line, and before that, you shall gather all information that they are going to ask you about.

Information Needed For Quote You shall do the following:

- Origin & Destination
- Truckload / LTL
- Dimensions
- Commodity
- Weight / Trapping Required?
- Pallet Exchange Required?
- Date of Pickup & Delivery
- Contact (5) carriers to get their quote on the Line Haul.
- Post the load and request rates from carriers that call you for the details
- Get an average price for the load and then contact your shipper with the rate.

When you quote dedicated lanes for shippers, you will need to do some research. Dedicated means constant loads weekly from the same origin to destination, and carriers usually love this type of freight, so they will give you a better rate than the normal spot quote line haul rate. Because of the demand, this type of freight is very competitive, and your quotes will be compared and considered against many others.

It is essential to offer your shipper a quote that actually can transport the freight especially that you are a non-asset-based freight broker. Most brokers will provide low quotes to shippers so that they can get the freight in hopes of brokering it out to carriers. When this happens, many of these freight brokers will not be able to move the freight since your quotes are not accurate. This is one of the main reasons shippers will not deal with many freight brokers. You must set yourself apart from the rest, and here are a few ways to do that.

Rates of Market prices:

Sometimes shippers will need carriers to move their freight due to a truck falling out or another vendor's inability to provide the service. That will be when a shipper will have to pay the going rate for a truck to move the freight, so there will be a relationship with a lot of carriers that will be possible. You can make huge commissions on these loads, as the shipper will most generally pay whatever is necessary to transport the load.

Do not gouge your shippers

Rates Calculation

Freight charges vary according to a number of variables, but the two main factors are the weight of the load and the distance it must travel. The truck's type affects the rates, regardless of the driver's need to make one or more stops to pick up the freight or to deliver it. However, rates for additional stops are usually negotiable.

You'll need to get an idea of the current "going rates" for the types of shipments that you can handle before you begin shopping for rates for specific shipments. This can be achieved by requesting copies of tariffs from several carriers and studying them. There are different methods to calculate these rates mentioned below. Load boards and calling for rates on posted loads is another way of getting information on current

market rates. The National Moto Freight Traffic Association (NMFTA) classes products according to four characteristics Weight, Handling, Storability and Liability. There are 18 freight classes that are beginning from class 50 (the least expensive) to class 500 (most expensive). For more information on NMFTA classes, visit: http://www.nmfta.org/Pages/welcome.aspx

1. Flat Rate: The broker can set up a flat rate for the shipper's load that might need to be hauled from one state to another. For e.g. the loads are to be shipped from Miami, FL to Houston, TX, then the broker can decide upon the flat rate to be $2200.

2. Rate per Mile: Rates can be determined based on the mile. For, e.g. the rate per mile is $1.5, and the carrier covers 2,500 miles, then the total cost to cover the loads will be $3750.

3. Rate per Unit: The shipper may prefer to pay the broker per unit price, like the payment for a carton of juice cans to be delivered $1.75

4. Rate per Hundred Weights: The shipper can also choose the payment option of pay per hundred weights. Say if $6.25 is the price per hundred weights and the total weight of the loads to be shipped is 32,000 lbs. Then the total amount the shipper will pay is $2000.

The broker should find if there is any extra cost involved in the shipment, such as extra picks, unloading fees etc. The broker should have good negotiation skills to ask the shipper for some add-ons like fuel surcharge etc., above the regular rate. With increasing fuel prices, more and more truckers want the fuel surcharge payment to be added to the deal.

The broker should have good knowledge about all loading techniques and regulations. He should be aware of the loading terminology like Full Truck Load (FTL) and Less than Truck Load (LTL). He should keep himself well informed to avoid any future problem related to loads transporting.

Commissions that you earn on each load is your main source of income. There are two methods to receive your payment: You can bill the shipper the amount you're going to pay the carrier plus the amount of your commission, or the carrier can bill the shipper directly and then pay you a commission from its revenue. The most common and efficient way to handle billing and commissions is to have the carrier bill you, and then you bill your customers. Freight rates are based on many factors, including

1. The distance that shipment will take.
2. The shipment's weight
3. The density of the shipping goods.
4. The commodity's susceptibility to damage
5. The value of the commodity.
6. The commodity's load ability and handling characteristics.

All of the above factors affect the classification of a commodity. The NMFC, or National Motor Freight Classification tariff, contains all product classifications. There are eighteen possible classes ranging from 50 to 500. The increase of the class increases the rate for every hundred pounds you will ship. Most less-than-truck-load (LTL) rates are stated as a rate per hundred pounds or per hundredweight. Rates of each hundred pounds are structured to decreases as the total shipment weight increase. For example, a shipment weighing 100 pounds may cost $41.00 per hundredweight, while a heavier shipment--say, 500 pounds--of the same commodity (moving to the same destination) may only cost $35.00 per hundredweight. But doing the math, we see that the total charges for the 500-pound shipment are higher (5x$35 is greater than 1x$41). For very light shipments, most LTL carriers state a minimum charge.

Carrier expenses such as fuel mileage, driver wages, IFTA (International Fuel Tax Agreement), fuel taxes as well as the toll roads play a critical role in the line haul rates you submit to your customers; this is simply because carrier's rates are based on mileage. Regardless of the line haul rate, which is broken into mileage, there are additional costs that need to be calculated, for example. If that very same $1,500 load had two extra stops,

you should add another $50 to $100 per stop to the gross line haul rate.

Carriers tend to use two major formulas to determine shipping rates:

1. the linear foot rule and

2. the cube rule.

The standard carrier linear foot rule states that shipments occupying 10 linear feet or more of trailer space are charged for 1,000lb per foot. Usually, this rule applies when there are at least five pallets single-stacked or 10 pallets double-stacked. For example, say, a 10-pallet order of stackable freight occupies 10 linear feet. If those pallets were not stackable, they would occupy 20 linear feet. In the former scenario, a shipper would be charged for 10,000lb; in the latter, they would be charged for 20,000lb.   Here's a simple rule of thumb to remember: for stackable pallets, take the number of pallets on the floor of the trailer and multiply by two; that's how many linear feet you should be charged for. For non-stackable pallets, multiply the total number of pallets by two to get the linear foot count. Review your invoices to see if this rule is being applied.

How To Calculate Linear Foot from a number of Pallets?

Example

Units: 16, Width: 42, Length: 48, Height: 42, Stackable: 1, Weight: 5000, Not Tunable:

Turn pallets resulting in width of 48. Number Across: 2

Base Linear Feet: (42 / 12) = 3.5

Linear Feet after accounting for 2 wide in Trailer = (3.5 / 2) = 1.75

Linear Feet after Stacking: (1.75 / 1) = 1.75

Linear Feet for all Units: (1.75 * 16) = 28

Here is a great link to calculate linear ft. To reiterate, linear feet = square feet / width.

http://www.wpg.org/Member/LinearFootCalc3.asp

What is meant by fuel surcharge?

A fuel surcharge aims to compensate carriers and balance the spiralling fuel expenses. In case the fuel cost has risen to $750 per gallon, then it's not feasible for a carrier to haul a load at the rate of $150 per mile. We try to resolve this issue by getting the clients to pay a fuel surcharge, which is then handed over to the trucking company.

How is fuel surcharge calculated? The average of most trucks is approximately 5 mpg. The base fuel cost should range from $1.10 to $1.20, irrespective of the existing cost of fuel. For instance, here, we will assume the base price to be $1.20. You now have to divide the fuel expenses for more than $1.20 for every gallon by 5 (which is the average mpg for the majority of the trucks).

If the existing fuel rate is $2.50 per gallon, then you will have to deduct the base price (In this case, $1.20). The amount which remains ($1.30) will now be divided by the average MPG (5 as decided in the example). Thus you get $0.26 cents which is your fuel surcharge.

Regional/National Fuel Prices

The fuel surcharge depends on the national average retail price of diesel fuel in a specific region from where the load begins. You can get the details about the average retail price from the Federal Government's Energy Information Administration which is updated every week on Wednesdays.

You can also call: (202)586-6966 or visit http://www.eia.gov/petroleum/ gasdiesel/ to find out more details.

Often freight brokers decide on a floating fuel surcharge with their clients. This surcharge is modified every month. It is better to ensure that you update your customers about the changes in the fuel surcharge, which will be applicable for the following month. In case you do levy a fuel surcharge, then sincerely ensure that it reaches the carrier. Never be overcome by greed, as it could spell doom for your business.

Fuel Surcharge Rate Confirmation

The fuel surcharge must be included separately on the rate confirmation sheet, and you must never levy any commission for this amount. It is better to have a detailed rate confirmation with all the overheads like the line-haul rate, the paid miles, the tarp pay, additional stops & fuel surcharge. Itemizing the confirmation sheet will give you better clarity in revenue sharing. You do not have to pen down the fuel surcharge on any other shipping documents like the Bill of Lading. But it is essential to include it on the load rate confirmation agreement as well as the invoice which you send to the client.

Freight Rate Variables

The freight rates differ from day to day. Besides this, they are not uniform throughout the nation. The freight rates depend on the supply & demand at that particular location, and as long as there's no sudden hike in the fuel rates, the rates you finalize should be stable for around a month. After you have finalized a line-haul rate, it is easier to keep the base rate stable and negotiate with the rate variables like the truck fuel surcharge.

The motor carrier will have to order the proper permits for all the states through which the load is going to be hauled. But you, too, should find out if the load requires any additional permits. The customer, too, should be fully updated on the same.

A load must have individual state permits in case:

Its width exceeds 8 feet.

Its length exceeds 53 feet, and it is hanging over the back of the trailer.

In case the GVW Gross Vehicle Weight of the truck exceeds 80,000 pounds after being loaded.

Because of the extra expense for the carrier, it is better that you get a good deal for such loads.

Extending Credit to Shippers

The credibility of information, efficiency of communication and control plays a vital role in managing credit in your small business. Before you can even begin to think about granting any kind of credit terms, it is essential that you research and get the correct information you need to obtain reasonable

assurance that you will get paid on time and in full. Transparent communications and an excellent flow of information, and complete and clear documentation will contribute to building positive business relationships with your customers and clients. Most importantly, having a strong contact relationship with the accounts payable and following up will be a key aspect in your collections and cash flow.

Freight Brokerage& Credit

It is a normal procedure to perform buying and selling operations on credit. Establishing and maintaining a clear credit policy and following the proper credit practices and procedures should be an integral part of your small business operation. Marketing and sales, production and delivery, and customer service are essential aspects of your business, and your credit and collections practice complete the operating cycle.

Three key concepts involved in credit are:

- Communication
- Control
- Information

To sell on credit is agreeing to deliver the products orders by your customers or to perform their requested services based on a promise to pay at a determined future date. Therefore you will need to make an informed decision about extending credit before committing your time and resources.

Clear communication with the customer will avoid any misunderstandings that may happen later. Once you have decided to extend credit to a customer, the terms should be documented so that they can be clear to both parties. It is also important that all your employees who work in sales and marketing, production and distribution, or accounting operate from the same base in terms of credit.

Your credit policy will only be effective if it is carried out in practice, and in order to have proper control, you'll need to perform constant follow-up. Guidelines should be consistently applied in the sales and billing phase and enforced through follow-up in the collections stage.

Common Credit Practices

You should take into your consideration when establishing a credit policy the factors that will be the standard practices in your line of business. It is most common in many businesses that customers with 30-day payment terms. In spite of the fact that you are not obligated to accept terms imposed by your customers, but it is extremely important to recognize these standards or common practices. Most businesses operate on a standard pay cycle, issuing payments once a week, for example, based on an accounts payable system that age invoices and calls up for payment for those that are due. In many cases, when the invoices are entered into the system, the due date will be assumed to be or will default to 30 days.

The 30-day payment period is an example, and it does vary according to business's nature, type of industry, general economic industries conditions, and individual companies' financial policies and practices. You will need to provide your small business cash flow permits; by making it easier for your customers to pay you, it may be acceptable and beneficial, to accept the standard terms of your customers as your company is new established.

However, you may be in a business that normally involves payment on cash terms, which means you receive payment for your sales essentially by cash, check, credit or debit card, or

electronic transfers of funds. Your credit policy would involve exceptions when you would extend credit to a particular customer based on a certain set of circumstances. Though even in the case of an exception, the same principles would apply in deciding whether to grant credit to that customer.

Considerations regarding the potential customer

Some of the questions that may form part of a credit evaluation of a particular company include the following:

- How long has the company been in operation?
- Are you familiar with the company?
- Is the company generally recognized in your market, industry, or community?
- Does the company have a physical address?
- Do you know the manager?
- Has the company undergone a change of management or a restructuring?
- Who are the owners?
- Has the company undergone a change of ownership?
- PAYDEX score
- Is the company in bankruptcy, or has it declared bankruptcy in the past?

Dunn - Bradstreet PAYDEX

The most important thing to know as a business is your Paydex score. A company's Paydex score is the business equivalent to your personal FICO score or personal credit score. Knowing what this number is and having the secrets to increasing your Paydex score can mean acquiring the financing necessary to start or grow your business and make the difference in achieving your business goals. On the flip side, not managing your Paydex score will cost your business.

The exact definition from Dunn &Bradstreet or D&B is: The D&B PAYDEX® Score is D&B's unique dollar-weighted numerical indicator of how a firm paid its bills over the past year, based on trade experiences reported to D&B by various vendors. The D&B PAYDEX Score ranges from 1 to 100, with higher scores indicating better payment performance.

Understanding Payment Patterns

100 -Anticipate – Payment detail may state: payments are received prior to the date of invoice (Anticipated) 90 -Discount -Payment detail may state: payments are received within trade discount period (Discount)

80 -Prompt -Payment detail may state: payments are received within terms granted (Prompt)

70 -15 Days Beyond Terms

60 -22 Days Beyond Terms

50 -30 Days Beyond Terms

40 -60 Days Beyond Terms

30 -90 Days Beyond Terms

20 -120 Days Beyond

UN -Unavailable

The payment details section may include the following comments on your payment patterns:

- Antic -payments are received prior to the date of invoice (Anticipated).
- Disc -payments are received within the trade discount period (Discount).
- Ppt -payments are received within terms granted (Prompt).
- Slow -payments are beyond vendor's terms. For example, "Slow 30" means payments are 30 days past due.
- Ppt-Slow means that some invoices are paid within terms, others are paid beyond terms.
- (#) -indicates that no manner of payment was provided; the number merely reflects the line where it appears in the listing. For example, (004) means it is the fourth experience listed.

Closing Deals

All small business owners either hate or completely ignore the cornerstone of the business; the sales process. The main idea of closing a sale is even less appealing. Sales and marketing are the foundational functions that keep every business alive and growing, and that makes every successful business owner make good deals. Selling is much more about educating and informing than pushing and listening. A truly good salesperson, regardless of what they are selling, is a master at determining their customer's needs and finding answers for them. The quicker business owner realizes the importance of selling and closing, as well as makes a positive business decision to educate himself on techniques and principles associated with selling and closing, so his business will grow.

The last and most critical step in the sales process is closing; ask your prospective customer for their business. Closing is a critical step; without thinking, many people do not close. They make the age-old mistake of thinking; their prospect will just automatically give them their business. Of course, this does occur occasionally. It's difficult to pay your bills every month if you rely on what may occur occasionally. Closing the sale is as important as crossing the finish line at the end of a race. All or many business owners do not like going into "close" mode, as they are fear rejection. You should not be afraid to close and ask for the business whenever possible. That is the purpose of

having the business in the first place. With practice, you will know when your potential customer's interest is high; make sure you take advantage of the timing by asking for their business. Never, ever be afraid to close. Even if your attempt at closing is unsuccessful, you shall tell your potential customer that you are able to offer them your service/product as you will have an instant indicator in order to know where they are in the sales process.

Frequently, customers will have an interest in asking about details related to your service. This is a guide an indication that their interest is high. This is the time that a nudge puts them over the buying edge. If they committed after your initial close, there is some type of objection standing in your way.

You must determine that objection or concern, then address it and go for the close again.

Trial Close

In order to close your prospective customer, you should define the level of interest by using a "trial close". A trial close is a very simple question that gets the customer to think about the possibility of using your services. Lots of car sales representatives may use a trial close with an interested buyer by, for example, asking them about the colour that they prefer. If the buyer answers with a colour, then the sales representative has known that the buyer's interest is high. Simply because the

customer has already imagined owning that car in a particular colour. Therefore using the close trial technique is very helpful in determining your prospective client's level of interest. In fact, trial closes builds interest from your customer by getting them to think of you as a service provider who has what they need.

Assumptive Close

Assumptive close is considered one of the most effective closing techniques. Simply it is a statement that implies that you will do business with your prospect. Similar to the trial close, the assumptive close has the same aim to gets the prospective customer to consider you as a service provider. It should also be used throughout the sales process to determine and build interest. Nevertheless, unlike the trial close, the assumptive close is normally posed as a statement. The close should be a very conscious part of the sales process and when you enter into a closing opportunity, confirm that you have:

- Successfully created enough interest in your service.
- Familiarize yourself with closing options.
- Have clear pricing objectives.
- Have mental and emotional clarity about closing.
- Have prepared a way to accept payment.

Have an agreement or contract ready if it is necessary Alternate Choice Close:

"Alternative choice close" is an extremely strong and very powerful closing technique, which gives your prospective client several options on any particular aspect of your service. The alternative choice close is formed as a question that prompts your prospective client to consider how to do business with you or not to do it with you. This is possible to do throughout the sales process.

You should limit your choices to two possibilities when using the alternative choice close. After the potential customer answers the question by selecting one of the possibilities, have them commit to specifics immediately after that. A free analysis or a free offer form is highly recommended to be added to your website. As it is going to help to initiate the sales process by letting you cultivate a contact with the potential client to determine their needs and to educate them on how you can become a solution to their needs. Closing and selling is not a way of manipulating your prospective clients but as an opportunity for you to show them that your service can serve their needs. It is vital that you are successful at closing and selling, and persuading your client that there is a great need for your service. Your job is to be proactive by making others aware that they need your service. As a salesperson, you know that there is always some resistance to change among those considering using your services.

Selling and closing are the tools by which you can overcome that resistance.

Additional Closing Tips:

- Ask for the order.
- Ask for the order again.
- Ask for commitment using the alternate choice close.
- Create a sense of urgency with temporary discounts and promotions.
- Keep your energy and enthusiasm high, don't lose steam at the end, don't oversell, ask for the order and quietly wait for a response.
- Move into closing seamlessly and without hesitation.
- Visualize yourself successfully getting the business.
- Ask for the order again.

Remember, you should not be hesitant or fearful in promoting your services proactively. As business owners, we know that most people need our services. Take it as a conscious mission to improve the sales and closing processes and then use as many of the techniques as possible in order to help more people and essentially grow your business.

Additional Closing Techniques

If it's a low-ticket retail purchase, most people won't say "Okay, I'll buy it!" out of their own initiative, especially if it's a purchase that will require a financial commitment. In order to be successful at closing a sale, you'll have to convince them by using these ten sales closing techniques. The idea behind closing a sale is learning to make him ask the right questions that will make the buyer want the product. This is not to say that sales closing techniques should be clever, manipulative, or deceptive. Rather, closing a sale should come as a natural conclusion of the selling process. Here is what many consider to some the top ten sales closing techniques that will make the customer say the magic words, "I'll take it!"

Affordable Close

Price is the key element of any buying operation; actually, it is the first objection most people have about buying a product, especially a major one like a car or house. But did you know that "I can't afford to buy it" is more an excuse than an actual objection? You'll need to restructure the payment scheme according to your client's budget in order to change his prospective mind; this is called the Affordable Close technique. To do that, you have to find out their budget and how much they can spare and present a payment scheme that can fit the buyer's capacity to pay. Supplement this by showing the price of not buying, e.g. the current car's cost of continued ownership.

You can also make the product more affordable by stripping it down to the bare minimum and selling the other options, accessories, or add-ons as separate products. Alternately, you can present a different product that fits their budget. Your very last option is to bring the price down to something the buyer is prepared to pay.

Opportunity Cost Close

The "opportunity cost" is the cost of not doing something as there is the cost for everything in the world of business. We can understand that the cost is not equal for the price as the price refers to what the buyers pay, but the cost may refer to the problems that may face you such as "hassle" and "dissatisfaction", which are not valued by money.

No Hassle Close

The No-hassle close is the way that makes you win the prospective buyer by making the purchase process very simple and avoid him any trouble or hassle matters. For example, you can fill all forms and papers for him.

Best Time Close

If your client says that he does not have the time now, then try to persuade him that it is the best time for that, as when the client went away, he will not be back again. So you should try to close the deal now. You can do that by showing him the

advantages of your product and how it will be suitable at this time.

Minor Points Close

You shall persuade the buyer to close the deal by closing the minor points that mean that you ask him about small details like the colour, delivery time, fitting options, etc., that may make him decide easier and help you to close the sale as well. At the same time, you should know the factors that may help him to take the decision.

1-2-3 Close

There are three main items in this technique Cost, Quality and time. There are two ways for doing this; they may be together to make a single point or may be separated in order to gain greater coverage. We all know that all customers want free, perfect and delivery on-time products.

Adjournment Close

We know that the relationship between the seller and client is very important as it will be a long-term relationship. So it will be very bad to push him to take a decision before he is ready. So you can make an Adjournment Close that usually is a great deal for your client to take time before he can decide what he really needs. The Adjournment Close is better and easier to manage when the salesperson is in a face-to-face meeting than waiting

on a call phone. So you will tell him that you will put his deal on the table and give him time to think.

Use this when:

1. You are seeking a long-term relationship, and if the client makes the wrong deal, that may affect the relationship.

2. You do not need to make the sale today, for perhaps you've made your quota, and this sale would be just fine for next month.

3. You are confident that the client likes your products and he will come back.

4. You know that they are not going to decide now.

5. Given more time, it is very likely that they will buy more if they are at the edge of a budgetary period and their current funds are low.

Balance-Sheet Close

It works through building Trust by seeming to be taking a balanced and fair approach. It can save customers from wasting their time, and it helps them to know their positive and negative sides, so their lists will be different.

Squeeze Close

Give the customer three different offers. First, offer them something that is well beyond their target budget number but

not quite so far beyond them that they would not consider it. Ideally, it is something they will look at wistfully but just cannot justify the purchase. Then, as another option, offer them a good deal that is within their price bracket. It may not have all the bells and whistles they wanted, but it is clearly a very good value for the price they want to pay. Lastly, offer a severely stripped-down deal in which very little of what they want is included. More than likely, they should, and probably will, go for the middle option.

Bracket Close

The Bracket Close works by contrasting the preferred option both upwards and downwards. Rejecting a higher option lets the other person feel good about not spending too much. By comparison, the option they choose seems quite obvious in comparison, and they may even feel you have saved them some money. Rejecting the lower option tells the customer to feel they are not cheap and can't afford something of value, such as the service you provide.

Charmer

Deal with your customers gently and express your admiration for their personalities. Boost their self-confidence and make them feel that they have the necessary expertise to determine what they want to buy. You have to entice the customers and massage their ego to become more concerned about themselves.

Link your customers to the product and let them feel that the product meets their personal needs. Praise their earlier decisions and express your confidence that they can take new successful ones.

Carrier "Set Up" Package

When starting a business with a new carrier, you will need to get them "Set Up" in your carrier database; you will need to collect the following information from the motor carrier.

Broker Carrier Agreement

This agreement will regulate the provided services by the carrier for your freight brokerage. It will also list the exclusionary rules of how the carrier should operate and also help prevent back solicitation of your customers. Company Profile

You'll need to have a "Company Profile" to obtain a better idea of the capabilities that the motor carrier possesses; the carrier's company profile should include the following information:

- Payment Information
- Factoring Company
- Type of Equipment
- Dispatch Contacts
- Operating Areas
- Emergency Contact Information
- Endorsements
- Insurance Contacts

5.8 Daily routine

Being a freight broker will involve a huge amount of phone time and being on your computer within your daily routine. You have to communicate with potential shippers efficiently to discover their needs. You will be very busy finding carriers or just providing lane quotes for the shipper to use at a later date. These communications are very important to build your database of contacts and getting your name out there to the shippers. The first two to four hours of your day are the most critical. You can maximize your time by receiving calls and booking loads for the shipments you posted the previous day; rather than spending that time performing freight inquiries, there forfeit is preferred to implement Inquiries in the afternoon when things begin to slow down. Customer freight inquiries should be looked at as another form of time management that can make you money.

- The initial load details that will be collected by each broker will generally be: commodity or cargo type, pick up and deliver locations, type of carrier required anticipated rate for the load and any special instructions to the carrier regarding the load.

- As soon as you collect the previous, you will begin entering these notes into your contact manager, indicating when and where this shipper's loads move and also the frequency of shipping. Remember to start as early as possible, preferably by 6:00 AM. These offices start work early as the shippers are usually preparing to arrange their freight early in the morning.

- After establishing your relationship with a shipper, getting loads wouldn't be a problem. The shipper will tell you what lanes and carriers are needed. You have to note everything about the load since this information will be relayed in detail to the carriers that are interested in moving the freight.

- The shipper will give you either a rate that they want to pay for the load, or they will ask you to submit a quote for the lane. Once you have the numbers nailed down, you now know what to offer the carrier to haul the freight. On average, freight brokers make about 10% of the load amount. Try to average 15%-20% of the load. It might take a bit longer to find a carrier, but it will work out better at the end of the day.

- In case you do not have a carrier already in mind for the freight, then you should start posting on load boards such as; Internet TruckStop, Get Loaded, or The DAT. However, they are not the only load boards on the Internet but are the load boards that receive the most traffic and most prospective carriers.

- Once the load has been posted, then you can move on to find more freight, or you may start calling your database for interest in the load. While calling the database, you will also start to receive calls from prospective carriers who saw the postings on the load boards. Once you have reached an agreement with a carrier to accept the line haul, immediately call the shipper to inform them that the load is "Covered" and that you have a truck.

- If you have reached a deal with the shipper, then you'll obtain from them the rate confirmation and load sheet for you to sign and return immediately. It might take a while to receive the rate confirmation; this is common as most shippers are extremely busy moving several loads.

- Now it is time to clear your carrier through the FMCSA to make sure they have no prior history of accidents and that they have the proper insurance. Once this has been done, you will then fax your "Sct Up" package to the carrier for him to sign and return.

- Once the carrier has completed your initial "Set Up" package, you will then prepare the rate confirmation sheet and loading order and fax that to them. They will also sign and fax that back to your office for your records.

- Now that you have received the signed rate confirmation from the carrier dispatcher, you have to call the truck driver and verify the entire load details and dispatch them to the location to pick up the load.

- The carrier should contact you daily with a status of the whereabouts of their truck. This is called a "Call Check". It is the standard operating procedure to impose fines to the carrier for failure to comply with your "Call Check" policy. This policy should be notated on the rate confirmation sheet.

- As soon as the load has been delivered, contact the shipper to let them know the status. It is the standard operating procedure to require the carrier to fax a copy of the signed bill of lading when the load has been accepted. Then you are aware of any problems with the load or to verify delivery to the recipient.

- If there have been any problems with the load, you should contact all parties immediately, i.e., Shipper, Carrier, and Recipient, and resolve them amicably. This is your responsibility as a broker.

Though this may all seem to be complicated and a very mundane procedure, however, but you have to follow those procedures strictly to ensure smooth deliveries and also returning customers. Keep in mind that all situations that may

arise concerning any given load can be resolved with the exception of force majeure incidents "Acts Of God".

Dispatching

Always be calm and speak professionally; never get into a verbal altercation with a driver while he is dispatched on your load, as you don't need to take the risk of getting into a situation that could potentially turn bad.

Dispatching means the process of assigning motor carriers to your loads. Once you and your client have discussed the line-haul rate, you will have to start searching for a motor carrier willing to haul the load. There are many ways to find motor carriers. You will have to complete some formalities like signing the set-up contract, preparing the rate sheet and scrutinizing the safety ratings of the motor carrier before you can start the dispatch process. It is important to complete all the formalities to prevent any legal or financial issues at a later stage.

If you are brokering a load, you will be following the roles and responsibilities of a contractor. At the same time, availing of the services of the motor carrier, you need to have an arrangement or 'set-up' with the carrier. 'Set-up' means the contract agreement which has been chalked out between you and the motor carrier. In case you aren't aware of the process of creating a contract, then you should seek assistance from a lawyer who will draft a proper contract with the help of any sample contract form.

There are numerous forms & agreements which have to be filled before you can begin to dispatch. Such forms and agreements are used during various stages of the dispatch process. However, it is important to know the purpose of these forms and agreements.

The majority of the companies include a lot of legal terms in their set up contracts to protect their prospecting endeavour. It is also necessary for the brokers to have a 'back end solution clause', which is informally called a 'non-compete agreement with their set up contract to avoid the possibility of the carrier hauling directly from the clients. Thus, as a freight broker, you are sure that the efforts of procuring a client have not gone to waste. In case the motor carrier ends up directly dealing with your customer, then it will be mandatory for them to share a certain percentage of the revenue they have earned from that customer. Thus, this is the best solution to safeguard your business.

Motor Carrier Snapshot/Safety Rating

In case you do not have any set-up agreement with a carrier and intend to dispatch for the first time, then it is better to find out more about the Motor Carrier Snapshot or Safety Rating. By doing so, you can find out a lot about the motor carrier. Some vital information you will get is the number of units on file with the FMCSA, the drivers they have employed and their safety snapshot. You will also get to know they're 'Out of Service' ratio.

A motor carrier can be termed 'Out of Service' by the USDOT in case it does not adhere to the regulations which have been laid down by the FMCSA. But this is not always accurate. For instance, in case a carrier has just one truck and yet was given a 100% Out of Service rating, it may mean that the truck was being handled by the owner himself and had once been declared 'Out of Service' due to a small or major issue.

This could have happened unintentionally due to ignorance about the law. Besides, if the carrier has two trucks, out of which one got an 'Out of Service' label, then it amounts to 50%, which indeed cuts a sorry picture. However, if the same carrier had 100 trucks, out of which one was labelled 'Out of Service', then the rating would be a mere 1%.

Hence, focus on looking for a carrier that has a low Out Service Percentage. However, this will not make sense unless you find out about the total number of units they possess.

After you dispatch the carrier, do not assume that everything is moving smoothly. You should keep in contact with the truck driver directly or the agent and dispatch personnel responsible for that carrier.

Typically, you would ask the carrier to contact you:

- When the truck is loaded
- Each morning or once daily while under the load
- Immediately after the load is delivered to the final destination

Have you ever heard the term GAP? It stands for Grab a Pen! Each time the carrier contacts you for a check call, grab a Pen!

Make a note of the following:

- Who you spoke with?
- Motor Carrier Snapshot/Safety Rating
- Broker/Shipper Agreement:
- The date and time (always use your local time zone)
- The driver's location (or nearest town if you're entering these notes into the software)
- The estimated time of arrival at the final destination

Your customer depends on you to know where their freight is and whether or not it's going to be on time for delivery. And if there is a change in plans, such as a mechanical failure or bad weather conditions, your customer may also need to notify their customer. If the motor carrier does not contact you, you should contact them each day while they are dispatched under your load. When contacting customers and carriers, consider the time zone in which they are located.

Dispatch Cancellations

Cancellation occurs when the carrier has already signed a rate confirmation agreement and agreed to transport your freight,

then, for whatever reason, chooses not to haul it. In case the carrier fails to pick up a load after agreeing to do so, you will have to find an alternative truck to service your customer. Motor carriers use backhaul loads to get back into their home or to an area where they have direct shipper contacts. Obviously, motor carriers can secure better paying freight from their own customers.

For this reason, carriers opt to pre-plan their trucks in a direction that will put them closer to their direct customer base.

Carrier Fines & Carrier Communication

Brokers will use a system of fines to impose on carriers to insure the successful transportation of the cargo and communication throughout the load. It is simply not enough to ask the carrier to do his job and move the load with no problems. A freight brokerage is not a daycare centre, so we may not put the carrier in "Time Out" if he fails to hold up to his part of the contract moving the load.

A freight brokerage will use carrier fines to help avoid a multitude of problems. Below is a list of infractions in which a carrier will be fined. I have also included a suggested amount to charge for each infraction.

Daily Call Check ($100.00 Per Instance) -It is important to impose fines on carriers who do not

Maintain communication with your brokerage. These fines are to be clearly listed on your rate confirmation sheet to the carrier. If these are not listed on your rate confirmation sheet, you have no legal recourse to impose the fine on the carrier.

Late Delivery (25% Of the Load) -This is generally only enforced if a shipper has placed time constraints on the arrival of the load. The above amount is on the high end of the spectrum. Fines could range from $100 -$1,500 per load.

Failure to Fax BOL's within a specified time ($100.00) -A number of shippers want the BOL's faxed to them within 4 -6 hours of the load being delivered.

Dispatching of Drivers (%10 of the load) -Fine is enforced if the carrier requires you, the broker, to dispatch his driver. This is the carrier's responsibility. Do not create additional work for yourself.

Truck No Show Fee - ($250.00) -I bill the carrier's company this fine if the truck does not show up to take the load. This is a rarity.

Failure To Load Complete Order -Occasionally, trucks will not load a complete order as prescribed by a shipper. It is my recommendation that you place specific quantities needed to be loaded on the rate confirmation sheet. If these are not on the rate confirmation sheet, the truck can literally leave half your order behind. This fine will vary depending on the load. This is on an as-needed basis. Freight's Types

LTL - Less than Truckload

Define LTL Freight?

LTL freight refers to Less Than Truckload, which usually weighs between 151 and 20,000 lb. (68 and 9,072 kg). The main task of Less Than Truckload carriers is collecting freight from shippers and consolidate that freight into enclosed trailers to the delivery place, where this freight will be further sorted for additional distances. Drivers usually make deliveries first, and then they make pickups after the trailer has been emptied; generally, most pickups are made in the afternoon, and most deliveries are made in the morning.

How does the LTL model work?

Pickup/delivery drivers, as a rule, have particular routes that they travel every day or several times a week, the driver has a good chance to develop a rapport with their customers. Once the driver has filled their trailer or completed their assigned route, the driver returns to their destination for unloading. The trailer will be unloaded, and the individual shipments have been then weighed and inspected to verify their conformity to the description contained in the accompanying paperwork.

All LTL freight is subject to inspection for this purpose, though not all freight is inspected. Freight that is shipped LTL (less than truckload) has an increased risk of damage or loss as the freight may be handled multiple times while passing through

freight terminals and being consolidated with other shipments on its way to the ultimate destination. Next, the freight has been then loaded onto an outbound trailer, which will later forward the freight to breakbulk, a connection, or to the delivering terminal. An LTL shipment may be handled only in transit, or it may be handled many times before final delivery is accomplished.

The times for LTL freight are more than that for FTL, as they are not related only to the distance between shipper and sender. But LTL transit depends on the making network of Terminals and Break bulks, which have been operated by the nominated carrier, and the carriers belong to agents and interline partners. For instance, if a shipment is delivered by the same freight terminal, or if the freight must be sorted only in transportation, the freight will be delivered the next day after pickups. If the freight must be sorted and routed many times or if there is more than a line haul that is required for transportation to the delivery place, and then the time of transportation will be longer. So, if the delivery is going to remote areas, the transit time will be increased.

There are several advantages for the LTL carrier. The most important one is that a shipment may be transported for a fraction of the cost. The second advantage is that the accessorial services are usually available from LTL carriers, but it is not offered by FTL carriers. These optional services include liftgate

service at pickup or delivery, residential (also known as "non-commercial") service at pickup or delivery, inside delivery, notification prior to delivery, freeze protection, and others. These services are usually charged at predetermined fees that are based on weight.

What's the difference between an LTL Common Carrier and a Volume Consolidator?

Common carriers usually handle small LTL 1-5 pallets less than 4500 lbs. Common carriers use the NMFC classification 50-500 to charge for freight. Usually, there is a maximum linear foot before it has to change to a volume spot rate quote…rule of thumb: if your freight is over 10 feet in length, double-check your LTL rates and possibly get a volume rate quote. If your freight is light and the linear feet you take up is more than 10 feet, you may be violating their low-density minimum charge rule.

Consolidators do exactly what the root word is; they consolidate freight. They charge based on the linear feet you take up in the trailer. So if you have 10 non-stackable pallets with dimensions of 48 x 48 x 96 you will be taking up 20 linear feet. You will be charged for 20 linear feet, not for classification. Some things to keep in mind, you are only entitled to 1000 lbs. per linear foot. So if your 10 non-stackable pallets weight 18klbs but only take up 20 linear feet, your price would be the same. But if your 10

non-stackable pallets weigh 21500lbs, you are entitled to pay for 22 linear feet because of the 1000lbs per linear foot.

Carrier Integration of FTL & LTL

Shippers that have a large volume of LTL freight may choose a Full Truckload Carrier to move the freight directly to a break-bulk facility of an LTL carrier. For instance, if a North Carolina shipper has a large number of shipments for Western US States such as CA, NV, OR, WA, and ID, then the shipper can realize significant cost savings by having an FTL carrier, known as a Linehaul carrier, transport the freight to a break-bulk facility nearest the centre of such shipments in terms of the carriers network. In this case, the shipper may choose to send the freight to a break-bulk in CA. The use of an FTL carrier to transport this freight will save you money because the freight will travel fewer miles in the LTL carrier's network, and a further benefit will be realized because the freight will not be unloaded and reloaded as many times. This reduces the incidence of loss and damage in transit.

Double Load vs LTL Load

As long as each piece of freight is within the standard legal dimensions, the weight of a shipment is the primary concern. Distinguishing a double load from an LTL load begins first with the origin, destination, and timeline similarities. Does the load pick up or deliver to points close to the other load? Are loading times flexible enough to make room for the other loads delivery

times? If so, the next things to examine are weight and load dimension. The main factor in determining whether a double load can be booked is the carrier's ability to handle the job with respect to the trailer, size, type, etc. If you maintain a good carrier equipment list, the chances you'll have to swiftly recognize when a double load is possible will greatly increase.

5.9 Freight classes

The National Motor Freight Classification (NMFC) is a standard that offers a comparison of commodities moving in interstate and foreign commerce. In concept, it is near to the groupings or systems that serve many other industries. Commodities are grouped into one of 18 classes—from class NO. 50 to the high of class 500—based on an evaluation of four transportation characteristics: density, storability, handling and liability. Together, these characteristics establish a commodity's "transportability." The four transportation characteristics were prescribed by the Interstate Commerce Commission (ICC) in 1983 and then mandated by its successor agency, the Surface Transportation Board (STB). Although the ICC no longer exists and the STB no longer regulates the classification process, by analyzing commodities on the basis of these characteristics and only on the basis of these characteristics, the NMFC provides both carriers and shippers with a standard by which to begin

negotiations and greatly simplifies the comparative evaluation of many thousands of products moving in today's competitive marketplace.

General Freight

Shipments that are larger than about 7,000 kg (15,432 lb.) are generally classified as "Truckload" (TL) in the United States of America since it is more efficient and economical for a large shipment to have exclusive use of one larger trailer rather than share space on a smaller LTL trailer. The total weight of a loaded truck (tractor and trailer, 5-axle rig) cannot exceed 36,000 kg (79,366 lb.) in the U.S. In ordinary circumstances, long-haul equipment will weigh about 15,000 kg (33,069 lb.); leaving about 20,000 kg (44,092 lb.) of freight capacity. Similarly, a load is limited to the space available in the trailer; normally 48 ft. (14.63 m) or 53 ft. (16.15 m) long and 2.6 m (102.4 in) wide and 2.7 m (8 ft. 10.3 in) high (13 ft. 6 in/4.11 m high overall). While express, parcel, and LTL shipments are always intermingled with other shipments on a single piece of equipment and are typically reloaded across multiple pieces of equipment during their transport. TL shipments usually travel as the only shipment on a trailer and usually deliver on exactly the same trailer as they are picked up on.

Truckload (TL) carriers generally charge a rate per kilometre or mile that depends on the distance, geographic location of the delivery, goods are being shipped, the type of required

equipment, and the time of required service. TL shipments usually receive a variety of surcharges very similar to those described for LTL shipments above. In the TL market, there are thousands more small carriers than in the LTL market; so the use of transportation intermediaries or "brokers" is extremely common.

Facilitating pickups or deliveries at the carrier's terminal is another cost-saving method. In this way, shippers avoid any accessorial fees that might normally be charged for lift gate, residential pickup/delivery, inside pickup/delivery or notifications/appointments. Carriers or intermediaries can provide shippers with the address and phone number for the closest shipping terminal to the origin and/or destination.

Shipping experts increase their service and costs by similar rates from many carriers, brokers, and online marketplaces. When the shippers get rates from different providers, they may find quite a wide range in the pricing offered. If a shipper uses a broker, freight forwarder, or another transportation intermediary, it is common for the shipper to receive a copy of the carrier's Federal Operating Authority. Freight brokers and intermediaries should be licensed by the Federal Highway Administration. Experienced shippers avoid unlicensed brokers and forwarders; because if brokers are working outside the law by not having a Federal Operating License, the shipper may face problems. Also, shippers normally ask for a copy of the broker's insurance certificate and any specific insurance that applies to the shipment.

Produce Freight

The appetite of America for food and delicacies keep Reefer's running continuously from all parts of the country. Produce Warehouses, Wholesalers and Supermarkets need to replenish their inventories daily with fresh vegetables to keep up with the demand of the American consumer. Produce is the easiest type of freight to get that. Your customer will be the Grower, Packer, Produce Cooler, Produce Broker or the Consignee himself.

Produce loads are generally very competitive for pricing that depends on the type of produce. Shippers will require minimizing the carrier load or paying on weight. Shippers will do this so they can be assured that the carrier loads are the maximum amount of product by law. Outlined below is how most shippers will require the carrier to load for specific types of produce around the country.

- **Rates** -Overall rates for the transportation of produce are most generally low throughout the country. Unless you have access to a core group of carriers, these types of loads will require a lot of work.

- **Claims** -To keep claims to a minimum, use carriers with a great deal of experience in hauling produce. These carriers will have newer equipment that is maintained accordingly, temperature thermometers, and good insurance.

- **Detention** -Inexperienced carriers will frequently attempt to bill you for detention because of the long periods of wait time to load for produce. This is because of product unavailability, a number of carriers loading or seasonal delays.

- **Carrier Fines** -Produce shippers and receivers are notorious for implementing fines for delays in delivery. These fines are incurred because the receiver has to purchase their product at terminal markets in their area. Shippers will then impose fines for the price differences to the carrier due to the delay.

5.10 Consigner Procedures

When produce or refrigerated freight is prepared for shipping, it is most generally fresh from the field. When your carrier arrives for their scheduled pick up, the product may or may not be ready due to product availability. They will be waiting in line until the product arrives at the shipping location.

Produce must be cooled down prior

When the shipment is loaded on trucks or spoiled, damage may occur during transit. This will occur because the outer layers of products that are palletized, whether bagged, boxed or loose, will cool down to the temperature of the trailer. However, they

will also serve as an insulation barrier against the product that is underneath the top layers. Encourage your carrier to exercise diligence as produce shippers file the most insurance claims on freight because the profit margins on their products are so slim, and freight charges are usually very high during peak seasons and areas.

Consignee Procedures

When produce or refrigerated freight is delivered, most generally consignees have a set of guidelines that they should follow before receipt of the freight. If these guidelines are not followed, the load could be rejected, and a claim situation could arise. Here is a scenario of a consignee receiving procedures.

The condition of the trailer will be examined. If there are any insects or rodent infestations, the load will be rejected. If the floor of the trailer is dirty, the load will be rejected.

Pulp temperatures of the product are taken and recorded from each pallet removed from the trailer. (Industry standard is tail, middle, and nose of the trailer.) These recorded temperatures are then compared to tolerant temperatures for the product. Product quality is examined on each pallet.

Refrigerated

When you are transporting refrigerated loads, there are several variables you need to be aware of prior to the loading of cargo and during the lifecycle of the load. The list below is containing items you need to be aware of that your carrier will go through while transporting your freight, and also that will happen if a problem occurs once delivered. Refrigerated, also known as reefer loads, require increased rates because it costs the carrier more money to run a refrigeration unit on their trailer to keep the goods from spoiling. You should try to negotiate an additional 20 to 40 cents per mile above your standard rate to help them cover the fuel and maintenance costs for that reefer unit.

- Your carrier must arrive Clean & Dry to load your cargo.

- Your carrier must arrive at the consignee Pre Cooled to the determined temperature for the load.

- When your cargo is loaded, your carrier will need to make sure that the cargo is not loaded above the danger line in his trailer. If this happens, the cool air will not circulate properly, and your load could be damaged.

- When your cargo is loaded, your carrier will need to make sure the air chute in the trailer is not blocked as the air will not circulate, and the load will run at inconsistent temperatures.

- Most shippers will require the load to run at consistent temperatures during transport.

- When your load delivers, whether it is produced or other food-grade products, the consignee will check the freight before he accepted it to make sure the load was transported correctly. If there has been evidence of a problem such as thawing, discolouration or wilting of your products, the consignee will likely reject the load. The carrier, at this point, does have the option of contacting the U.S.D.A. and requesting an on-site inspection of the cargo. This is at the carrier's expense. The cost of this inspection will generally range from $200 -$250.00. If the U.S.D.A. determines that load has not been compromised or that the evidence of spoilage is not the fault of the carrier, then the consigner can not reject the freight.

- If the freight has evidence of spoilage and the load is rejected, the consignee will have to notate this on the "Bill of Lading".

- Once this happens, your shipper will then want to possibly move the freight to another location in the area if they can find a buyer for the product depending upon the condition of the goods. In both cases, you and the carrier are now in charge, and you re-negotiate the new freight rate for the load to the new location or back to the original consigner of the product.

- If the carrier has been found at fault, generally, the load will be rejected by the consignee. The carrier will then be responsible for disposing of the freight. A claim will be filed by the shipper to the carrier's insurance company, and they will instruct the carrier on how to get rid of the contents of the trailer.

Time-sensitive loads, also known as Expedited loads, are handled by team drivers. You should secure rates comparable to that of a reefer load. If it is both refrigerated and time-sensitive, set your per-mile rate accordingly. If you plan to coordinate dry van or refrigerated freight, there are two terms you should familiarize yourself with lumper charges.

What are Lumper Charges?

A freight lumper is basically a dockworker or a driver assistant whose work involves loading and unloading trucks. Often they are hired independently by shippers as well as receivers for loading or unloading their trucks. In fact, companies are more comfortable outsourcing these activities to lumpers. Typically lumpers deal with delivering the products from inbound carriers, which would have to be unloaded by the drivers.

Truck drivers have a very busy and hectic schedule, and they seldom get any free time. So if they hire a lumper for the unloading process, then they can take some rest while the trailer is unloaded. They can also get ready for their next assignment. The drivers who are required to segregate the load, split it, or modify it to make it fit in the warehouse of the consigner often leave this task to the lumpers.

Due to insurance liability, the drivers aren't allowed to use forklifts and similar motorized equipment for unloading their trailers.

For dry vans and frozen or refrigerated freight, the consignee provides the driver with a pallet jacket for manually unloading the trailer. In a Driver Unload, the driver has to personally unload the trailer, and if needed, segregate it before storage.

When it comes to Driver Assist, the driver will have to help in the process of loading and unloading. In both cases, the carrier is compensated.

Often carriers let their truck driver's work as lumpers or driver assistants to make some quick money. However, some restrict their drivers in being a part of the loading and unloading process. At times carriers are operated by the owners who do not agree to unload the trailer themselves, and so they have to hire and compensate a lumper or a driver assistant to complete the task.

Requirements for Freight Delivery

Make it a point to ask the customer whether the load is a Driver Unload or a Driver Assist, and pass the information to your carrier. However, if you fail to do so, then the driver will assume that he can take a rest at the destination. Besides, the driver will not be prepared to unload the trailer and segregate the containers which contain the boxes. This is an unpleasant situation and is sure to tarnish your reputation since truck

drivers tend to take communication flaws to heart. They prefer to be well prepared, and hence you should do the needful and find out the proper details before updating the driver or carrier.

Dry vans and refrigerated shipments often hire lumpers or driver assistants. Hence if your freight includes this, then you should find out whether the customers need a lumper service or not.

Lumper service rates are not static, and it depends on the type of work they are required to do. Besides, the amount depends on how much they are expected to load & unload. You do not have any say in the negotiation. The remuneration is decided by the carrier or the driver on reaching the destination.

CHAPTER 6: LOCATING AND SETTING UP

One of the most attractive features of a freight brokerage is that the physical start-up costs are minimal. You don't need a warehouse or loading dock like a carrier or freight forwarder. Because your customers are unlikely to visit your site, you don't need an attractive welcome room or beautiful offices. In reality, although having a commercial site has its benefits, a freight broker is an excellent company to start and operate from home.

MCD Transportation was founded by Cathy Davis in her house, but it expanded quickly enough to need commercial premises after just eight months. The location of your business is determined by your resources and objectives. Many brokers start out from their homes with the intention of expanding into commercial space once they have a few customers, which is a great approach.

The most important advantage of establishing a home-based company is that it drastically lowers the amount of startup and early operational cash required. But there's more to think about than just the money upfront. Do you have a dedicated office space, or will you be working at the dining room table? Are you able to set up a comfortable workplace with all of the necessary tools and equipment? Is it possible to divide your workspace from the rest of the home so that you have privacy while you're working and a place to escape "the office" when you're not?

You must be in a handy location so that you can physically contact shippers and potential shippers. If you want to employ administrative assistance, your office must be big enough to accommodate their requirements, and parking must be accessible.

Establishing a business at a commercial location, on the other hand, necessitates a larger initial investment than starting a business from home. If you take this route, your choices are quite wide, and your decision should be mainly driven by the market and growth objectives you've established for your company. Consider executive suites, light industrial parks, and office towers.

Unless you have a very big house, you'll find that renting a commercial space enables you to build a more efficient and practical setup than you could in a spare bedroom. Just be cautious while looking for a place to live. Because rental prices and lease periods differ, it's important to shop around.

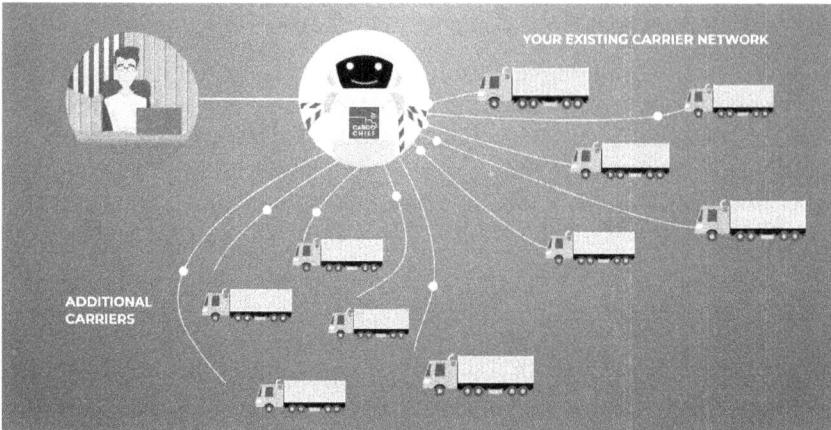

Put It in Writing

Whether you want to establish a single home-based company, a small family firm, or a transportation empire, you'll need a documented business plan to get started. This allows you to think about what you're doing, identify your strengths and limitations, and brainstorm solutions to problems before you encounter them in real life. Writing a business plan is more than just a job; it lays the groundwork and establishes the vision for your firm.

Worst-case scenarios should be included in your company strategy. You'll be better off planning ahead for what you'll do if things don't go as planned. Consider problems like equipment failures, absent workers (even for good reasons), uncollectible bills, and other difficulties that come with running a company.

The Agent Option

Some brokers may choose to hire agents in order to expand their business. Agents are independent contractors that represent your business in a certain region. This allows you to provide a local presence even if you don't have enough business to warrant establishing your own location.

Along similar lines, rather than beginning out as a broker, you may want to try starting out as an agent. Many brokers have representatives all throughout the nation (and a structure like that may be part of your long-term plan). Because agents aren't required to fulfil all of the criteria of brokers and work from home, their starting costs are low, usually consisting of a computer, phone, and fax machine. The agent's responsibilities are comparable to those of a broker, but the agent works under the broker's supervision, and the broker is responsible for problems such as paying carriers and maintaining the necessary surety bonds.

6.1 Naming your company

The name of your business is an essential marketing tool. A well-chosen name can help you succeed. If you choose a name that is ineffectual, you will have to work more to advertise your business and let people know what you have to offer.

Your business name should clearly state what you do and appeal to your target market. It should be succinct, memorable, and catchy. It should also be simple to speak and spell; individuals who are unable to pronounce your business name may utilise you, but they will not recommend anybody else to you.

Cathy Davis considered a variety of names before settling on her initials. Ron Williamson came up with RJW Logistics Inc. by combining his and his wife's initials. He wanted a name that no one else was using. Many freight brokers name their businesses after the area in which they operate.

Take a methodical approach to name your business. Once you've narrowed your options down to two or three, do the following steps:

1. Make sure the name is useful and practical. Is it clear and concise in expressing what you do? Is it simple to pronounce and spell? Is it memorable for the right reasons? To assist you in assessing the name's effect, ask a few of your friends and acquaintances to participate as a focus group.

2. Look for possible market disputes in your area. Check to see if any other local or regional businesses in your market area have a similar name that may lead to confusion.

3. Verify whether or not it is lawful to do so. Depending on the legal structure you select, you may accomplish this in a variety of ways. Typically, sole proprietorships and partnerships operating under a name other than the owner(s) must register their fake name with the county, city, or state. Even though it isn't necessary, it's a good idea since it ensures that no one else will be able to use the same name. It may sometimes be as easy as submitting a "doing business as" application (dba). Corporations are often known by their corporate names. In any instance, be sure the name you want is accessible by contacting the relevant regulatory body.

NAMING YOUR TRANSPORT BUSINESS

8 Vital Dos and Don'ts

Don't Use More than 3 Words

✓ Lightning Logistics
✗ First Call Auto Transport

Do Make it Easy to Pronounce

✓ Apple Express
✗ Thorough Transport Inc.

Don't Limit Yourself to a Local City Name

✓ Jet Delivery
✗ Tupelo Transportation

Do Poll FB Friends on Your Top 3 Choices

VOTE

Do Conduct a Trademark Search

uspto

Do Get the .com Domain Name

✓ marketexpress.com
✗ marketexpress.biz

Don't Use Hyphens in the Domain Name

✓ roadrebel.com
✗ road-rebel.com

4. Make sure it's safe to use on the internet. Consider coming up with something new if someone else is currently utilising your name as an internet address.

5. Check to see if the name clashes with any other names on the trademark registry in your state. Your state's Department of Commerce can assist you or point you in the right direction. You

could also examine the United States Patent and Trademark Office's trademark registry (PTO).

Once your selected name passes these criteria, you must safeguard it by registering it with the proper state agency; your state Department of Commerce may assist you with this. You should also register the name with the PTO if you want to conduct business on a national basis.

6.2 Choosing a legal structure

The legal form of your freight brokerage will be one of the first choices you'll have to make. This is a critical choice. It has an impact on your financial responsibility, the amount of taxes you pay, and your level of control over the business. It also has an impact on your capacity to recruit investors and eventually sell the company. Legal structure, on the other hand, should not be confused with operational structure.

The proprietor of a sole proprietorship, the partners of a partnership, and the shareholders of a corporation are the owners. The limited liability company (LLC) is a business form that combines the tax benefits of a sole proprietorship with the liability protection of a corporation. The laws governing LLCs differ by state; for the most up-to-date information, contact your state's Department of Corporations. Owners of sole proprietorships and partnerships have complete control over how their businesses are run. In a corporation, shareholders usually elect directors, who then elect executives, who then hire others to manage and work for the business. It is, however, completely feasible for a company to have just one shareholder and operate as a sole proprietorship. In any event, how you want to run the business should not be a significant consideration when deciding on legal forms.

So, how do you choose a legal structure? The first point, according to Bernstein, is who is making the legal structure decisions. If you're establishing a business by yourself, you don't have to consider anybody else's preferences. "However, if there are many individuals engaged, you need to think about how you'll interact in the business," he adds. "You should also think about asset protection and minimising your responsibility in case things don't go as planned."

Another thing to consider is your target audience and how they will perceive your structure. "There is a tendency to think that the legal structure of a company is related to the sophistication of the owners, with the single proprietor being the least sophisticated and the corporation being the most complex," Bernstein adds. Because your target market will be other companies big enough to transport significant quantities of goods, incorporating will almost certainly improve your image.

Regardless of your image, the greatest benefit of establishing a company is asset protection, which, according to Bernstein, is the act of ensuring that assets you don't wish to invest into the firm aren't held responsible for corporate debt. However, in order to benefit from the protection provided by a company, you must preserve its identity. That includes keeping the company distinct from your personal finances, even if you're the only shareholder, and adhering to your state's regulations for annual meetings and other recordkeeping obligations.

Davis formed on the advice of her accountant and attorney; the C corporation was the greatest fit for her business in terms of tax and responsibility. You may form a company and own 100 per cent of the stock, giving you the liberty of a single proprietor while yet enjoying the advantages of a corporation.

Setting up a company, LLC, or partnership does not need the assistance of an attorney. According to Bernstein, there are lots of excellent do-it-yourself books and kits on the market, and most state regulatory bodies have recommendations you may follow. Even so, having a lawyer go over your papers before filing them is usually a smart idea, simply to be sure they're comprehensive and will enable you to operate as you wish.

Finally, keep in mind that your legal structure choice isn't final, but switching from simpler to more complex forms is easier than vice versa. According to Bernstein, the usual trend is for a company to start as a sole proprietorship and subsequently expand into a corporation. However, if you need the asset protection of a company from the outset, you should do so.

6.3 Insurance

You don't need to worry about insuring your clients' products since you never really take ownership of them. It is the duty of the carriers to offer coverage for the value of the freight they are transporting. In general, the base freight cost includes a specific level of value (which varies by carrier), and if the actual worth of the items exceeds what the basic rate covers, the shipper may buy extra insurance from the trucking business.

Even if you don't have to worry about freight insurance, your business still has insurance problems to deal with. If you work from home, don't assume your homeowner's or renter's insurance covers your business equipment; it probably won't. If you live in a business building, expect your landlord to demand evidence of income. Every year, sit down with your incur certain levels of liability insurance when ance agent and examine the lease you signed. In any scenario, you'll need insurance to protect your equipment and supplies, which will vary as your business grows, as well as workers' compensation if you have employees.

Typically, home-based freight brokers want to ensure that their equipment and supplies are protected from theft and damage caused by natural disasters like fire or flood, as well as that they have some liability protection in the event that someone (a customer, supplier, or employee) is injured on their property. Most of the time, one of the new insurance packages developed specifically for home-based companies will suffice. Also, since you'll most likely use your car for work, be sure it's properly insured.

If you choose a commercial site, you'll need to satisfy the landlord's general liability insurance requirements. Supplies, equipment, and fittings should all be covered. Consider purchasing business interruption insurance after your company is up and running to restore lost income and cover associated expenses if you're ever unable to function due to covered conditions.

It's also a good idea to get cargo insurance in case anything goes wrong. This is cargo coverage that kicks in if the carrier's insurance doesn't completely cover the value of a damaged or destroyed shipment.

6.4 Professional advisor

You may be the boss, but you can't expect to know everything as a company owner. You'll need to seek expert advice and help from time to time. It's a good idea to build a rapport with these experts before you find yourself in a crisis.

Request referrals from friends and colleagues while looking for a professional service provider. You may also seek recommendations from your local chamber of commerce or trade organisation. Find someone who is knowledgeable about transportation in general, as well as the brokerage aspect of it in particular, and who seems willing to collaborate with you. Before making a commitment, check with the Better Business Bureau and the relevant state licencing body.

You'll most likely require the following expert service providers:

- Attorney: You'll need an attorney who knows and practises business and transportation law, is trustworthy, and values your company. There are numerous attorneys ready to compete aggressively for the honour of representing you in most areas of the United States. Interview a few and choose one with whom you feel most at ease. Make careful to obtain a written agreement and to explain the price structure ahead of time. Remember that competent business attorneys aren't cheap; if you want sound counsel, you'll have to pay for it. Before you sign any contracts, leases, letters of intent, or other legal papers, consult with an attorney. They may also assist you with bad debt collection and personnel rules and procedures. Of course, if you have any questions about the legal implications of a scenario, contact an attorney right once.

- Accountant: Of all your outside advisers, your accountant is most likely to have the biggest influence on your company's success or failure. If you're starting a business, your accountant should provide you with advice on tax problems. Your accountant can aid you in organising statistical data about your firm, charting future actions based on previous performance, and advising you on your overall financial strategy for buying, capital investment, and other issues connected to your business objectives on an ongoing basis. A competent accountant may also act as a tax adviser, ensuring that you are not only in compliance with all relevant laws but also that you are not paying too much in taxes.

- Independent insurance agent: A competent, independent insurance agent can help you with all elements of your company insurance, from general liability to employee benefits, and can most likely also manage your personal lines. Look for an agent that works with a variety of insurers and is familiar with your industry. This agent should be willing to explain the intricacies of different kinds of coverage, consult with you to identify the most suitable coverage, support you in developing risk-reduction initiatives, and expedite any claims.

- Banker: You'll need a company bank account and a banking connection. Don't simply go with the bank where you've always done your personal banking; it may not be the ideal bank for your company. Before choosing where to locate your company, interview multiple lenders. Maintain a connection with your banker after your account is established. Sit down and examine your accounts and services on a regular basis to ensure you're using the best bundle for your needs.

- Consultants: There's a reason why the consulting business is growing. Consultants may offer impartial advice on any area of your company. (Keep in mind that as a broker, you'll wear a consultant's hat on sometimes while dealing with clients.) Consider employing a business consultant or a marketing expert to help you with your marketing strategy. When it comes to hiring workers, a human resources expert can assist you to avoid making expensive errors. Because many freight brokerages are family companies, consulting with an expert in family dynamics in business and succession planning may be beneficial. After

Cathy Davis' death, her daughter, Donna J. Wood, became president (she had previously served as vice president), and her sister, Dionne R. Kegley, became vice president of the Smyrna, Tennessee–based firm. Davis had worked hard to develop a succession plan that would ensure a seamless transfer when the time came. The cost of consulting varies greatly based on the consultant's experience, location, and area of specialisation. If you can't afford to employ a consultant, try calling the closest college or university's business school and hiring an MBA student to assist you.

- Computer expert: Your computer is your most important physical asset, so if you don't know much about computers, hire someone to assist you to choose a system and software—someone who will be accessible to help you maintain, repair, and extend your system as needed.

You'll need a library of resources and reference materials in addition to your "live" expert advisers. There are so many details in the freight broker industry that you can't possibly remember them all. Broker and carrier directories, as well as a distance guide and company directories, will be required.

Create Your Own Advisory Board

Even the president of the United States is not supposed to have all the answers. That is why he surrounds himself with advisors—experts in certain fields who offer him expertise and information to aid in his decision-making. A similar approach is used by savvy small-business entrepreneurs.

You may gather a group of volunteer advisers to meet with you on a regular basis to provide advice and guidance on your Trucks account. Because fewer than 7% of all vehicles aren't official or legal entities, you have a lot of flexibility in how you set it up on US roads and highways. Despite this, they pay 38% of the entire government budget. Advisory boards may be set up to assist with the day-to-day operations of your firm as well as to keep you informed about different commercial, legal, and financial developments that may impact you. To create an advisory board, follow these guidelines:

- Create a board that fits your requirements. A legal counsel, an accountant, a marketing specialist, a human resources person, and perhaps a financial advisor is all recommended. You may also wish to hire successful entrepreneurs from other sectors who are familiar with the fundamentals of business and can look at your operation from a new perspective.

- Even if you don't know them well, ask the most successful individuals you can find. You'll be amazed at how eager individuals are to assist another company in succeeding.

- Be specific about what you're attempting to accomplish. Tell your potential advisers what you're looking for and that you don't expect them to take on a managerial position or accept any responsibility for your business or the advice they provide.

- Don't be concerned about remuneration. Members of advisory boards are seldom paid more than lunch or supper. Of course, if a member of your board performs a direct service, such as reviewing a contract or preparing a financial statement, they should be paid at their regular rate. However, as a member of the advisory board, this is not one of their responsibilities. Keep in mind that your advisory board members will most certainly benefit in a number of concrete and intangible ways, even if you don't send them a check. Being a member of your board will expose them to ideas and views they may not have encountered otherwise, as well as extend their own network.

- When conducting meetings, keep in mind the dynamics of the group. You may choose to meet with everyone at once or in small groups of one or two people. It all relies on how they interact with one another and what you want to achieve.

- Request honesty and don't be upset if you get it. When someone points out something you're doing incorrectly, your pride may be wounded, but the knowledge will be helpful in the long term.

- Both failure and success may teach you something. Encourage board members to share their errors with you so that you can prevent them.

- Value the contributions that your board members make. Let them know you understand how busy they are and promise not to squander or abuse their time.

- Have a good time. After all, you're asking these individuals to give their time, so make it as pleasant as possible.

- Pay attention to every piece of advice you get. Stop chatting and pay attention. You don't have to take every piece of advice, but you should listen to it all.

- Provide the board with comments. Let the board know what you did and what the outcomes were, whether they were good or poor.

6.5 Basic office equipment

As tempting as it may be to stock your workplace with a plethora of smart devices intended to make your job simpler and more enjoyable, you're better off buying just what you need. Consider the following fundamentals:

- Typewriter: While most typewriters are now housed in museums, they are nevertheless helpful for companies that deal with pre-printed and multipart forms, such as contracts and shipping papers. Even though these forms are increasingly being completed electronically, you may need to fill one out by hand on occasion, and a typewriter is preferable to handwriting. A decent electric typewriter costs between $100 and $150.

- Computer and printer: A computer can help you plan shipments, calculate rates, keep track of customers, manage your finances, and create marketing materials. You don't need the "latest and greatest" in computer power, but you do need a system that can manage big digital files and enable you to browse the internet without being slowed down. Your computer will cost between $1,500 and $3,500, with a high-resolution colour display monitor costing between $100 and $300 and a printer costing between $300 and $1,000.

- Software: Think of software as the brains of your computer, the instructions that teach it how to do the tasks you need. Many applications are available on the market to handle your accounting, customer information management, and other administrative needs. You could also check at the programmes tailored especially for freight brokers. Before making a final choice on software, do a thorough analysis of your requirements and research the market's many offerings. Many software firms provide free trials that allow you to "test drive" their products before purchasing them.

- Modem: Modems are now a common component of computers and are required to access online services and the internet. For a successful company operation, a high-speed internet connection is required. A high-speed phone connection, cable service, or satellite will usually be accessible, but not all of these alternatives will be available in every location. The kind of modem you'll need will be determined by how you'll access the internet, and costs will vary based on the service you need. Shop around for the greatest combination of service and pricing.

- Data and equipment protection: You'll need an uninterruptible power supply (UPS) to keep your computer running in the case of a brownout or power outage, as well as a surge protector, to keep your system safe from power surges. These products may be purchased individually or as a package. You'll also need a data backup system that enables you to transfer information from your computer to a secure place. Carbonite (contact information in Appendix) and other online data backup services offer cheap, effective backups that are simple to obtain if you need them.

- Photocopier: A photocopier is an essential part of every contemporary workplace, and even the tiniest freight brokerage needs one. In almost any office supply shop, you can buy a basic, low-frills, no-frills personal copier for less than $400. The cost of more sophisticated models rises in lockstep with their complexity. Consider leasing if you expect a high volume.

- Fax machine: Despite the fact that e-mail has significantly decreased the number of papers sent, fax machines are still commonplace in workplaces. A stand-alone machine with a dedicated phone line is a smart investment for a freight brokerage. A fax machine should cost between $100 and $150.

- A postage scale is a worthwhile purchase unless all of your mail is similar. A precise scale eliminates postal guessing and pays for itself fast. It's a good practice to weigh every piece of mail to avoid having things returned due to inadequate postage or overpaying when the weight is unknown. Mechanical postal scales, which usually cost from $10 to $25, may suffice for light mailers (one to 12 items per day). Consider a digital scale if you're averaging 12 to 24 items each day. They're a little more expensive—generally between $45 and $175 (or more for really complex units)—but they're far more precise than a mechanical scale. If you ship more than 24 items per day or regularly utilise priority or expedited services, consider investing in an electronic computer scale that weighs the item and then calculates the cost through your preferred carrier, making comparisons simple. Electronic scales that can be programmed vary in price from $70 to $250.

- Postage metre: With a postage metre, you may pay for postage ahead of time and have the precise amount printed on the mailing piece when it's used. Many postage metres can print in one-tenth-cent increments, which may result in significant savings for bulk mail customers. Meters also have a more professional appearance than stamps, are more convenient, and may save you money in a variety of ways.

Something Old, Something New

Is it necessary to purchase entirely new equipment, or would secondhand equipment suffice?Of course, it depends on the equipment you're considering.

Buying secondhand office equipment (desks, chairs, file cabinets, bookshelves, and so on) may save you a lot of money. Remember that only a few people will ever see your workplace, so focus on utility rather than aesthetics. You may also be able to save a lot of money by purchasing secondhand office equipment, such as your copier, phone system, and fax machine. You'll generally be better off purchasing new technology-based goods, such as your computer. Don't attempt to operate your business with out-of-date technology.

You'll have to look around for excellent secondhand equipment. Dealers of secondhand office furniture and equipment are a good place to start. Also, look for things for sale on craigslist.org and in the classified section of your local newspaper, as well as notifications of bankruptcies and businesses going out of business.

Postage metres are rented rather than sold, with monthly prices beginning at about $30. A licence is required, which may be obtained from your local post office. The United States Postal Service licences just five firms to manufacture and lease postage metres; your local post office may give you contact information, or you can find more information at usps.gov. You may also print postage from the USPS website or Stamps.com on your own computer.

• Paper shredder: As people become more concerned about their privacy as well as the need to recycle and save landfill space, shredders are becoming more popular in both homes and workplaces. They enable you to effectively delete incoming unsolicited direct mail as well as critical internal papers before discarding them. Shredded paper may be compacted considerably more securely than paper thrown in the trash, saving landfill space. Light-duty shredders cost about $20, while larger-capacity shredders cost between $80 and $200.

6.6 Security

You must ensure that your facility is safe and secure for you, your workers, and guests, whether you intend to work from home or in a commercial setting. Of course, you'll want to safeguard your supplies and equipment.

To decide what sort of security measures you need to take, start by looking at the crime history of your region. Check with the local police department's community relations department or crime prevention office to see whether your planned or current site has a high crime rate. Most would happily offer free information on how to keep your company secure, and many will even come to your location to talk about particular crime-prevention measures. Many also provide workplace safety and crime prevention training courses for small companies and their workers.

Electronic surveillance equipment is becoming more affordable even as its capabilities grow, and installing such security systems may qualify you for insurance savings. You may also improve the efficacy of your security system by putting notices declaring the existence of alarms and cameras in your windows and around your business.

If you own a business, make sure the parking lot is well-lit for those times when you or your employees will be arriving and departing before dawn and after dark. If you're alone at a workplace late at night, request additional patrols from the police.

6.7 Telecommunication

It's critical to be able to interact swiftly with your consumers and carriers. Also, whether you have telecommuting workers or utilise home-based independent contractors, being able to contact them promptly when needed is critical. You now have a broad variety of telecommunications alternatives thanks to advancements in technology. Small and home-based enterprises have their own divisions at most telephone providers. Contact your local service provider and request a consultation with someone who can assess your requirements and assist you in putting together a service and equipment package that will meet your demands.

Keep Your Customers out of Voice-Mail Jail

Voice mail is a common contemporary corporate convenience that may also be a useful communication tool. However, bear in mind that the freight business moves at such a fast speed that there isn't always time to return calls, so answer the phone personally whenever feasible—and demand that your staff do the same—and handle conversations as swiftly and easily as possible. • If you utilise an automatic answering system, be careful to inform callers how to get in touch with a real person. That information should ideally appear very early in your announcement. Your greeting, for example, might be something like this:

- Thank you for getting in touch with ABC Freight Brokers. You may now input the extension of the person you're phoning if you know it. At any point throughout this message, call 0 to contact an operator. Press 1 to send a dispatch. Press 2 to start tracing. Press 3 for billing and 4 for a business directory.

- Whether you're a one-person show or have a large team, update your voice-mail announcements on a daily basis. Callers want to know whether you're in the office or not and if they can expect a response in five minutes or five hours. Avoid expressing the obvious, such as "I'm either out of the office or away from my desk." You'd be answering the phone if you were at your desk. When you're not available, always let callers know how to contact a real person. Here's an example of a personal voice-mail message:

Jane Smith is my name. I'm at the office today, Monday, June 1st, but I'm currently unavailable. I'll call you back within an hour if you leave your name, phone number, and the purpose for your call. If you need urgent assistance, dial 0 and ask the operator to connect you with Bob White.

Do You Need a Toll-Free Number?

Freight brokers used to need toll-free numbers so that out-of-town shippers, consignees, and trucking firms and their drivers could contact them without having to make a long-distance call. Businesses and individuals, on the other hand, are increasingly opting for flat-rate long-distance packages to eliminate the expense of long-distance calls. The majority of truck drivers nowadays use mobile phones with free long-distance calling plans. You may wish to start without a toll-free number and see how customers react before deciding whether you need one.

6.8 Transportation Brokerage Software

Technology has made it simpler than ever to establish a freight brokerage, and there are many software programmes developed especially for brokers on the market. A limited list of resources may be found in the Appendix. You may also purchase off-the-shelf word processors, spreadsheets, accountancy applications, and other software features to assist you in running your company.

6.9 Inventory

Because service is all you sell, you won't need much in the way of inventory—but what you do need to have on hand is crucial.

You'll need to make sure you have enough marketing materials on your hands, such as brochures and sales goods. You'll also need plenty of administrative goods, such as checks, invoices, stationery, paper, and other office supplies. Use the following "Office Supplies Checklist":

• Scratchpads

• Staplers, staples, and staple removers

• Tape and dispensers

• Scissors

• Sticky notes in an assortment of sizes

• Paper clips

• Plain paper and toner for your copier and printer

• Paper and other supplies for your fax machine

• Letter openers

• Pens, pencils, and holders

• Correction fluid

• (to correct typewritten or handwritten documents)

• Trash cans

• Desktop document trays

• Labels

6.10 Company vehicle

Despite the fact that you won't be carrying freight personally, you'll spend a lot of time engaging with clients at their places of business and meeting with truckers at their terminals and offices. You'll also need to attend networking and professional events. You have the option of driving your own car or having your employer buy or lease a vehicle for you to use for work.

Choose a four-door sedan-type car that is spacious and comfy since you may have clients and/or coworkers travelling with you. It should also have a large trunk so you can transport documents and supplies (and a set of golf clubs, if you play).

Remember that your car is basically your mobile workplace, and others will evaluate you based on how it looks. Maintain cleanliness both indoors and out. To prevent a buildup of road filth, wash it on a regular basis and keep garbage and papers out of it. If you smoke, be sure to clear the ashtray on a regular basis and apply a deodorizer to keep your non-smoking passengers comfortable. (Sure, it's your vehicle, and if you want to smoke, it's your choice, but keep in mind that purchasing choices are often based on emotional reasons, which are then rationalized afterwards.) If a nonsmoker is upset by a smoker, he or she will find a method to avoid doing business with him or her.)

CHAPTER 7: STAFFING YOUR COMPANY

You can start and run a brokerage as a one-person show, but to grow, you're going to need employees. If you find the idea of interviewing, managing and hiring employees somewhat intimidating, you are not alone - that's a common feeling among entrepreneurs. But this is a people business, and the people you hire will be critical to the success of your company, so it's in your best interest to do it carefully and wisely.

This chapter discusses some of the hiring issues specific to freight brokerages.

Pay scales in the transportation industry are affected by geography and market. For example, an experienced dispatcher in Chicago could easily earn double what the same position would pay in Parkersburg, West Virginia. Another point to consider is that the pool of knowledgeable, experienced people is relatively small, so the wages in this industry will likely be higher than in many other industries. Do some informal networking in your community to determine what the going pay scales and commission ranges are before deciding how much you're going to pay. Whatever you decide to offer in the beginning, from the day they're hired, tell employees what they must do to get a raise without having to ask for it, then follow up by increasing their pay rates when they've earned it.

It's a good idea to hire people before you desperately need them. Waiting until the last minute may drive you to make hiring mistakes, which can cost you dearly, both in terms of cash and customer service.

When you first begin hiring people, you may want to consider bringing them on as part-timers until your business grows to the point that full-timers are required. One of the biggest keys to getting and keeping good people is flexibility, and you'll find plenty of talented folks who, for whatever reason, don't want full-time work. If you can accommodate them, you'll both benefit. And as the workload grows and you need a full-time person doing that particular job, either change the status of your part-timer or, if that won't work, be creative. Consider hiring a second part-timer, setting up a job-sharing situation, or some other solution that will allow you to retain a valuable person and still get the work done.

7.1 Basic positions

Because the service you offer is pretty straightforward, you don't need a wide range of job titles in your company. Here are the basic positions you'll need to fill as you grow:

- Broker: A broker does the necessary tasks for the essential services you provide. This person needs to understand all the details involved in arranging a shipment and have good communication skills. A background in trucking is helpful. Unless you have a full-time bookkeeper or accountant, you or your brokers will have to bill shippers and pay carriers. You can pay brokers either a salary or a commission based on their sales.

- Secretary/receptionist: In most freight brokerages, this individual answers the telephone, routes calls, takes messages (if you don't have voice mail), greets visitors (though they'll be infrequent), and handles routine word processing and correspondence.

- Customer service/account representative: This is an inside person who handles all customer service duties, including quoting rates, taking pickup orders, tracking shipments, assisting customers with claims, and dealing with any service issues that arise.

- Bookkeeper: This individual keeps your financial records and may also handle billing and payables.

- SALES REPRESENTATIVE: A sales rep may work inside on the phone, outside face-to-face, or a combination of both. This person's job is to identify and secure new business and help maintain existing business.

- Sources for prospective employees include carriers, customers (use caution here; you don't want to lose a client because you stole an employee), and professional associations. Become familiar with online job search sites and consider posting your positions with those sources. Put the word out among your social contacts, as well—you never know who else might know the perfect person for your company.

7.2 Evaluating Applicants

When you actually begin the hiring process, don't be surprised if you're as nervous at the prospect of interviewing potential employees as they are about being interviewed. They may need a job, but for you, the future of your company is at stake.

It's a good idea to prepare your interview questions in advance. Develop open-ended questions that encourage the candidate to talk. In addition to knowing what they've done, you want to find out how they did it. Ask each candidate the same set of questions, and take notes as they respond so you can make an accurate assessment and comparison later. If candidates claim to have experience, use industry jargon to see how well they understand it; the freight business has a language of its own that most outsiders won't be able to speak.

When the interview is over, let the candidate know what to expect. Is it going to take you several weeks to interview other candidates, check references, and make a decision? Will you want the top candidates to return for a second interview? Will you call the candidate, or should they call you? This is not only a good business practise; it's also common courtesy.

Always check former employers and personal references. Though many companies are very restrictive as to what information they'll verify, you may be surprised at what you can find out. At least confirm that the applicant told the truth about dates and positions held. Personal references are likely to give you some additional insight into the general character and personality of the candidate; this helps you decide if they'll fit into your operation.

7.3 Calling all people

Picture the ideal candidate in your mind. Is this person unemployed and reading the challenges all businesses face well into the twenty-first century?

Before you hire your first employee, make sure you're prepared. Have all your paperwork ready, know what you need to do in the way of tax reporting, and understand all the liabilities and responsibilities that come with having employees.

One of the easiest ways to do this is through E-Verify, a federal system that verifies worker eligibility that's mandatory in some states. It may only be used for new hires (not existing employees) and provides immunity from a discrimination claim by a U.S. citizen or resident aliens. To enrol in E-Verify, go to dhs.gov/E-Verify.

Be sure to document every step of the interview and the reference-checking process. Even very small companies are finding themselves targets of employment discrimination suits; good records are your best defence if it happens to you.

Be sure your employees are legal. Under federal law, you must verify the identity and employment eligibility of employees; complete and retain the Employment Eligibility Verification Form (I-9) on file for at least three years, or one year after employment ends, whichever is longer; and not discriminate on the basis of national origin and citizenship status.

7.4 Benefits

Many of the employees you want could be working for major freight carriers or large manufacturers and enjoying "big company" benefits.

You can't afford to offer a strong benefits package. The brokers we spoke with provide paid vacation and holidays, health and life insurance, retirement plans, bonuses, profit-sharing, and flextime.

As a smaller company, you have a degree of flexibility large companies don't always have. For many people, especially those who have children at home or care for elderly parents, flexible working hours can be a tremendous benefit.

Give your employees subscriptions to industry trade magazines and newsletters, and encourage them to use and share the information they learn from those publications. The cost is nominal, and the result is that you'll increase their value to the company as well as their sense of self-esteem.

Williamson says that, in addition to tangible benefits, you need to create a pleasant working environment. "This is a high-stress business, and we try to make the job fun," he says.

7.5 Keep People in Perspective

There's no business where the slogan "people are our most valuable asset" is truer than in transportation, and taking care of your people is certainly important. But it's also important to keep the relationship of the individual to the company in perspective.

"When you

hire people, you can never let them think they're more important than the company," says Indianapolis freight broker Chuck Andrews. When he started his company, he hired a few people who brought the business with them; they had an inflated opinion of their value to the company and used that to attempt to manipulate Andrews. Don't give in to this brand of professional blackmail. Of course, it's possible that when you lose certain employees, you may also lose some customers—but it's also possible that you won't, and it's highly unlikely that the loss of one person can destroy your business if you've built it properly.

7.6 The High Cost of Turnover

Employee turnover is an important issue in the transportation industry, especially in sales and customer service positions. Remember, this is a relationship business, and when you have employees who've built strong relationships with customers and carriers, you have employees who will be the constant target of recruiting efforts by other companies.

Some of the costs of turnover are fairly easy to calculate; others are essentially unquantifiable. When someone leaves, you have the hard costs of paying overtime to other employees to get that job done until a replacement is found, recruiting (advertising, screening, interviewing, etc.), and training. Those numbers are fairly easy to figure. Harder to calculate is the cost in customer relations and goodwill. You may even lose a few customers who opt to follow the departed employee to a different broker or carrier.

Bill Tucker says the key to keeping turnover down is not to see your relationship as an employer-employee one, but rather as a partnership. That certainly includes bonuses and profit-sharing programs, but it goes beyond pure financial incentives. Employees need to participate in the decision-making process; they need to be encouraged to contribute ideas and solutions.

People also need to be treated with fairness and compassion. It isn't realistic to expect people to leave their personal lives at home. When employees need you to be flexible about family issues—whether it's taking a few hours off to watch a child perform in a play or dealing with an elderly parent requiring full-time nursing care—it's not only kind but wise for you to provide as much assistance as possible. Along with doing the humane thing, you'll be building a level of employee loyalty that can't be bought for any amount of salary.

Why Train?

Training is an area of managing people that you can't escape. Many of your employees come on board with at least a basic knowledge of the work they must do. But even the most experienced need to be trained in your particular operation and procedures.

The transportation industry has an abundance of training opportunities, from formal courses of study at colleges and universities to special conventions and workshops to monthly professional association meetings. It's a good idea to support a variety of training opportunities. For example, MCD Transportation provides both formal and on-the-job training and maintains a company library with current publications. Employees are encouraged to work on their professional certification, and the company pays for related studies. The company also pays for costs related to membership and participation in professional associations.

Training Techniques

Whether done in a formal classroom setting or on the job, effective training begins with a clear goal and a plan for reaching it. Training falls into one of three major categories: orientation, which includes explaining company policies and procedures; job skills, which focuses on how to do specific tasks; and ongoing development, which enhances the basic job skills and grooms' employees for future challenges and opportunities. These tips will help you maximize your training efforts:

- Figure out how people like to learn. There is no such thing as a one-size-fits-all solution when it comes to training. People absorb and process knowledge in various ways, so your training approach must accommodate their preferences. Some individuals can read a handbook, while others prefer vocal instructions, and yet others need a demonstration. While working with a group, using a mix of techniques is the ideal strategy; when working one-on-one, adapt your delivery to the requirements of the individual you're teaching.

- When it comes to certain workers, determining how they learn best is as easy as asking them. Others may not be able to inform you since they are unfamiliar with themselves; in these instances, try out different training methods to discover what works best for the individual employee.

- To train, practise, and reinforce, use simulation and role-playing. Simulation is one of the most successful training methods, which includes teaching an employee how to do something and then enabling them to practise it in a safe, controlled setting. Allow the employee to role-play with a coworker to rehearse what they should say and do in different scenarios if the job requires interpersonal skills.

- Act as a positive role model. Don't ask your workers to accomplish more than you're willing to do. When you always do things the way they should be done, you're an excellent role model. Take no shortcuts that you wouldn't want your workers to take, and don't act in any manner that you wouldn't want them to act. However, don't think that just doing things well would be enough in teaching others how to do them. Training is not a replacement for role modelling. It helps to reinforce training. Employees are unlikely to get the message if you just role-model and never teach them.

- Keep an eye out for training possibilities. Once you've completed basic orientation and job skills training, you'll want to keep an eye out for ways to improve your employees' ability and performance.

- Make it believable. Use real-life scenarios to teach whenever feasible, but don't tell consumers they're being used for staff training.

- Be prepared for questioning. Don't presume that your workers will know what questions to ask. People frequently don't comprehend enough in a new environment to create inquiries. Anticipate their inquiries and be prepared to answer them.

- Request comments. Finally, encourage workers to provide feedback on your performance as a trainer. Convince them that it's OK to tell you the truth at the same time you're evaluating their work. Inquire about their impressions of the training and your methods, and utilise the feedback to enhance your own abilities.

7.7 Noncompete and Confidentiality Agreements

To protect yourself against an employee leaving you to start his or her own firm that directly competes with yours, you may want to ask everyone who comes to work for you to sign a non-compete and confidentiality agreement. Noncompete agreements typically consist of time, geography, and industry restrictions, and their enforceability varies by state. For example, they're generally illegal in California, but in New York, they're enforceable if the restrictions are "reasonable." Have the language of your non-compete agreement checked by an attorney familiar with employment law before you ask anyone to sign it. Confidentiality agreements help in protecting your proprietary information, such as customer lists and other intellectual property.

Keep in mind that even though your employees sign non-compete and confidentiality agreements, they may choose to violate them. Then you'll have to make the decision whether or not to take the issue to court.

Ron Williamson sued one former employee, a salesperson who started his own company. "We won, but we lost," he says. "It cost me about $32,000, and we settled out of court through arbitration and recovered about $12,000 of that. I had to go to my customers and ask them to testify against this person. Noncompete are tough, and they take an incredible amount of time [to enforce]."

That may be, but his willingness to sue helped when another employee left the company. He started to violate the terms of his agreement but backed off when he realized Williamson would take action.

Now that we've covered human resources issues, it's time to discuss marketing.

CHAPTER 8: MARKETING

Remember in Chapter 1; we said that just about everything must move at least part of the way to its destination by a truck? With that in mind, it's safe to say that almost every company is a potential customer for you. But if you take that approach, you'll have a tough time coming up with an effective, not to mention affordable, marketing plan.

What's wrong with just going after anybody in the world who might ever have to ship something by truck for any reason? Because that market segment includes literally millions of companies and individuals, and it's impossible for any small business to communicate effectively with a market that size. Can you afford to send even one piece of direct mail to 1 million prospective customers? Of course not. But when you narrow that market down to, for example, for 500 or 1,000 customers in a particular area, conducting a successful direct-mail campaign is much more affordable and manageable.

As you create your marketing strategy, keep the following questions in mind:

- Who do you think your prospective consumers are?
- How many of them there are?
- Where they are?
- What is the present mode of freight transportation?
- Is there anything you can give them that they don't already have?
- What are you going to do to convince them to do business with you?
- What kind of services do you provide?
- How do you stack up against your rivals?
- How do you want to convey your image?

The aim of your marketing strategy should be to inform potential consumers about your company's existence and service quality, preferably via a comprehensive approach.

Market Size in 2019

$ XX.X billion*

Incremental growth

$ 41.47 bn

2019   2024

The year-over-year growth rate for 2020 is estimated at

4.19%

Market growth will ACCELERATE at a CAGR of over

4%

33%

of the growth will originate from North America

Vendor classification*

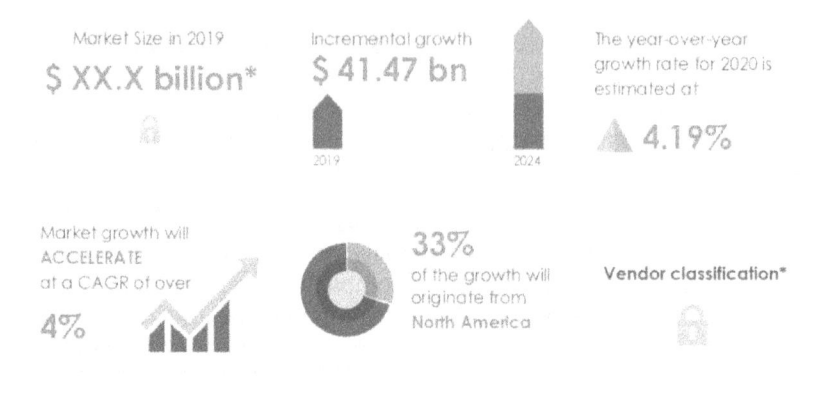

8.1 Market research

Market research provides businesses with data that lets them identify and reach particular market segments and solve or avoid marketing problems. A thorough market survey forms the foundation of any successful business. It's impossible to develop marketing strategies or an effective product line without market research.

The goal of market research is to identify your market, find out where it is, and develop a strategy to communicate with prospective customers in a way that will convince them to use you.

Begin by focusing on two broad areas: the people and firms you work with directly (such as carriers and shippers) and the general business trends that affect the industry as a whole. With this information, you will be able to move on to more specific research that will help you determine your target market, where to locate your business, what services to offer, and your geographic scope of operations.

8.2 Choosing a niche

There are many compelling reasons to choose possibly the best market niche. You may customise your service package and marketing activities to suit the requirements of a particular market segment by focusing on that group. You'll also get a reputation for competence, which will bring in new clients.

One of the most rewarding aspects of working as a freight broker is that you develop long-term connections with the majority of your clients. Motor carrier freight service is seldom a one-time buy; once a client joins your team, you'll almost certainly see a lot of them again. Most shippers, on the other hand, use several carriers and brokers, so you'll need to spend time learning as much as you can about their volumes and requirements and providing consistent service so they'll feel comfortable returning to you and you can grow your share of their business.

You may create a speciality based on geography (either shippers' locations or freight destinations), cargo type (agricultural, perishable, large, bulk commodities, etc.), load size, particular industries, or any other unique shipping need. Consider what kinds of shipments and/or shippers you like dealing with when deciding on a speciality. Then do some market research to see whether there is enough demand for the services you wish to provide. If there is, go ahead and implement your marketing strategy. If there isn't, think about how you might change your speciality to one that brings in enough money.

8.3 Communicating with your customer

Once you've selected a niche, you'll need to consider how to let the shippers in that niche know about you. This is the essence of marketing. Don't be discouraged if your marketing efforts don't produce an immediate response. This is a relationship business, and it takes time to build your reputation and the rapport you need with the shippers. Also, remember that your marketing efforts support your primary sales efforts but rarely generate a sale on their own. Even so, they deserve your attention.

All your promotional and advertising materials must clearly indicate your status as a broker, must be under the name by which you're registered, and may not directly or indirectly represent your operation as a carrier. With that legal caveat out of the way, be sure all these items are professional and letter-perfect. Consistency is important; your business card, envelopes, stationery, labels, invoices, promotional items, etc., should all have the same logo, use the same typeface, and be on the same colour and type of paper (where appropriate, of course—your invoices and stationery will likely be on different stock).

Small but useful giveaway items—such as pens, mugs, scratch pads, and baseball caps—are effective in supporting your marketing efforts. Customers aren't likely to choose a broker based on these items, but it's important to keep your name in front of them in a positive way. Be sure they clearly and consistently identify your company and tell you how to contact you.

Your telephone directory listing is important so shippers can find you. Check with your local phone company to find out its advertising deadline and directory distribution date, and, if possible, plan to launch your business in time to be included. For most freight brokers, a Yellow Pages display ad won't be worth the substantial investment that goes along with it; however, you might want to give your listing some distinction by having it set in bold type or including a line or two indicating your specialities or market niche. Be sure your company is also included in online directories because the use of printed directories is declining.

Broadcast (radio and television) advertising is generally not effective for freight brokers, but some print advertising will help build your credibility and name recognition. Look for publications that shippers in your target market read; if you're not sure what they are, ask some of the shippers you'd like to have as customers. Your ads don't have to be wildly creative; in fact, a better approach is to simply say what you do and why you do it well in an abbreviated format and then include your company name, your logo, and how to contact you. Keep the design of the ad clear and uncluttered; don't cram so much text into it that no one will read it. Some great places to begin your print advertising are in the newsletters of your local transportation organizations.

You'll also want a brochure that describes what you do. A basic 8½x11-inch three-panel piece is sufficient. It should include your company name, address, phone and fax numbers, website and e-mail addresses, other contact information, your logo, a detailed list of the services you provide, a brief description of your background to establish credibility, and a benefits statement that tells shippers why they should use you.

Use a professional graphic designer and copywriter to produce your ads and brochures and have them reproduced by quality offset printing. Don't just run them off on your laser printer or a photocopy machine; your prospective customers will be able to tell, and you'll look like an unstable, fly-by-night operation.

8.4 A web presence is essential

It's essential that you have a professional and functional web presence. This means a well-designed, eye-appealing, user-friendly website that will provide information to prospective customers and carriers as well as be search-engine friendly.

There are a number of fairly simple web design software packages on the market that are relatively inexpensive and easy to learn, making it tempting for many small- business owners to try to handle this process in-house. But that's not a great idea. The difference between a professionally designed site and one created by an amateur can range from subtle to obvious and can have a significant impact on a company's image.

A good web designer will seamlessly blend together a design that communicates the company's vision with user-friendly navigation and search engine optimization to build a site that truly accomplishes what the client needs. Poor design is at best a waste of time and money, and at worst detrimental to your company's image. I tell my clients that they're the experts in their fields and have valuable insight and input in the development of their sites, but they need to focus on their core business, whatever that happens to be, and let me focus on the development of their websites because that's my core business."

Resist the temptation to add a lot of bells and whistles to your site just for the sake of having them. Everything on your site should have a reason for being there. Once your website is up, be sure to maintain it with current information and news items, so your customers have a reason to visit it regularly.

8.5 Know thine enemy

One of the most basic elements of effective marketing is differentiating yourself from the competition. One marketing consultant calls it "eliminating the competition" because if no one else does exactly what you do, then you essentially have no competition. However, before you can differentiate yourself, you first need to understand

who your competitors are, and why your customers might use them?

As a freight broker, you'll be competing with other brokers, freight forwarders, carriers, and probably some types of transportation consulting firms. To a degree, you'll also be competing with your customers' internal traffic departments.

Finding out about your competitors isn't difficult. In many cases, you'll know their people from your own industry networking, perhaps from previous jobs or professional associations. Your customers and potential customers will usually be open about what they like and don't like about other service providers. The key is to pay attention, take notes, and use what you learn in your own marketing efforts.

8.6 Outsourcing opportunity

As you plan your marketing strategy, consider how the trend of outsourcing can help your brokerage. Outsourcing is the practice of contracting with an outside firm to handle tasks that aren't part of a company's core business. For example, as a freight broker, your core business is to link shippers and carriers, so you may choose to outsource such tasks as certain accounting procedures, some of your marketing functions, or perhaps the technical work involved in building a website.

Many companies are outsourcing all or part of their shipping functions. Brokers are in an excellent position to offer themselves as an outsourcing resource, essentially functioning as the customer's traffic department. You can relieve your customers of all the work related to transportation and traffic management, and in addition, save them money and improve their service.

"A number of our smaller customers use us for their entire shipping and receiving business," says Bill Tucker in Cherry Hill, New Jersey. "Not only on the traffic management but also some of the purchasing and acquiring of products." This type of consulting service doesn't require a particular license—just knowledge and the ability to provide the service.

Of course, it's not a good idea to go to the traffic manager and pitch yourself as a supplier who wants to take over his job. You'll have a much better chance of succeeding if you approach a senior person in the organization whose interest is in finance, such as the CFO, vice president of finance, or even the president of the company. If the traffic manager is someone who wears multiple hats, take the sales approach that your goal is to make his life easier.

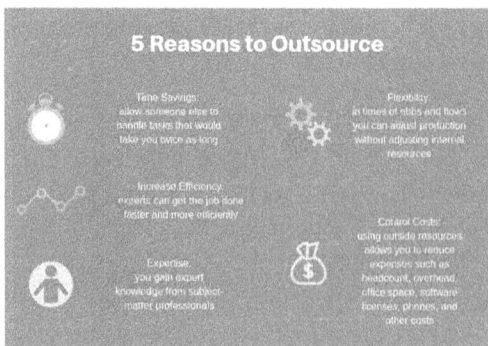

8.7 Join the right groups

Professional associations offer a variety of networking and educational opportunities. If you're serious about being a freight broker, you'll belong to several organizations, some industry-exclusive and others more general.

Some of the associations you may include (see the Appendix for contact information):

- Transportation Intermediaries Association
- Delta Nu Alpha
- National Association of Small Trucking Companies
- National Association of Women Business Owners (for the women-owned brokerage firms)
- Local transportation and traffic clubs
- Your local chamber of commerce
- A lead exchange or small local networking group

It's a good idea to belong to the local transportation clubs in all the cities in which you do business. For example, Indianapolis-based broker Chuck Andrews belongs to three transportation associations in Indianapolis where his company has its headquarters, plus clubs in Chicago, Cincinnati, and other major areas where he does business. He doesn't attend every single meeting, but he goes to the ones he can, and his name and company are listed on the membership rosters. "We get phone calls out of the blue from people who see our name on those rosters," he says.

Done correctly, marketing can really give your business a boost—especially in the beginning when you need it most.

CHAPTER 9: SALES

The freight industry involves the buying and selling of an intangible service, which makes it a strong

"relationship" business. Success as a freight broker requires that you do a tremendous amount of both face-to-face and telephone sales.

Don't let the word "selling" scare you. Most of the world's top sales professionals will tell you they dislike "selling." What they mean is, they don't buy into the stereotype of the slick, fast-talking character on the used car lot or the door-to-door peddler who wedges a foot in the door and won't leave until you buy. But that's not "selling" in the professional sense of the word.

When you sell as a freight broker, you convince shippers that you have the capability to help them with their shipping needs better than anyone else—and if you don't believe that, then you need to be in another business. You're not going to brow-beat them into using you, nor are you going to manipulate them into buying a service they don't need. You're going to provide the best professional service that meets their needs at a competitive rate, and communicating that is a major part of the sales process.

9.1 Phone or face to face sale

You might dislike the telemarketers who call your home at precisely the moment you're sitting down to dinner, but when it comes to selling your own service, a telephone call is a powerful tool. RJW Logistics has a sales rep who generates $2 million a year in gross revenue just by calling people on the phone.

The transportation industry used to be a "good old boy" system of casual, drop-in sales calls that consisted primarily of telling a few jokes, leaving behind some scratch pads, and asking for a shipment by saying something like, "Got anything going; my way?" Today's transportation professionals don't have time for unexpected visitors with no clear agenda. Collectively, they're spending billions of dollars each year to move materials, and they need those goods to arrive on time, in good condition, at a reasonable and competitive price.

This is not to say that you shouldn't be friendly and personable—in fact, your personality plays an important role in the growth of your business. But each sales contact should have a clear purpose that ultimately provides a benefit to your customer. Most customers appreciate a systematic, sophisticated approach that doesn't waste their time.

In today's intensely competitive environment, the majority of brokers mix telephone and face-to-face sales, using the phone to pre-qualify and set appointments, making a personal call, and then following up on the phone and by mail.

9.2 Qualifying prospects

The first step of the sales process is qualifying the prospect, which is a sales training jargon for determining how much business the potential customer has and who makes the decision as to who's going to get it.

This is not as hard as it seems. It really involves asking a few simple questions. If you networked your way into the company, you probably have a good idea of the answers. If you're cold-calling, simply ask the receptionist or operator, "Can you give me the name and title of the person in charge of choosing carriers for your outbound shipments?"

It's important to ask for both the name and title before you ask to be connected with that individual. Of course, sometimes operators will transfer your call, but when they don't, you begin the conversation with the advantage of knowing whom you're talking to and the ability to call that person by name.

Once you're on the phone with that person, confirm that you are indeed talking to the decision-maker. The receptionist may have referred you to the

shipping clerk, who fills out the freight bills, calls carriers, and handles some tracing functions—but who doesn't actually make the decisions.

Don't be shy about asking this question. Most companies these days operate "lean and mean," and workers don't have time to listen to a sales presentation they don't have the authority to act on.

As we've said, you need to identify the real decision-maker (and keep in mind that there may be more than one in many companies), but don't ignore the decision influencers. As the name indicates, these are the people who are in a position to influence the decision-making process. They could be telephone operators, receptionists, administrative workers, shipping and receiving clerks—even high-ranking corporate officers.

Think about this: Say you and another broker are competing for a major piece of business from a particular company. The plant manager is making the decision, and his goal is to find someone who can work well with his shipping clerk so he can delegate the details and focus on other things. You and the other broker are offering similar rates and service packages, but the other broker took time to talk with the shipping clerk, maybe even took him to lunch, and established a relationship you don't have. With all else being nearly equal if the plant manager asks the shipping clerk for input in the decision, whom do you think he's going to recommend?

This doesn't mean you need to wine and dine with every shipping clerk at every company you deal with or that you need to send all the receptionists flowers and candy. What it means is that you respect their roles in the process, and you communicate with them to find out what they need and how you can best meet those needs.

9.3 Determining sales

Once you've confirmed that a business has freight you can handle and you know who makes the routing decisions, you need to find out what they need before you begin telling them what you can do.

It's a waste of their time and yours for you to do this any other way. For example, why bother to spend time telling them about the wide variety of equipment you can pro-vide only to find out 20 minutes later that they only need standard trailers? Besides wasting time, that sends a clear message that you're far more interested in making the sale than you are in your customer.

So how do you find out what a prospective customer need? Simple: Just ask. Say something like, "Before I tell you about our services, I'd like to ask you a few questions and find out exactly what you need. Can you tell me about your outbound freight?" Most of the time, you'll get more information than you need. Have a notebook handy and take notes while your customer talks; don't count on being able to accurately remember all the details of weights, commodities, and destinations. Most importantly, never say no to a customer. When they need something you can't provide, offer them an alternative.

9.4 why do you ask?

When a customer (or a prospect) asks you a question about your capabilities, find out what's behind the question before you answer it. This lets you answer in the most positive and appropriate way possible.

Consider this scenario: You're in Charleston, South Carolina, making a presentation to the traffic manager at a mid-sized manufacturing firm. She asks, "Do you work with any carriers that go to Des Moines?" The short—and honest—the answer is that you do not. So rather than lie, you say, "No, I'm sorry." And you've lost every ounce of sales momentum you've built to that point.

But suppose you respond to her question with a question of your own. You might say, "Why do you ask?" or "Do you have shipments going to Des Moines?" If she says the reason for her question is that she ships a truckload a week to Des Moines, you can ask more questions about the move and her needs and offer to get back with her after you've had a chance to find a carrier with a more competitive rate and service package than she has now. But if she says, "No, we don't ship out there, but one of our senior managers just left us to take a job with a company there, so I was just thinking about that city," you can avoid a flat no answer and, instead, emphasize your flexibility and willingness to shop until you find what your customer wants.

9.5 Steak or sizzle?

If you've ever taken a basic sales course, you've probably heard, "Sell the sizzle, not the steak." What that means is you need to understand the difference between features and benefits—and focus on the benefits.

A feature is an aspect of the service you provide; the benefit is what the customer gains from that aspect. For example, that you will call the shipper with delivery notification within two hours of the freight being unloaded is a feature. That the shipper has the peace of mind of knowing that the freight has been delivered on time and in good condition is a benefit. That you have access to thousands of carriers is a feature. That by using your firm, your customers are assured of getting the equipment they need when they need it is a benefit.

Before you ever call or visit a prospect for the first time, put together a presentation that includes needs identification and benefits selling, and practice it. Don't worry that you'll sound rehearsed; the reality is that the better you know your stuff, the more natural and confident you'll appear.

9.6 Does anyone object?

Another long-time sales training phrase is "handling objections." That sounds more daunting than it really is.

In most professional sales situations, an "objection" comes in the form of a question, and whether it's a question or a statement, it's usually a request for more information.

For example, a prospective customer might say something like, "How many carriers do you have agreements with?" or "I know you're new; I'm not sure you have the experience I need." Both of these statements might be seen as objections, but what they really are is a chance for you to tell the prospect about the benefits he or she will gain by using you.

It's important to keep in mind that while freight may not appear particularly glamorous, for most companies, the efficient and timely movement of cargo is critical to their ongoing operations. Selecting a broker or carrier isn't a decision most shippers make lightly or casually. You'll find your customers very much involved in both the sales process and the ongoing service. You've chosen a highly interactive business, and you can expect your customers to view you and your staff as the service.

9.7 Ask for the business

One of the most difficult parts of a sales call for most people is the close —but it shouldn't be. If you've been paying attention—if you identified your prospect's needs and determined that you can satisfy them, if you've focused on benefits rather than features—then asking the prospect to make that final commitment should be a natural evolution of the sales call.

Here's one approach that works well: Find out what internal procedure the customer would have to change to give you his or her business. This is a simple matter of asking, "If you were to decide to let us handle your next load to Phoenix, what would you have to do?" When the prospect answers the question—perhaps with something like "I'd have to tell the shipping clerk to call you"—ask if you can have the shipping clerk step in so you can answer any questions that person might have.

If the prospect resists, find out why. Say: "We've agreed that we have the services you need, that our rates are competitive, and that we're in a position to provide some extras you're not getting now. Is there any reason why you shouldn't call the shipping? clerk in now to give us a chance to prove ourselves on the next shipment?"

Prospects rarely say no without some sort of an explanation—an objection—that you'll have a chance to overcome. And even if you don't get the business—and you won't get it all—you'll at least know why.

Once you've devised your sales strategy, you'll be selling like a pro. Now you'll need some insights on financial management, the subject of the next chapter.

CHAPTER 10: FINANCIAL MANAGEMENT

One of the great things about the freight broker business is that it doesn't require a tremendous amount of startup cash to purchase facilities and equipment— you can be up and running with just a computer, fax machine, and phone. However, it does require a substantial amount of cash or a significant credit line, virtually from day one. Precisely how much depends, of course, on your business volume, but you need to have sufficient cash on hand to pay your carriers on time, and that will likely be weeks before your shippers pay you.

This fact cannot be stressed enough: Cash flow management is critical in this business. If you don't pay your carriers on time, they'll stop accepting your loads. And though the industry is huge, in many ways, it's also like a small town—everybody knows everybody else's business.

If you're not paying your bills on time, it won't be long before every carrier—and maybe even the shippers—find out about it. In a relationship business like freight brokering, a good reputation is essential, so protect yours by paying your bills on time.

You should monitor your cash flow constantly. Look at your receivables and payables on a daily basis. Cultivate fast-paying customers, and be sure your sales staff is explaining the need for prompt payment to new customers.

Ideally, you'll open your doors with enough cash in the bank to pay all your expenses and your carriers until revenue from your customers (shippers) starts coming in. More practically, you may need to look at short-term credit options, such as unsecured commercial bank loans, borrowing against your accounts receivable, or selling your accounts receivable (a process known as factoring, which is explained later in this chapter). You may have a tough time with conventional loan sources because, by traditional lending standards, most freight brokers wouldn't be considered bankable. Even if you have a record of paying your bills on time, you'll likely need a revolving line of credit significantly higher than whatever assets you have to offer for collateral.

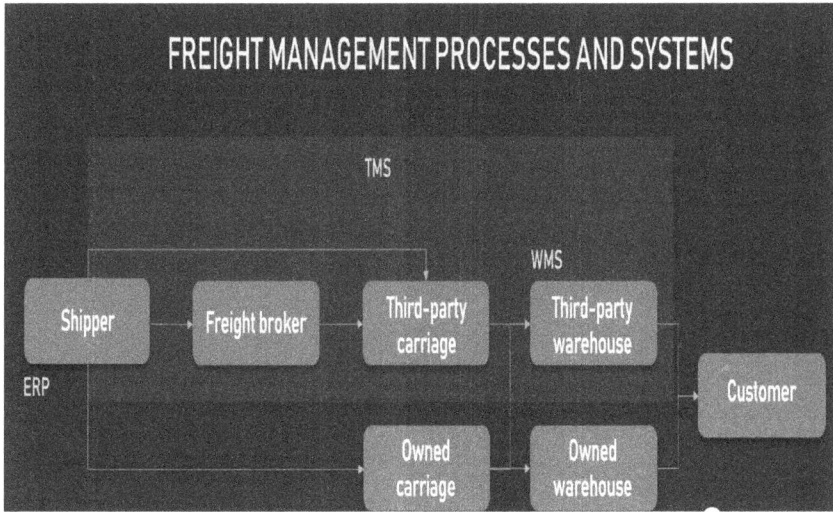

FREIGHT MANAGEMENT PROCESSES AND SYSTEMS

10.1 Setting credit policies

Because you're billing your shippers, or sometimes the consignees, you need to set credit policies and procedures. When you extend credit, you do so under the assumption that the customer intends to pay and is capable of paying and that nothing will prevent him or her from paying. Most of your customers will be honest and dependable when paying their bills, but that doesn't mean you should blindly extend credit without first gathering and verifying information.

Each new customer should complete a credit application, and you should check the information he or she provides. This is standard practice in business. If a customer objects to complete a credit application, seriously consider whether extending credit to that customer is a safe thing to do. Look at it this way: When you extend credit for a service, you're essentially granting an unsecured, interest-free loan. Once the goods have been moved and delivered, you can't take back the service—and you (depending, of course, on the terms of your carrier agreement) are responsible for paying the carrier whether or not the shipper pays you.

Thanks in large part to the old Interstate Commerce Commission regulation that required payment of freight bills within seven days, most shippers have systems set up to pay freight bills faster than other invoices. "In the old days, it was regulation," Tucker says. "Today, it's entirely contractual among the parties. But carriers usually have pretty narrow margins. [Trucking companies have] a serious financial burden to carry. [They have] to pay the driver, buy the fuel, buy the insurance, and make the loan payments on the equipment—all before the driver goes out the door." Cooperative shippers understand the economic realities of trucking and that if truckers are going to stay in business, they must be paid promptly. But you'll still have customers who will take as long as you allow them to pay. It's your responsibility to set your terms and make those terms clear to your customers.

You can include your terms (essentially when payment is due) on your credit application and have customers sign an acknowledgement that they know, understand, and agree to abide by your policies. On each invoice, clearly indicate the date the invoice will become past due.

10.2 Warning signs

Just because a customer passed your first credit check with flying colours, don't neglect to re-evaluate his or her credit status—in fact, you should do it on a regular basis.

Tell customers when you initially grant their credit applications that you have a policy of periodically reviewing accounts so that when you do it, it's not a surprise. Things can change very quickly in the business world, and a company that's on sound financial footing this year may be quite wobbly next year. An annual re-evaluation of all customers on an open account is a good idea—but if you start to see trouble in the interim, don't wait to take action. Another time to re-evaluate a customer's credit is when they request an increase in their credit line.

Some key trouble signs are a slowdown in payments, increased complaints, and difficulty getting answers to your payment inquiries. Even a sharp increase in volume could signal trouble; companies concerned that they may lose their credit privileges with you may try to milk you while they can, and if they aren't paying other brokers or carriers, they may have already lost some credit privileges and be looking to replace those sources. Pay attention to what your customers are doing; a major change in their customer base or product lines is something you may want to monitor.

Tucker says the process of providing good service to customers will also alert you to potential credit problems. "Just in the course of my relationship with the company, I talk to the president, I talk to the salespeople, I talk to the manufacturing people, I talk to the traffic manager, and even the guy who loads the trucks," he says. Changes in a company's transportation needs and patterns can be early indicators of a problem. So, what does Tucker do if he spots a red flag? "It depends on the details and on how serious it is. We may be [able to] help them solve their financial or market problem. But you also have to keep them at arm's length if they are getting into trouble. You have to either quietly be 'running out of trucks' or tell them the salesperson will be in there every Friday to pick up a check. It's our job to protect the money in every way we can, including refusing to extend more credit and walking away from the business. Sometimes you just have to do that. But you have to know when, and you have to be able to evaluate those things. And we stay close enough to the customer, so we can at least minimize the hit."

Most customers accept routine credit reviews as a sound business practice. A customer who objects may well have something to hide—and that's something you need to know.

10.3 Cash flow controls

Certainly, cash flow is important to any business, but it's critical to a freight brokerage. You need to keep sufficient cash on hand to pay your regular operating expenses and your carriers, but not so much that you miss out on revenue from alternative investments. In addition, you need to take steps to protect your company from internal theft.

Before you hire your first employee, set up internal controls to safeguard your assets and assure maximum cash flow management. One such control is to require proper authorization of transactions. Be specific as to which individuals are authorized to carry out what tasks, and hold them accountable for their actions.

You'll also want to establish a separation of duties, so the person responsible for the custody of an asset isn't also responsible for recordkeeping for that same asset. This prevents someone from stealing and then changing records to cover up what he or she has done.

Be sure the records you keep are sufficient to satisfy financial and tax reporting requirements, as well as the federal regulations governing freight brokers. However, you should limit access to both assets and documents to prevent unauthorized use or theft; keep access on a needs-only basis.

Finally, set up a system to independently verify individual performance. Someone who was not involved in the work should check it for accuracy. This will help uncover intentional theft and fraud, as well as unintentional errors.

Beyond techniques to protect your assets, you'll also need systems to maximize them. Consider these:

- Set up a sweep account. This is a bank service that lets you earn the maximum interest on all the money in your accounts, even if it's just overnight, without penalties or concerns of bouncing checks. The system is set up, so funds are automatically moved— or swept—in and out of the appropriate accounts each day. If your banker is reluctant to set you up with this type of account, shop around for one who will.

- Use a lockbox for receivables. Another bank service, a lockbox, works like this: Your customers mail their payments to a post office box that your bank rents in your company's name. The bank sends a courier several times a day to clear out the box, checks are immediately deposited into your account—literally within hours of their arrival in the mail—and you get a report outlining all the transactions in as much detail as you want, as frequently as you want. Lockboxes mean you no longer have to run to the bank with deposits or spend your (or one of your staff members') valuable time opening envelopes, recording payments, and preparing deposits.

- Accept electronic payments. Talk to your banker about getting set up so you can accept payments through electronic transfers. Many companies prefer this payment method because it provides you with greater control over cash flow and reduces handling time and expenses.

- Invoice on a timely basis. You can't expect customers to pay until you've issued an invoice, so get your invoices out as soon as you know all the appropriate charges on a given shipment. Be sure you include all necessary documentation (copies of bills of lading, delivery receipts, etc.) for your customers to pay promptly.

- Enforce your payment terms. Be prepared to follow up on late bills as soon as they become past due. Initial reminders don't have to be ugly or obnoxious, but you want to make it clear that you expect your customers to pay by the terms to which they agreed when they applied for credit.

The Power of Compensating Balances

One way to measure the value of a company is its profitability. When it comes to the value of a company to a banker, the measure is in compensating balances. Though your ultimate net profit may be pennies on each revenue dollar, you're still funnelling large sums of cash through your bank account as you collect from shippers and pay carriers. Banks are very interested in companies with large cash flows. Even though the money doesn't really belong to you, you have temporary control over it. It will spend a certain amount of time in your account, and that time can be important to a bank. As you build your relationship with your banker, be sure to point out how much cash you expect to move through your accounts—it's called compensating balances—and ask what types of services and/or concessions the bank can provide you because of it.

10.4 Managing payables

Due to the nature of the industry, paying carriers on time is critical. In fact, Bill Tucker says you're a financier of sorts for the carriers you use because you'll likely be paying them before you're paid by your shippers.

While carriers make up the major portion of your payables, you have other bills to pay. Certainly, on-time payment of all your bills is essential to building a good credit rating and maintaining a good reputation. But by the same token, it isn't good cash management to pay your bills before they're due. If your suppliers are willing to extend terms of net 30, then it's OK for you to take 30 days to pay that bill—it's not necessary to pay it 10 or 15 days early. Keep your money working for you in your accounts for as long as possible.

10.5 Facts on factoring

Factoring is the sale of accounts receivable to a third-party funding source for immediate cash. In a typical factoring arrangement, the client (you) makes a sale, delivers the product or service to the customer, and generates an invoice. The factor (the funding source) purchases the right to collect on that invoice by agreeing to pay the client the face value of the invoice less a discount, typically 2–6%. The factor pays 75–80% of the face value immediately and forwards the remainder, less the discount when the customer pays.

Because factors aren't extending credit to their clients but instead to their clients' customers, they're more concerned about the customers' ability to pay rather than the financial status of their clients. That means a company with creditworthy customers may be able to factor in even though it couldn't qualify for a traditional loan.

Though the principles arc the same, factors, vary based on the type of businesses they handle, the amounts of invoices they purchase, and the specific services they provide. Choosing a factor is like choosing a bank —you have to find the right match.

Though factoring is almost as old as commerce itself, it was used primarily by very large corporations until the mid- 1980s. Since then, awareness of factoring has grown, and more companies are incorporating this weapon into their cash management arsenal. Even so, there are still plenty of misconceptions about factoring.

Though factoring is often confused with accounts receivable financing, it's important to understand that this isn't a loan, and it doesn't create a liability on your balance sheet. Rather, it is the sale of an asset, which in this case is an invoice for goods or services received by the customer.

Factoring is also considered one of the most expensive forms of financing, and while it may appear so at first glance, that's not necessarily true. The factor's fee is generally higher than the interest rates a traditional lender charges, but you need to also consider that factors provide a wide range of services that banks do not. They can help with credit checks, take over a significant portion of the accounting function for you, and generate reports to help you track your financial status.

Once you get a handle on money matters, you should be well on your way to running a successful freight brokerage. Good luck!

CHAPTER 11: TALES FROM TRENCHES

By now, you should have a decent understanding of how to get started and what to do—and what not to do—in your own freight brokerage. But nothing beats the voice of experience when it comes to teaching. As a result, we asked seasoned freight brokers what factors have aided their success and what they believe leads businesses to fail. Here's what they had to say to us.

11.1 Use Advertising and Marketing Techniques That Work

Keep track of your marketing efforts so you can focus on the strategies that work while avoiding the ones that don't. Small gift goods, such as pencils, notepads, hats, and T-shirts, perform well, according to Cathy Davis, a freight broker in Smyrna, Tennessee. Personal and industry information in company newsletters also get a positive reaction. She believes that contributions to fundraising events may be beneficial (depending on the event and how well it is publicised) but that the effect of website sponsorships is debatable. She suggested creating a three-panel printed brochure that could be easily attached to letters, bills, and cheques.

You may also increase your brand awareness by putting advertisements in association newsletters and yearly association and industry directories on a regular basis.

11.2 Prepare for the Future

It's natural that your main emphasis right now is on getting started, but you also need to consider the future. Create a succession plan that is evaluated and updated on a yearly basis. Know how leadership will be passed on in the event that it is required, whether via voluntary or involuntary departures.

Don't Reinvent the Wheel.

Look for excellent ideas and items that are currently being used by others that you can integrate into your business. Get ideas from other brokers, carriers, shippers, and even completely unrelated companies; nothing you do has to be unique. When Ron Williamson, a freight broker in Bloomingdale, Illinois, hired someone to build a proprietary computer system, he learned the hard way.

Get Rid of Carriers That Don't Perform.

Every trucking business will have a service issue now and again, but if the problems become chronic, you should remove the carrier from your roster. "If you have continuous issues with your carriers, you won't retain your clients for long," Ron Williamson explains. Of course, he admits that you will most likely not know who the good and bad carriers are at first. While being understanding and giving a carrier a second opportunity is one thing, you must draw the line before the issues impact your own company.

Maintain a Broad and Diverse Customer Base

You'll need enough clients that losing one—or even a few—will not be disastrous. When Cathy Davis managed her freight brokerage, one of the greatest errors she made was allowing one client to control too much of the income. She was left trying to replace that company when that client abruptly pulled away.

Get in the Spotlight

Because the freight sector is so heavily reliant on relationships and reputation, it's beneficial to keep oneself in the public spotlight as much as possible. Being the winner of accolades and having bylined pieces published in trade magazines had a positive effect on Cathy Davis's company.

11.3 Be Open to Evolution

Though a freight brokerage may be very profitable on its own, it can also lead to the growth of other transportation-related businesses, such as consulting, truck purchasing, and becoming a carrier. Bill Tucker, a freight broker in Cherry Hill, New Jersey, for example, provides a broad variety of logistical services.

CHAPTER 12: FAQ'S

1. What is the definition of a freight broker?

The Federal Motor Carrier Safety Administration (FMCSA), a component of the United States Department of Transportation, has defined a freight broker as a property broker. It refers to the licenced people or businesses that assist a shipper and an authorised motor carrier in successfully moving freight.

2. What are the qualifications for becoming a freight broker?

To work as a freight broker, you'll need four legal documents:

1. A Broker's Authority, which may be obtained for $300 from the FMCSA. You fill out Form OP-1 and submit it to the SEC to get your broker's licence.

2. A bank or bonding business may provide you with a Surety Bond or Trust Fund. The price is determined by your own credit. A $75,000 bond or trust is needed of you. BMC-84 or BMC-85 is the form that was submitted with this.

3. Processing Agent, which costs about $50 and comes with form BOC-3.

4. Register as a unified carrier (UCR)

3. Is this a field that is expanding? Is there a demand for it?

There are about 15,000 certified transportation brokers in the United States as of this writing, although many are inactive. In 1970, there were only around 70 brokers. Thus this is still a relatively young business. Freight brokers are thought to contribute about 10% of the shipping industry's income or around $40 billion out of $400 billion. Freight brokerage and logistics, according to a recent publishing in the Wall Street Journal, are the fastest-growing segment of the transportation business.

4. Is there a method to enter the business without needing to get a bond and licence?

Yes. You may start a freight agency or work as a freight broker agent with minimal risk and without needing to acquire your own licence. In such a scenario, you'd work as an agent under the supervision of another broker, and your earnings would be shared with the broker.

5. What tools will I need to get started?

You'll need a computer with high-speed Internet, a fax machine, a phone, and phone service with cheap unlimited long distance if you want to start a freight brokerage or agency. If you're starting a brokerage, you'll almost certainly need to invest in transportation software. If you're an agent, you'll utilise the software provided by your broker.

6. Is this a work-at-home opportunity?

Absolutely. The majority of agents and brokers operate from their homes.

7. How long would it take for my company to break even?

Building up your client database will take time, just like starting any other company. Typically, it takes three to six months of hard effort to see a significant return. Sometimes it takes a lot less time, and sometimes it takes a lot more. However, after you've established a client base, they'll almost always have leftover shipping, so the offer will keep repeating itself. Many variables influence your degree of success, including your level of drive, perseverance, and genuine desire to assist your clients to succeed.

8. What is the average salary for a freight broker or agent?

Again, your profits will be decided by your own skills and will to achieve. You may earn anything from $40,000 to well over $100,000 as a full-time broker or agent.

$200,000 and above. As you progress, your potential becomes practically limitless.

9. Where do I look for customers?

We go through this topic in-depth in the session, giving you a variety of methods for finding your shippers, including periodicals, reference books, and Internet sites.

10. What factors should I consider when deciding whether to open my own brokerage or work as an agent?

There are many variables to consider while making this choice, which we will discuss in-depth throughout the session. Money, time, and experience, among other things, are three key variables. In any case, you'll need three to six months' worth of living costs or supplementary income to get your company off the ground. If you want to establish your own brokerage, you'll need more money for cash flow and start-up expenses.

CONCLUSION

There are many stages involved in becoming a freight broker. To begin, you must first create a strong business strategy and register the appropriate corporation to carry out that plan. Then, to acquire all of your registration and licences from the FMCSA, you must follow our step-by-step instructions. You're ready to start promoting and brokering after you've received your UCR. The current median salary for a freight broker is more than $42,000 per year, which is a welcome relief. When you add in the stated high work satisfaction, it's easy to see why this sector is booming and why you should join it! This guide provides you with all of the resources you'll need to get started in this fascinating profession. Once you're up and running, you'll reap the rewards that drew you to become a freight broker in the first place: work freedom and a bright future.

That is exactly why freight brokerage is so fascinating. You schedule freight deliveries by tonne and are always looking for the most efficient method to transport everything. Everyone benefits when you perform your job properly.

BOOK 2: TRUCKING COMPANY BUSINESS STARTUP

The most complete Step-by-Step Guide to successfully & quickly start your own trucking company business from scratch

INTRODUCTION

We have constantly been observing for a while now that there is this wave of startups. We see everyone trying their hand at entrepreneurship. These businesses range from small home-based setups to huge business setups. No one formula can determine a business to take off and flourish. With the observation that startups are launched at a great speed, most of them disappear as soon as they come into existence. One rule, however, can be successfully applied. Start a business based on the demand in that given time.

If you look at current times, we observe great potential in logistics, especially the trucking industry. According to a survey conducted by the American Trucking Associations, there has been a generation of $700 billion in revenues for 2017.

This industry has huge potential. It is observed that trucking businesses are creating a huge profit for the economy in general as well. It can be observed that people who are venturing into the trucking business are expected to get great profits and success in the trucking industry.

This book will find a detailed description of the trucking industry and how you can start a trucking business. All the necessary details and requirements are discussed in the following chapters.

CHAPTER 1. STARTING A TRUCKING BUSINESS

In this chapter, we will look at the step-by-step process of starting a trucking business. Before moving further, we should understand that starting a trucking business might seem easy from afar, but it could be quite daunting when you bring in the details. When we think about a trucking business, we only think of buying a truck and delivering stuff to doorsteps. There is a lot more to a trucking business, and it takes a lot of hard work and effort to start and then maintain a decent trucking business, let alone a successful one. We will discuss all the points important to set up and start a trucking business.

Given the world's circumstances today, with the pandemic still having its effects worldwide, it seems pretty overwhelming to even start a new venture or business. A person has to be extra cautious when even thinking about starting a new business. There are a lot of things to be considered once you start a business. A few being, the research, the market survey, bureaucracy, the expenses and a huge amount of paperwork that has to be done. All this and much more can confuse someone who is a first-timer. You will often be at a point where you will find yourself deciding not to move forward with your plans. But the urge to become a business owner will keep on itching you time and again. If you are that sort of a person, you should try to make your mark in the business field.

Now let us come to the main focus, the trucking business. The good news about this business is that it is one of the very few businesses which remained unaffected even during the pandemic. The corona virus was not able to affect this business.

It is one business that generated revenues amid the corona virus pandemic. It has been observed that the trucking business has shown to be stable, and the growth rate has been steady as well. The demand for truck drivers and loaders has increased over the past two or three years.

If you are still confused about whether or not to start a new business, this chapter will help you decide in a much better way.

The business is on the boom these days, and when a certain industry is on the rise, it is likely to gain profits in a shorter period than other businesses that might be stable but are not in demand. The ATA (American Trucking Associations) survey reported that in the year 2019, there were approximately 3.6 million truck and van drivers hired. Compared to the year 2018, this was an increase of 1.7 percent. Now that we have established a guarantee of employment with the trucking business, we know that the profits are also steady with this business.

According to another survey by ATA, there have been 791.7 billion dollars with primary shipments only in 2019. These further proofs that even in 2021, the trucking industry is expected to be strong as ever. It only leaves you with the question of how and where to start.

The first step in creating any business is to focus on your business strategy and develop a business plan. First, you will have to set up a plan and calculate the amount of money you have and how much you are willing to invest.

Another aspect is that you have to take a calculated risk; you will have to measure how long you can sustain the business without profits.

For this, you will have to create a detailed plan for how you will go about the business and where you will start.

Now let us imagine that you have started your own business, and your start-up has taken off; you will need proper software and technology to match the competition in this digital age. It will ensure your chances of success. Now, let us focus on where to start:

1. Come up with a Business Plan:

The first and most important step in starting a business is to create a solid business plan. The business plan should be detailed and well written and should cover all the aspects of the business. It should include every detail about how the business will be and how you have planned for the performance and functions. The sources of investment and your plans regarding the financing should be mentioned in the business plan. This detailing in the business plan will have two advantages. The first one is obvious that you will be able to run your business smoothly and successfully. The other advantage is showing this business plan to prospected investors or banks where you want to apply for a loan. A well-written business plan will create a good impression on the investor and the bank, and the chances for loan approval will be brighter.

Now, we should discuss how to write a good business plan and the key features in the business plan. Following are the points that should be mentioned in the business plan:

- The plan should start with your main business name and the objective of the business. Along with this information, the plan should mention all the services you are willing to provide.

- You should mention any research and any market survey you have conducted regarding the business.

- It would be best to mention why your company is better than the competitors and your business's edge.

- Then you will have to put in details about your target market.

How you are going to fulfill the needs of the customers.

- You should mention that how you plan to expand your business and increase your profits and revenue.

- You should mention the members you will need for your company. The number of employees you wish to hire, and you should mention the reason to hire the number of people you wish to hire. You should mention the roles of the people you will hire.

- In the end, again you should mention the main objectives of this business. Highlight the services your business will provide. Also, mention your clear plan on how to meet your targets and goals.

You should always keep in mind that your business plan should be written, considering who the business plan is written for. The other name for the business plan is also a business proposal, so it should be written as such. You should also mention timelines in your business plan. It should be mentioned that the goals and targets are expected to be achieved in the given period. There should be supporting surveys and explanations to back your claims so that the business plan seems stronger.

The plan should not look artificial; the deadlines and targets set should be realistic. Whit this, we come to the next step of our business. The next step is to showcase and determine what business strategy you are going to use. In short, you should explain your business structure. Business structure means how you are going to form and establish your trucking and transportation business.

1. Build the Business Structure:

Now, this point depends totally on your preference and requirement. You will first have to decide what kind of trucking business you want to establish. Next, you will choose from the available, tried and tested business models, the one that fits your needs. For this purpose, you will have to do an extensive study on how others formed their businesses. It will be better to study the cases of people who started businesses with the resources comparable to the kind of investment you are ready to put in. For the establishment of a company, there are four kinds of business models that are mostly considered. Namely:

- Partnerships

- LLC (Limited Liability Corporations)

- Sole Proprietorship

- C Corp (Corporation).

With each kind of business, structure come different types of rules and laws by which they are governed. Each business structure has a few pros and a few cons. You will have to choose which kind of business you want to set up, and the advantages and disadvantages will be according to your requirements.

It is an important step and should be taken wisely. In the following paragraphs, we will discuss each type of business model that will make it easier for you to decide.

2. Partnerships:

As the name suggests, this kind of business plan is for those who wish to start a business with single or multiple partners. If you intend to start a company independently, this kind of business model is not for you. However, if you are willing to start a partnership, the USA Small Business Administration mentions that there are two types of partnerships, limited partnerships and limited liability partnerships. Limited and limited liability partnerships are quite similar, but the difference is that there is limited liability given to each partner in the limited liability partnership.

It means that one partner is not responsible for the actions of the other partner or partners. In this way, the partners are protected from any debts against the partnership.

3. Sole Proprietorship:

This kind of business structure is most suitable for someone involved in the business as a single owner. So, you will have complete control over the business, and all the decisions regarding the business will be yours. With this advantage, there lies a disadvantage as well. With this business model, your assets and liabilities will be connected to the business liabilities and assets. You will be responsible for your debts and liabilities yourself, which can damage your assets. You will have to find a way to protect your assets and keep them disconnected from your business.

4. Limited Liability Corporations (LLC):

In the United States of America, this is the most common and most popular business model for small businesses and startups. The benefit of starting an LLC is that they are made according to state law, and limited liability protection is provided to the business owners. It means that in this kind of corporation, you get a few tax benefits. The owner has to pay taxes, and there is a tax exemption at the limited liability corporations (LLC) level.

5. The Corporations (C Corp):

According to the United States Small Business Administration, corporations are legal and separate entities separate from their owners. Just like a person is liable for tax, can make a personal profit and is legally liable. Similarly, the corporation will also be taxed, able to make a profit and held accountable legally in any case of default. From the perspective of business owners, this is the safest kind of business model for them. It provides a great deal of security, and your assets are not connected to the corporation in any way. The only downside to this kind of business model is that to form a corporation is more expensive, and the costs to form such a corporation are significantly higher than all the other business structures discussed above. The corporations have to pay income tax on all their profits, which is not the case in the other three business models. Although this is the safest kind of business structure with the costs, the owners will have to arrange for proper record keeping, proper operations processes and procedures, and a significant amount of reporting. There is a lot of paperwork involved in this type of business structure. For this purpose, more staff will have to be hired as well.

With an overview of the available business models, you will be able to make a sound decision about the path you would want to follow. You can also consult an accountant for their expert advice and explain your requirements and financial state to them. If you want to keep your assets and business separate, it is always better to avoid partnerships and sole proprietorships. It is an important decision, and the foundation of your business will rely on this. This decision should be taken wisely.

6. Obtain Licenses and Permits

After the initial business plans and business structures, you will need several permits to start a trucking business. The drivers will require a license for each kind of vehicle you plan to use in your business. If you plan to serve as a driver for your own company, you should know that you require a related divers license. It is different from the license you obtain for driving a personal car. You require a different type of license to transfer goods, known as the Commercial Driver's License (CDL). The CDL also has different types. The categories are usually A, B and C. the letters A, B and C are based on the type of vehicle, vehicle size, and the kind of goods you will be transporting. For the exact license you need to acquire, you should consult the DMV for your state. It will give you a clear picture of the rules, regulations and requirements. You should also know that to obtain such a license, and you will be required to take practical classes, written tests, health inspections and then pass the road test to obtain the license finally. It is always advisable to obtain a license before starting your business venture.

Also, when hiring any drivers for your company, always do a complete background check and check for the required license so that there are no ambiguities once they start working for you.

Other than driving licenses, you will also be required to obtain different permits for different transportation assignments. For example, you must obtain a permit following federal law and the respective state's laws to transport cargo. You will have to follow a set of rules determined by the law to carry out cargo transportation. There are several permits you will have to obtain. To ship different goods, there are different requirements. After that, you will also have to obtain a Motor Carrier Authority number and a Federal DOT number. This number will track the location of your trucks and cargo. This number will also be used for inspection to ensure that your business complies with the federal and state laws of the United States of America. The Motor Carrier Authority Number has to be obtained for your vehicles and the kinds of goods transported through them. These numbers are crucial to ensure your compliance with the laws. You will have to file for these numbers with the Federal Motor Carrier Safety Administration (FMCSA). Once you have filed the applications, you will have to wait for 10 days which is the mandatory wait time. Anyone who feels that you should not start the trucking business can challenge your applications in this period.

You will have to obtain working insurance for your business. The next permit you will be required to apply for is the Unified Carrier Registration (UCR). This registration is to certify that you have obtained the necessary insurance for your business.

The insurance must be following the laws of the state you are operating your business from.

You will have to obtain additional permits if your trucking company plans to operate throughout the country and Canada; you will have to obtain another permit. You will have to apply for an IRP, which is the International Plan Tag. It is an additional license plate that allows you to transfer goods throughout the country and Canadian territory. You will have to renew your International Plan Tag every year, and there is a fee for the renewal of this tag.

The fees change over time, and you will have to confirm the related fees and renewals from the DMV office or website. Sticker. Another permit you will have to obtain is a fuel permit or a fuel sticker. In the official language, it is known as the International Fuel Agreement. This sticker is required if you intend to transfer goods from one state to another where the jurisdiction changes. Also, this sticker is essential if you run operations in Canada as well.

The utility of this sticker is to make it easy to report the consumption of fuel by the vehicles that travel and transport goods from state to state. This sticker is easy to obtain, all you have to do is apply for the International Fuel Tax agreement sticker with the correct details about your vehicle and intended use, and you will get the sticker within a few days.

7. Get insurance:

Along with all the other kinds of permits and licenses, you will also need several kinds of insurances for your trucking business. Insurance is expensive but necessary and a legal requirement by federal law.

You cannot function in the trucking industry without necessary insurances. You will find all the rules and regulations and the relative fees for the insurances in the FMCSA. You will have to obtain more than one insurance for your trucking business, so you should carefully research what kind of insurance you will require. According to the Federal Law, you will require four types of insurances for your business in the trucking industry before you can even start to drive:

- All the trucks that you have leased or you own should be insured. It is known as Primary Auto Liability. Under this, all your vehicles should be insured. It protects and covers the insurance holders if the third party has had an accident and is injured. This kind of insurance coverage starts from $750,000 to $5,000,000, depending on the vehicle, the goods used to transfer the route, and the risks involved. All factors are taken into consideration before getting insured.

- There is another kind of insurance you will have to obtain, known as General Liability. You will have to obtain this insurance for every state you wish to operate in. this insurance protects the business owner or the employee if they accidentally cause damage to any property or cause any other kind of bodily damage.

- The third kind of insurance is known as physical damage insurance. It kind of insurance will protect the owner in case of theft, vandalism and case of natural calamities. If you have this insurance, you can obtain a new vehicle or truck if the vehicle gets damaged due to such an event. For unforeseen conditions, this kind of insurance is necessary.

- If you want to use your vehicle for other purposes apart from business use, such as for personal usage, you will need insurance. This kind of insurance is known as bobtail insurance which allows you to use your vehicle personally off duty.

These four kinds of insurances are necessary for the trucking business alone. If you have obtained these four types of insurances, it is easy for you to get on the road, but you might also want to consider other types of insurances from a business viewpoint. These kinds of insurances may include medical insurance for your employees if they get injured during the job or insurance for yearly check-ups for your drivers. You might also want to get insurance for the cargo you intend to transfer to get some protection and coverage for expensive items or big shipments. You might think that paying the insurance premium is a waste of money, but insurances come in very handy in times of need. You never know when an adversary might hit you, and in those conditions, your insurance will provide you with the financial and mental protection you would require.

8. Raise Money for the Star Up:

To start any business, you need finance. Buying trucks and obtaining the required permits and insurance cost a hefty amount. Sometimes you have some of your own money you are willing to invest, but you still require a loan or a partner or a line of credit. In most cases, you will start your business with a loan. Starting a trucking business is no easy feat, but it will be easier for you if you start small. The scale of your business determines what kind of investment and funding you need. For this, you must have a clear picture of what you expect from your business; the business plan is of utmost importance. The loan you might be granted from a bank will determine how well you have planned your business, how realistic your plan seems, and how promising this business idea looks on paper. The same is the case with any other investor you might be pitching your idea to. You should be clear about how much initial investment is required and how much will be required to keep the business afloat until you start making profits. If you do not have the right type of investment or obtain a lower loan, this will create problems to move further ahead, and you will see yourself failing in no time.

9. Getting hold of your Vehicles

For a trucking business, the most important component is the vehicles. The number and type of vehicles you buy directly depend on the type of business you plan to start. First, you will have to decide what kinds of goods you are going to transport. Either you will operate in a single state, or you want to operate across the country if you are planning to operate beyond the USA. After that, you will have to plan what type of items you will transport and deliver. If you plan to deliver perishable items or goods that require certain conditions, like medicines or frozen foods, you might want to buy a refrigerator truck. Another important consideration would be whether you will be doing day trips or plan to do overnight trips. In case you are planning to do overnight trips, you might want to consider a truck that has space for you to sleep as well. If you are starting a new business, buying second-hand trucks or leasing used trucks is advisable to save some money. The only important consideration, in this case, would be that the condition of the vehicles is acceptable. Often, it is seen that people try to save money by buying used vehicles, but they end up spending more on maintenance because of the quality of the vehicle.

10. The Management of the Trucking business:

Once you have obtained all the necessary licenses and permits, it is important to select your core team. It is a crucial step in business building a business. What most people try to do when starting a business is that you try to do everything yourself. It may seem to be a formula in which you save money by not hiring staff, you might be able to manage in the initial stages of your business, but this might become a nightmare once your business starts to flourish. Also, sometimes it is better to leave some tasks to the professionals. Now in the trucking business, the most important component is drivers. If you plan to use one truck and drive yourself, you must get the CDL, but if you want more than one truck and start your work at a slightly higher scale, you will have to hire drivers. It is always better to look out for drivers with prior experience. But drivers with experience these days are in huge demand and may charge a sum of money. So, you might be interested in hiring drivers without experience. When hiring people without experience, it is always smart to hire someone who already has CDL to save you from costs to get the driver CDL. Apart from drivers, there are a couple of people you should hire:

- Hire an office manager who can take care of all the administrative work and deal with the huge amount of paperwork with the trucking business.

- Next, you might want to hire an accountant or a bookkeeper for all the record-keeping and accounting work. This person will manage all your taxes and manage the payroll.

- Once your business has taken off, you will want to expand. For that, you will require a person who manages your marketing. It is an era of digital networking. So, you should hire someone who has expertise in the digital advertising field as well. You might want to hire more than one person to manage customer service and marketing on different platforms.

It is the basic team you will have to hire for your small trucking start-up. Now, you should always keep in mind that it will take time to create the perfect team, and the downside of this is that the only way to get your team is by hit and trial. There is no fast fix to getting the right people for your business. The only thing you can control is, before hiring anyone, you should do a complete background check and ensure that you can trust this person with the given tasks.

11. Find the correct Programmes and Technology for your business:

The trucking business is one where you do not have the conventional desk and char set up. Most of the employees are out and about. With the advent of technology, you can use the already created applications to manage your trucking business successfully. In this way, you can always remain connected with all your staff members and ensure that the business is running smoothly throughout the place. Using an app makes things much simpler and easier. The employees feel at ease with managing the tasks, and they will be more motivated to work if the work is in systematic order. It will ensure higher productivity.

The most common application most people are using these days is the Connect am app. It is an app for business and employee management app. It is suitable for the trucking business because you can access the app anywhere; this removes the need for the conventional desk and char setup. The functions you will be able to control remotely include:

1. Scheduling dispatch orders.

2. Allot tasks to the employees

3. Control workflow

4. Manage and monitor clock in timings and clock out timings. It will enable to calculate the number of hours a person is working.

The advantages of using such an app for your trucking business are:

- You can offer online courses and pieces of training for your employees. It will ensure that all your staff members are up to date with the latest rules and regulations of the business. This training will also provide information about the safety and standard operating procedures. The rules and regulations change and are updated time and again, so with such online training, the employees will be able to learn and function better without having to attend physical workshops and pieces of training.

- The owner will be able to schedule all the tasks digitally. It will be easily communicated to the entire team without informing and updating every person individually. You will be easily able to make changes and corrections, and update schedules and the employees will be able to see as soon as the schedule is updated. The employees may confirm their availability for the tasks, and the information will be updated and visible to everyone.

- You can manage the location and positions of trucks. You can colour code the type of trucks so that it is easy to interpret where each of your consignments is and the current status of delivery and transfer.

- There is a feature for live chat for all the members of the company. So, whoever is using the application can send and receive messages and updates. If there is any delay or problem someone faces, you can deal with it as soon as possible. The important announcements can easily be made through this application. The business owner can be assured of all workflow and status of work at any time. You can easily send appreciation messages to the employees through this feature as soon as the given task is completed.

- A feature included in the app is a time tracker and location tracker with geo fencing. With this, the drivers can easily update their location and the completed orders. This way, the owner can also keep track of their employees and each order's total time. This information can be useful for future projects and estimations.

- There is another important feature in this application. It is known as the workflow feature. This feature is more useful for administrative work. With the help of this feature, you can keep your internal operation records. The drivers can put in information regarding completed orders. Automatic reminders can be put within the app so that the drivers are reminded of the monthly maintenance and inspections of the vehicles.

- Most of the work can be achieved online through the app. So, the data and can be constantly updated.

- You can create forms, instructions, and circulars within the app in PDF, and they can easily be signed and updated by the employees as soon as they see them.

- The employees can give a real-time location update and any new information that needs to be delivered via the app.

- Th best feature about this app is that all the data is stored online, and there is no limit for data storage. You will be saved from tons of paperwork you would otherwise require in a business.

A business management app is the need of the hour. You might feel that it is not as beneficial at your business, but the utility will be understood as soon as it starts growing and flourishing.

In this chapter, we have targeted all the basics to start the trucking business. We have already determined that the trucking business is high in demand, and there is a lot of profit in this kind of business given the current scenario of the world. The need for transportation services is on a high. Now you know that to start a trucking business, you will need a solid business plan. Take your time to research the market. What is it that is required, and what is it that you want to do. You must be fully invested in what you want to do and how you want to contribute. So always consider this as well. There are many options for the trucking business; most of them will make you profit but differentiating between good and better is the driving force. And the driving force is always the person who conceived the idea. So always consider your liking as well as a gut feeling. The next most important thing is market research. Do thorough research on the actual demand of the market, what the customers want. Businesses are always customer-driven, they demand, and the business provides. You will have to determine and devise the best business plan to cater to the customers. The next thing is getting the finances. You should ensure that the business plan is attractive enough for the investors or the banks where you will be applying for loans. A good business plan and an informed presentation to the prospected investors is always a plus point. It might be possible that the plan you come up with is brilliant, but you cannot sell it to the investors. So, presentation and precision are mandatory when putting forward your business plan. Next, you should be clear in your mind about the size of your business and the business structure you will be choosing to carry forward. It will make it easy for you to determine the kind of permits and license you will have to apply for and obtain. One thing to always consider is that some permits have their fees. Dome permits have a one-time fee, and some have an annual fee. It is important to note that these costs are usually on the higher side.

Next, you will have to decide what kind of vehicle you are willing to use for this business. The first decision will be whether you are buying a new truck or going for a used truck. A new truck is always the best option in terms of quality and durability. It also comes with some sort of warranty from the manufacturers as well. The downside of using a new truck is obvious. The costs of new vehicles are on a much higher side. In starting a new business, you always want to keep the costs limited and in control. So, it is advisable in most cases that you go for a second-hand truck or vehicle. The only thing you will have to take care of will be the quality. Most of the time, second-hand vehicles look fine until you start using them. It is always advisable that you bring a professional mechanic or someone who understands the vehicle's working with you to inspect the used vehicle before purchasing it.

Once you have decided what kind of vehicle you want to buy, you will have to decide what kind and size of truck you will have to buy. This decision is directly related to the kinds of goods and items you are planning to transport. You will have to do thorough research on the special requirements of each of the items to take this decision.

Next comes the staff. You will want to keep your budget to the minimum at the beginning of the business, but you cannot ignore that you need staff to manage different aspects of the business. Business owners usually make one mistake because they think they will manage everything themselves and not need any staff members. It is the biggest mistake some people make. Sure, when you start a business, you can manage everything single handily, but once the business starts to take off, you will not juggle all things. If you start as a one-man company, there are chances that you will have problems when you do have to hire people because you will have to train them, and there will be the business to manage, and there is always a shortage of time. In the flip scenario, if you start with a team, they will get many opportunities to learn. With a low workload, they can be easily trained without affecting the work and projects. And by the time you get more business and there is an increased workload, you already have a trusted team, and your workflow can be managed easily.

Last but not the least, you have to be up to date with the latest technology in business. You should invest in an app for business management. The digital era and the trend of a table and chair office setting are already considered a thing of the past. You should have a business management app to control your business even if you are not physically present to oversee the operations. With the help of an app, all the data, paperwork and conversations and mails between the company and the employees will be automatically saved, and the hassle to keep records is reduced. You and your employees can keep in touch even if you are not there physically. This type of business setup is the best for a trucking company because most work involves transport, and most employees are almost always on the go. Apart from the business management app, you can also keep a bookkeeping app. It will ensure all your payments to the staff and payroll will be run smoothly. All the payments received can be monitored, and all the money matters can be streamlined. This way, an automatic digital record can also be created to avoid discrepancies within the business. You can manage the accounts yourself or hire an accountant to keep and evaluate your financial records.

CHAPTER 2. OUTLINES OF STARTING A TRUCKING BUSINESS

We know that trucking is a business that gets profits. The American industry relies heavily on the trucking industry. When Americans are switching from the conventional ways of life and depend more on online purchases, this industry is not going anywhere in this date and age. It's only going to bloom further. There are different types of people who want to venture into the trucking business. Some people are drivers who see an opportunity as a business owner, and some people want to make investments and get profits, and some are new to the business market and try their hand at business to gain profits and earn a steady income. All these groups can start a trucking business, but the most important feature is research and knowledge. You need to read and discover as much as you can about the business before starting even a one-truck business. You need to talk to people who are in this business, read case histories. Learn how to make a business plan and see what has worked in the past and what has not worked. Also, look at businesses that have failed in the past and learn from the mistakes. Be ready for loss. Go in with a positive attitude but be ready for adversary as well.

Having put out all the risks involved, we must suggest that business in the trucking field is a good option and the best time to start is now when you have strength and energy in you.

Once you have established a steady income, you can always hire staff and overlook the business when it is time to retire. This plan seems perfect, but the foundation that has to be set should be strong for this plan to work.

Now that we have already established that trucking is a good business option, we shall discuss the basic outlines of the business structures. The essentials to start a trucking business and where to start.

- Arrange for Commercial Driver's License

It has been discussed in the previous chapter as well. In this chapter, we are going to get into details of this. Either you want to drive yourself or hire a driver; whoever drives the vehicle needs a CDL. First of all, no one can operate a commercial truck for business purposes without a CDL. It is the requirement of the Federal Motor Carrier Security Authority. There are a few requirements for the CDL:

1. The driver should have his social security number.

2. You will have to provide proof of your identity.

3. The person applying for the license must have valid residency in the United States of America.

4. You need to be above 21 to apply for CDL, which makes you eligible for transportation interstate.

5. First, you will apply for the CDL with the FMCSA.

6. Next, you will have to get your eyesight tested.

7. You will have to pass another knowledge exam to get the Commercial Driver's Permit.

8. Next, you will have to take a before-trip inspection test with the vehicle provided by them.

9. After passing that test, you will put in the fee for the CDL and hopefully obtain a driver's license.

• Obtain Trucking Authority

It is another way to say that you need to get yourself registered before starting this business. In the trucking business, it is termed as filing for your trucking authority. Plan to transport in vehicles with a weight of more than ten thousand gross vehicle weight, and your business will cross state borders. You will have to apply for a trucking authority with the Federal Motor Carriers Security Authority. After getting the authority, you will obtain a Motor Carrier Number, more commonly denoted as MC#. It will enable you to move your vehicle across states as well. For this, first, you will have to find a nice and unique name for your company. Then check online so that it is confirmed that this name is not already taken by someone else. Then you will have to apply for the MC# with the FMCSA. You have to mention that you will be transporting good interstate as well. Usually, if there are no other problems, you will get the MC# quite easily.

• Find Process Agents

It is one requirement that a lot of people do not know about. The trucking business deals with different states. As it is known the in the USA, all states have their laws and regulations.

So, for carrying out business in a different state, you need legal representation in each state you wish to operate in. Process Agents are your legal representatives, to be precise. You will need a process agent in each state you operate your business in. For example, you carry out business in two states, so you will have to find two process agents. For the trucking business, you cannot skip this step. It may seem like a hassle, but in reality, the legal representatives make your work much easier. They are familiar with the state laws and better equipped to deal with situations that may suddenly arise.

You may think it might be difficult to find process agents for yourself, but it is not that difficult. The FMCSA requires the processing agent, so on their website, you will find a link to legal representation throughout America, and you can choose the required state from there. They are professionals and know their job pretty well. When you present your business proposal for acceptance in court, the process agent will walk you through the procedure and be your legal representative. Your legal representative will be helpful in situations that you sometimes face in other states. They will appear on your behalf and manage the proceedings. It is the process agent who will complete your BOC-3 paperwork.

- Decide on the Business Structure

Next, you will have to decide on your business structure. As discussed in the previous chapter, you have an option of four types of business structures in the trucking industry:

1. Limited Liability Corporation
2. Corporation
3. Partnership
4. Sole Proprietorship

Deciding about this point is difficult because each setup has its advantages and disadvantages. It also depends on your current financial stability. The best person to consult in such a situation is an accountant. It is an expert person who will evaluate your current situation and advice you accordingly. The accountant will evaluate your current financial health and explain to you regarding the taxes and other matters.

Many people opt for a sole proprietorship to save taxes. Another advantage of this kind of business model is that it is the cheapest. When people look to start a new business, saving extra money is what they have on their minds. The only drawback of this business model is that you will be held completely responsible for whatever happens if something goes wrong. It means that you could be sued for all your business and personal assets. In the case where you form a corporation, your assets will be secured. But forming a corporation is much expensive, and many people are not willing to go through this route.

- Obtaining All the Permits and Licenses

As discussed in the previous chapter, you will have to get hold of several licenses before you start your trucking business. In this chapter, we will jot down point by point regarding the legal requirements.

1. Frist, you will have to apply for your DOT number. The DOT number is the US Department of Transport Number.

2. Next, you will apply for your MC#, also known as the Federal Authorities.

3. You will have to file for a BOC-3 in court through your process agent.

4. File for your IFT. It is the International Fuel Tax sticker. You will have to obtain this for all your vehicles.

5. Buy the required insurance policies. You will have to get policies for cargo as well as primary liability.

6. If you plan to transport goods and items beyond the United States of America, get a UCR permit and the International Registration Plan's IRP. For this, you will also have to get relative car plates for your vehicles.

7. You will have to obtain a special Employee Identification Number for IRS, irrespective of whether you filed as an LLC or a corporation or filed as a sole proprietor.

8. You have to install electronic logging devices on all your vehicles. All these devices must comply with FMCSA.

Please make sure you take care of all these important permits and licenses. Take care that some of the permits have to be renewed annually.

- Insurance

It is an important part of the trucking business. Obtaining insurance might seem expensive, but it is required in case of misfortunes and accidents. We have observed that truck and large vehicle accidents account for a substantial amount of damage and accidents. The compensation values are quite high, and even medical bills may take a toll. For this reason, investment in insurance is essential. Insurance will protect you against bearing the cost of huge loss to vehicles and their repair.

Apart from that, the insurance will cover for harm and injuries that might be caused due to the truck or carrier. There are specific requirements mentioned on the FMCSA website for trucking industry insurance. Refer to those and find insurance that suits your requirements. It is always advised to look around few options, and then it will be easy to choose the best option for yourself. As discussed in the previous chapter, you will have to get more than one insurance for the trucking industry. These are a few different types of insurances that you will have to invest in:

1. The primary Liability: the minimum requirement for this kind of insurance is $750,000. In some cases, the requirement is even up to $1000,000 for the coverage.

2. Insurance for Physical Damage: This type of insurance cover is required for accidents considers as no-fault.

3. The cargo insurance: the minimum coverage for this kind of insurance should be $100,000.

4. You will have to get insurance when you are handling the goods and products of a company other than yours. For accidents in such conditions, you must get insurance.

- Buy or Lease a Vehicle

To buy a truck or trailer is no easy thing. Either you can buy a truck or not depends on your credit scores. A lot of people do not have credit scores that are up to the mark. There are options for such people as well. So basically, in the trucking business, there are three types of ways in which you can get the vehicle:

Operators: this is the simple and most straightforward way. You get the vehicle on lease, and you pay for all the kinds of permits required. The truck remains in your possession for the whole leasing period, and you take care of all the maintenance in the whole leasing period. You pay all the required taxes, and at the end of the leasing period, you give back the vehicle.

Lease-Purchase: This is almost the same as the first type of lease, but this is applicable for people with lower credit scores. The only difference is that you will have to pay a higher leasing premium in this case. All the other features remain. You keep the vehicles, you pay the taxes, you get the permits, and in the end, you turn in the vehicle.

The Close of Terminal Rental Adjustment: in this case, you will have to put in a down payment at the starting of the lease. And keep on paying the lease; at the end of the lease, you can pay off to own the vehicle, or you can turn in the vehicle and then the company that leased it to you can sell it, and the balance can be shared.

- How to Find Business

Once you complete all the requirements for your business, you should start looking for business options. Gone are the times when you had to go door to door to get business. Now is the digital age; you can find work by clicking on the keyboard or your smartphone. Here we will discuss an amazing app that helps you find work and all the other amazing features in this work finding app.

The app is known as the Tuckshop app. It is an amazing app to find the work. With hundreds of options, you can easily choose the best option for yourself. This app has different features, which we are going to discuss one by one:

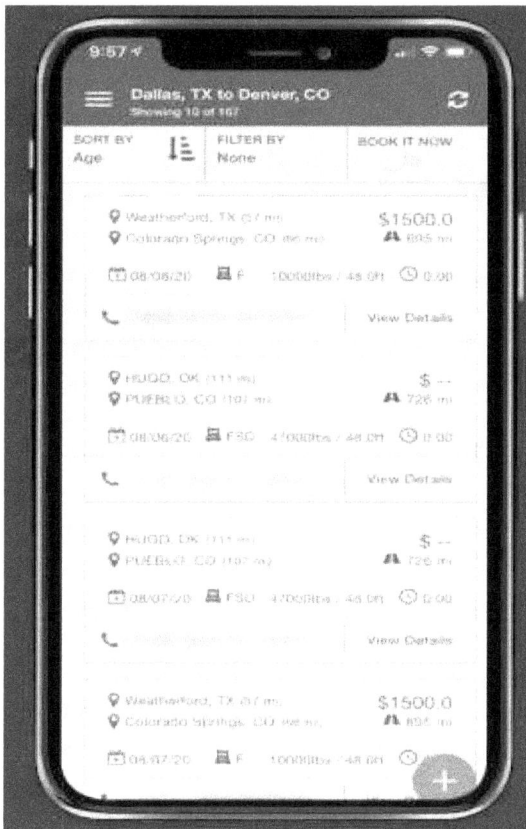

1. Searching A Load

So, in this app, there is a feature of Book it now, which you click, and it will give you options for loads and trucking jobs throughout the United States of America. You will have to select your specific state where you want to function and easily find suitable jobs. Once you book a project, then you can negotiate and discuss the details.

2. Distances and Mileage

The app provides you with the correct maps and routes in different states. It will mention the mileage and fuel usage by different vehicles as well. It is an important feature that you can consult before making the trip to know the time and all the important information regarding the route you want to take. You can also find the exact information according to the type of your truck or the lane you are going to move in. You can even customize the features according to the weight of the load you will carry and the truck's height. This feature will give you an overview of your trip, and you can plan accordingly.

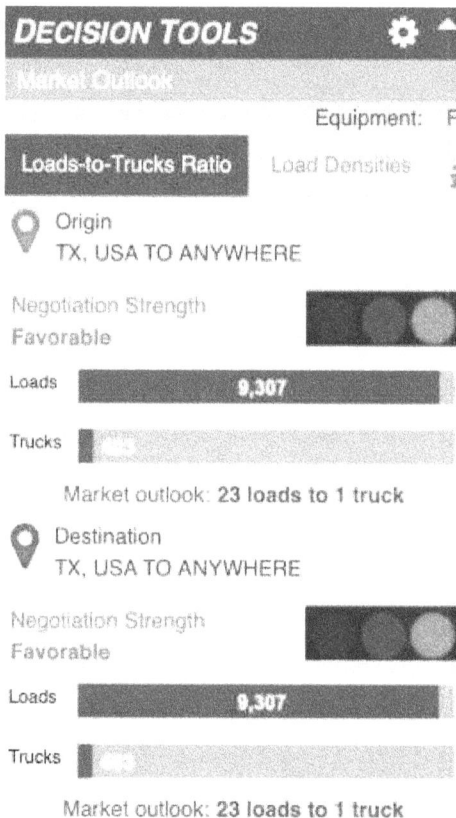

3. Decision Tools:

It is another feature of the app. In this, you can look at jobs and negotiate better with the prospected business brokers or partners. You can view how many drivers have looked at the given gig and evaluate your negotiation according to the demand of the job. You can even choose jobs according to the destination you would want to go to next. This app makes decisions much easier for you and opens numerous options for you.

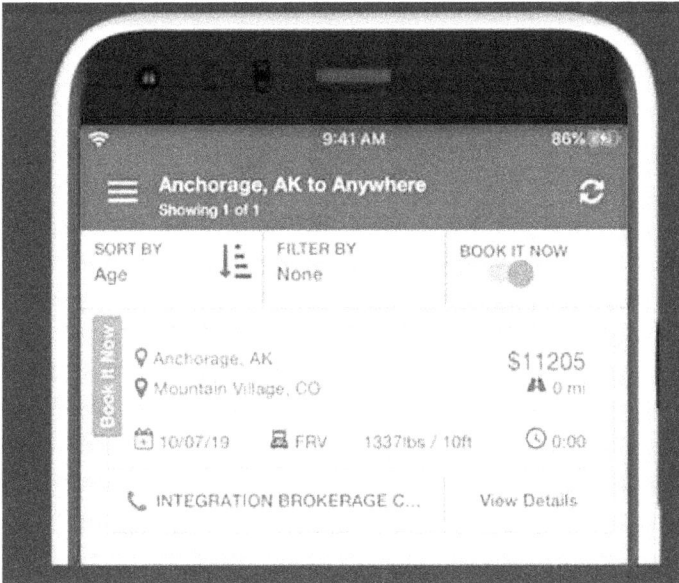

1. Book It Right Now Feature

It is another feature where you can look for a trucking project or job, and you can instantly book for that job. You can use this app from a computer, laptop or even a smartphone or tab and easily click Book it and sign up for the job. Getting a job is as easy as clicking on the button. The only thing to be careful of is that before booking any job, research it fully.

Either you will be able to do this, the distance and the price. People often cannot meet deadlines because they take up much more work more than they can complete. So always be careful of this that only take up that much work which you can easily do.

2. Fuel Desk

It is another feature included in this app. What you can do is that first of all, put in all the travel details. The tool will calculate the nearest route and the fuel requirements. It will also suggest nearby refuelling stations for your convenience. All this planning will make your trip quite smooth. This feature will also estimate the IFTA data for you to find all the fuel rates easily.

3. Background Checks

There is a feature in this app known as the credit of the broker. You can check the credit history of the broker or the person who has advertised the business opportunity.

You can check if this is a genuine person or a fraud. You can search the company name and check if it is legal. Check for the validity of the DOT number.

4. The Price of the App

For this app, there are three plans which are Basic, Advanced and Pro plan. The Basic plan costs approximately $39. The Advanced plan costs $125, and the Pro plan costs $149.

If you start your company at a small scale, it is best to get the basic plan, and you can always upgrade to the pro plan when your business expands and grows. If you buy the pro plan, you will get a few more features that might be helpful for you.

1. Right now, Updates:

It means that you will be updated as soon as new job listings are posted in your locality. In this way, you can quickly apply for the advertised job and give it to the driver.

It saves a lot of time. Rather than looking for loads, you are informed as soon as a suitable job is posted in yours. You can easily sign up for a job as soon as it is advertised.

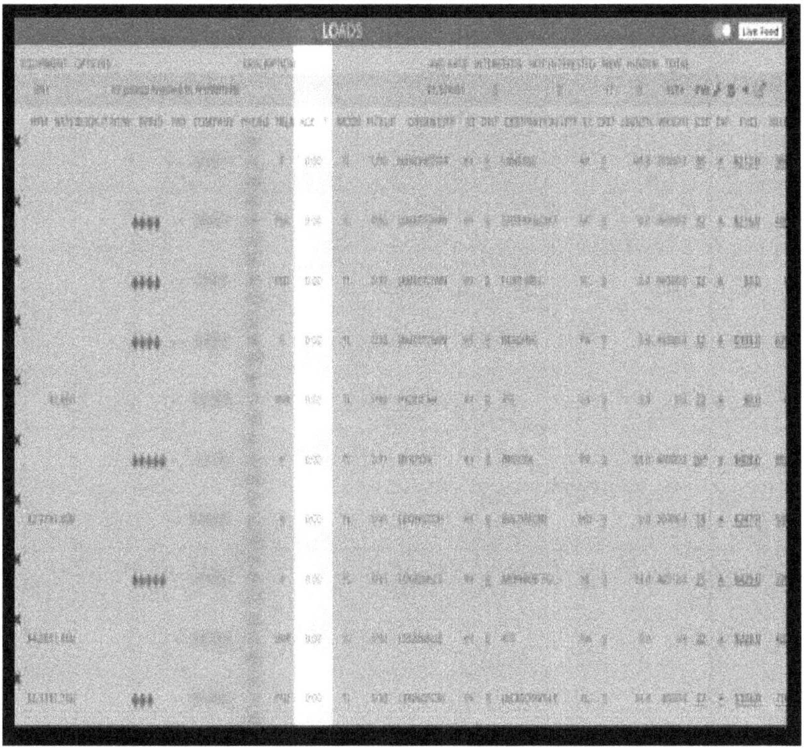
LOADS
Live Feed

2. The Rate Estimation

This feature will give you the exact rates, and you will get an idea about the rate trends in real-time. You will be in a better position to negotiate your fee for the correct job.

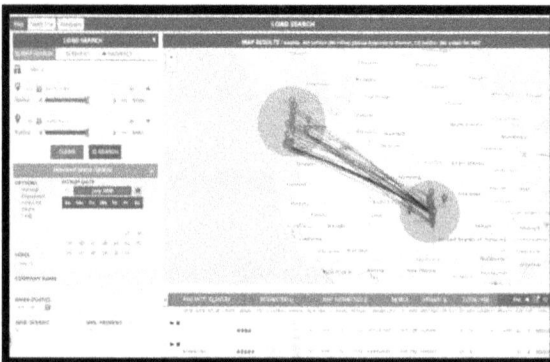

3. Heat Map

This feature helps you see the new job postings, accurate distances, and accurate routes. It will help you to successfully plan the route and the trip in a much convenient way. You can also search for different jobs at the same time by setting the tool for more than one kind of search

BEST PAYING LOADS		
#	RATE	RPM	ORIGIN & DESTINATION
1	$1,100	$3.87	Mount Vernon, WA / Keizer, OR
2	$1,000	$5.43	Seattle, WA / Aloha, OR
3	$850	$3.90	Everett, WA / North Plains, OR
4	$829	$3.80	Sumner, WA / Albany, OR
5	$800	$2.90	Lynden, WA / Portland, OR

4. Find the High Paying Loads

It is a feature known as the best payment load. You can set and customize the app to find certain kinds of jobs with a certain rate of pay. The app will notify you any time such a job is posted, and you can easily respond. To get high-paying jobs, you will also have to comply with the criteria set for high-paying jobs. If you plan your trip, you can also estimate the pay rates according to the accurate route.

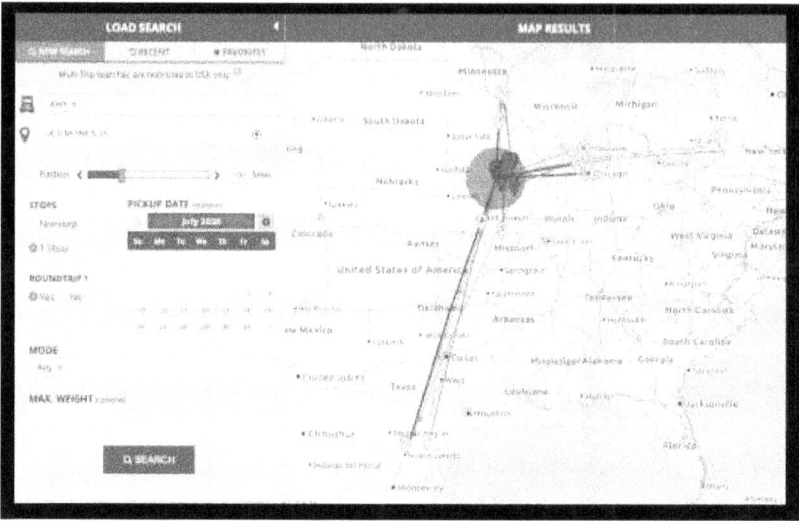

5. Multi-Trip Jobs

If you are interested in regular dispatch jobs, you can get information regarding multi-trip jobs. You can customize your load search to multi-trip loads. In this way you can plan for your drivers and also the drivers can mention their availability and working hours according to these loads.

Take Care of Finances

It is a tricky topic for a lot of people. Many people who want to start a business are ready to put in the hard work, but the problem is that not everyone is good with finances. Finances are a tricky business. To start a trucking business, you need an initial investment, and to keep the operations running, you need more money. The trucking industry is a booming industry, and with the world trends shifting to online shopping and big stores closing in favour of the online system, there are more and more opportunities for truck operators and drivers, and the best thing you can do for yourself is your boss. Work at your own pace and on your terms. But, no one said it would be easy, and the most difficult part of this is the business will be the finances.

To own one truck, you will need approximately $80000. And after that, you have permit fees, and staff pays as well. For the first-time business owner, it is going to take a little time. It is always advisable to hire an accountant to manage your business to manage the accounts and limit cash outflow. You can also buy apps like QuickBooks to manage your accounts.

You will have to apply for loans and leasing. For this, it is best to apply to smaller banks and credit unions. The big banks will not be interested in smaller business investments. You can look for private investors and lenders as well. Your business plan should be perfect for getting a loan, which was discussed in the previous chapter.

The best advice would be to hire a good bookkeeper or accountant, and as soon as your company starts making money, you should also hire a legal advisor for taxes.

CHAPTER 3. THE SECRETS OF A SUCCESSFUL TRUCKING BUSINESS

It is an age of start-ups. We hear about start-ups now and then. People are taking risks and prefer to work for themselves rather than in an organization. The sole reason for this is that you can gain more profits if no one binds your business venture clicks and you. You can work at your pace, and time is flexible. These advantages seem to be very attractive, but a lot of hard work and planning are required. We rarely hear a success story. Most business ventures fail very soon. The main reason for this is that the people only see the advantages and heavily ignore the disadvantages of this business.

1. Strategies for Successful Business

This chapter will discuss strategies that will help you keep your business afloat and eventually gain profits. The trucking industry is flourishing these days, but there is another downside: many people are venturing into the industry, and the competition is very high. There are few features that we will discuss to make our business a success and avoid failure.

1. Information and knowledge to be comprehensive

Now, this is a big one. We all know that being informed and up to date with information is the need of the hour and is of utmost importance. For this, you will have to make decisions and make change as to the systems used in the past. It is the digital age, and we have to be upgraded according to the requirements of today's world.

In the past, all the relevant data was noted in ledges and notepads. Then came computers. But now, the requirement of the world is instant information. For a successful trucking business, instant information and software are required to be easily accessible on the go. This kind of software makes a lot of sense for the trucking business because most workers and employees are on the go, and there is no concept of the table and chair set up.

You will need software that can display all the relevant information on your smartphone or tablet screen.

Information such as the payables and receivables should be easy to access. The invoices should be generated promptly.

The orders being received and the orders being accepted should be updated in real-time. Similarly, the orders completed should also be updated promptly. The flow of information throughout the system should be smooth and sound.

With the trucking business, you might be requiring more than one kind of customized software. One for your internal management, which is between the owner of the business and the staff and another software for the dealings with the clients. The management software will take care of the internal matters such as scheduling of trips, the timings of the drivers and payroll. The other software will be needed to manage the payments, lending and other financial issues and deadlines related to the client. It will keep the system streamlined, and you will have a clear picture of the business and assess your growth in a better way.

Remember that it is always good to progress with the needs of the time, and you cannot deal with the problems and challenges of the present with the tools created for the past.

2. Proper Coordination Between Departments

As discussed in the previous paragraphs, we need proper software for the business's proper functioning and streamlined flow. It is correct, but the management of this software and its coordination and integration is equally necessary. We have earlier mentioned that you might be needing more than one software. But they have to go hand in hand. The information should be updated on both the software simultaneously so that business flow does not disturb. Just installing the software will not do the job. You will still have to regulate it and update it yourself. Suppose the software is not integrated and updated properly. In that case, it will create confusion. Confusions will lead to missing deadlines, missing parcels, and frustration among the employee and the owner, which will extend to the client. Getting good software is not good enough if it is not being used properly. Having mediocre software and using it effectively is better than having the most sophisticated system and not managing it well.

Once the system is integrated perfectly, it will become easy for everyone to work in such an environment. The drivers will be informed and updated, the owner knows the condition and position of work, and the client will be happy with the end product. For this purpose, you should have a manager and an accountant whose sole responsibility will be to take care of the smooth flow of the business. The business manager should also be responsible for the queries and questions from the customers and the partners. The purpose of the business manager will be to overlook the whole system and solve any problems that the staff or the client is facing due to miscommunication.

3. The Customer is Always Right

The business is always dependent on the jobs you will be getting; if you get good projects, you will make more money. When you venture into the business, you will notice that the clients look for the cheapest deals. They will try to bargain with you about everything. When a person starts a business and wants to get work quickly, a person falls for such tricks. The clients who run after the cheapest deals are not worthy of your time. There is another type of clientele who are willing to pay good price for better service. Your target market is those customers.

The reason for this is that if you accept the cheapest offers, you will have to compromise on quality and profit. It does not seem to be a favourable situation. In this way, you will be decreasing the quality of your service, and you will not be able to pay the drivers well who, in case of getting better opportunities, will think about leaving your job. The profits will be low, and you will not be able to keep the operations afloat. A big part of this business is to keep the vehicles up to date, and if you are not making profits adequately, you will not be able to make good profits. You will be able to deliver low-quality service, your clients will be unhappy, your staff will be unhappy, and the vehicles you use will be of poor quality because of low maintenance.

So, the most important task is to have clients who demand quality at reasonable prices. If you demand very high prices then also you will not be able to get good business. There are 3 qualities of a good trucking business:

- Decent rates
- Safe transport
- On-time deliveries

If all these requirements are met, it will be possible to make your name in the business. As trucking is a competitive business and there are many options available to the client, you will have to put forward your best performance to get and retain clients.

Another aspect is customer satisfaction. You should always be mindful of customer satisfaction. During the dealing, till the order is complete, you should take care of customer service. You should clear all the queries and confusion that the customer is facing. This way, you will build your connection with the customer and get business from the same source again, and you will be given good reviews and recommendations as well.

1. Staff Satisfaction

Often, we hear about customer care, and most business owners focus on customer care only. In this way, we tend to forget our team. Our work and accuracy rely on our team. It is necessary to nurture and evolve our team for better results. Hiring a person does not mean that the job is done then and there; you should constantly focus on their development to more responsible and valuable assets to your company. It would help if you also focused on the employees remaining with your team and not moving to greener pastures. It can only be ensured in one way, and this is employee satisfaction. The first rule is not to underpay for their services. Try to pay their salaries in time. There should be on-the-job training provided to all the staff members to perform in a better way. Incentives should be provided. For trucking companies, drivers are an asset. You cannot, in any case, run a trucking business without truck drivers. You should take special care of the drivers, and you should be willing to give them enough off time, you should pay them and encourage them when they carry out their job well. There should be on-the-job training provided to drivers to keep up to date with the new technology and handle situations better. Remember the golden rule that you can only get rewards if you are willing to respect your staff members and employees.

2. All Payments on Time:

When we talk about payments, it always seems simple, but most of the conflicts and confusions occur due to money matters. For a trucking business, you must pay your drivers on time. If this is not the case, you may lose a good and reliable driver. Talking about this seems that this is a simple equation, but most of the time, the drivers are suffering and fighting for payments. Most of the time, confusion is created because the business system is not steady. There should be a proper system installed where the rates and working hours of each driver are mentioned. The rates for overtime, flat rates, and loaded and unloaded truck transport rates should all be mentioned. The payments should be generated as soon as the order is completed, and the driver should be compensated. There should be no problem and hiccups in this flow. The pay should be directly credited to the driver's account.

It has been observed that drivers throughout the United States are paid well, and there are jobs available for drives at all times. So, it is necessary to retain your trusted drivers. One way to retain an employee is in-time payments, and this is still the most important point when people stay at their jobs. If the money is right and the money is steady, most employees will remain loyal to their respective companies.

3. Effective Dispatch System

As the drivers are the business, the dispatchers are the circulatory system of the business. They are responsible for the correct locations, loading and unloading of the goods and items. They assist the drivers and manage the required equipment to load or unload the items. To carry out their work effectively, the dispatchers need to be informed and updated in real-time. They should have software that has a dispatch interface and the order interface to manage both tasks easily. The dispatch software should be well integrated with the accounting software so that both the parties are aware of the finances and there are no confusions in the system, and the workflow is not disturbed.

The task of the dispatchers is to guide the drivers to the most effective routes and ensure that the deliveries are according to the schedule and are on time. They make sure that the drivers are functioning effectively by guiding them and assisting them throughout the process. They ensure that the drivers reach the destinations in time. If you do not have an effective dispatch system, there will be confusion and misunderstandings. There are also risks of late delivery and lost shipments. It is why there is a need for a transparent and effective dispatch system.

4. Well Handled Cashflow

It is also an important aspect of a good business. It would be best if you kept the cash flowing. There should be available liquid assets at all times. To nurture the business, you will need a constant inflow of cash. In many cases, the company is showing a profit, and the expenses are also well handled. But their problems are occurring because the cash flow is not constant. It is mostly because of the uncollected receivables. Due to these small problems, a lot of businesses have failed. Often the billing is not handled properly, and there are outstanding payments to be made, and due to workload, a lot of payments are not received. It may cause the business to lose money and lose the smooth business flow. Often, fraudulent companies do not pay on time, and with time passing, these companies vanish with the money they owe, and they cannot be tracked down. This way, a lot of money and thousands of dollars are wasted and lost due to negligence.

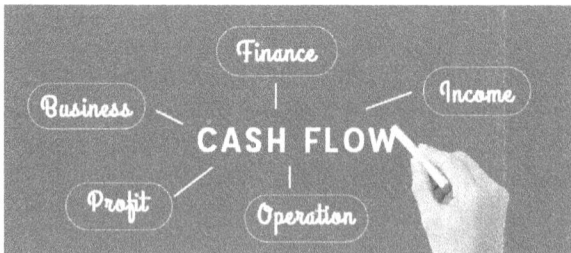

The first step is to have good quality software for accounts management and employ a bookkeeper or accountant to manage and update all payments and reduce the chances of error. No payments must be done without proper checks and balances. The drivers and suppliers should neither be overpaid nor underpaid. The system should limit collecting its payments, and remainders should be issued to receive the payment. As soon as you complete and order, your payment should be cleared within a week. Late payments create gaps in the cash flow, and then the whole business and all the orders are affected.

5. Generation of IFTA Reports:

One thing about the trucking business is that it is a deeply regulated business. In the United States of America, if you want to invest in a trucking business, you have to see that there are multiple permits you will have to obtain, and you will also have to pay taxes regularly. An International Fuel Tax Agreement states that the company should file taxes in each state where they operate and where they have a license. You have to obtain permits in every state where you operate, so you will be bound to pay taxes in all those states.

The government also demands the business owners to maintain their vehicles and file their reports every three months to ensure the quality of the vehicles.

There is a lot of accounting work involved in the trucking business; the taxes and tax reports can seem to be a bit overwhelming. Most of the time, small businesses hire a firm or an individual to manage their taxes. It might be good to hire outside and expert help to manage the IFTA reports and taxes.

Another thing you can do is to make use of the extremely easy-to-use telematics solution. It will enable you to manage the assets and your employees easily. The IFTA software can be used to calculate the number of miles travelled and to which states. It will also lower the risk of any fine imposed by any state, ensuring a better audit report.

6. Good Trucking Software

If you are thinking to start a trucking business or already have one, and you are thinking of expanding your operations, a good option will be to invest in a good trucking solution app. The software can speed up your business response, and in turn, you will become more effective in your approach and can easily attract more customers. It will all culminate into a better business and a systematic layout. With a clean and systematic layout, you will have more time to concentrate on the business's operations and less time on the administrative side of the business.

For the trucking business and especially start-ups, there is very good software known as the Truck Pulse, which you can use. This app is compatible with both the android and iOS interfaces. It can be used by all staff members, the drivers, the administrative staff and the owner. The best part about this app is that it is in line with the requirements of today's world. Most of the bigger companies in the trucking industry also use software to keep their business operations streamlined.

The right **fleet management solutions** can reduce operating expenses and improve efficiency. Suppose you are thinking about starting a trucking business or already have one but want to expand your business. In that case, having a good trucking software solution can make a big difference in how quickly you become successful and efficient in this extremely competitive market.

A good trucking software solution created by someone who understands the demands of the industry will be loaded with features like managing and dispatching shipments, real-time tracking, freight bid management, and so much more.

When looking for a trucking software solution, you should test it out to ensure a user-friendly interface and a scalable architecture. The software should be customizable to suit your company-specific requirements.

2. Support the Right Market Niche

The hard effort pays off and becoming an owner-operator is one of the trucking industry's most difficult and rewarding jobs. Most truckers, I believe, anticipate being their boss at some time; if this is the case, you should start thinking about it earlier in your driving career.

"Earlier" in this context refers to your first week of CDL training in Tacoma — or wherever you reside. While becoming an OO (owner of a small business) may not be for everyone, you should get started as soon as possible if you believe you might like to go down that path.

Don't be afraid to inquire about becoming an owner-operator with your trainers. Keep the knowledge in your memory bank and utilize what you've learned to retain your eyes open through your first few years as a truck driver — you won't be an owner-operator for a while.

Keep a look out for possible niches for your hauling firm throughout those early years as well. Niche markets and businesses offer a clear and quick path to success.

- Definition of Niche Marketplace

A niche marketplace is essentially a market that is focused on a certain topic. Individuals in niche markets have highly particular demands and expectations, and niche markets are usually underserved.

There are specialized markets in many sectors. There is a range of retail businesses catering to specific markets in every shopping centre or downtown.

You wouldn't expect to see children's toys in the window of "Country Florist" if you passed by. They operate in a specialized market.

Trucking niche marketplaces are typically developed rather than discovered. To make it happen, you'll need to discover what appears to be a neglected specialty.

Shipping logs from a forestry firm in one region to a port in another is an example of a specialized truck market. If you & your vehicle are authorized for port accessibility, you may be able to make numerous shipments in this area each week while being at home for the majority of the time.

- Best Way to Identify Trucking Niche

As previously stated, you'll almost certainly need to define your market; you don't want to be "all things to all people." It's simply not feasible. As you examine the trucking business and plan your transition to owner-operator, consider the following concepts. They'll show you how to find your specialty.

Geographic Range — how far do you wish to travel from home? If you want to be near to your family, short-haul flights are usually the best option. Long-haul truckers may make a lot of money, especially as owner-operators, but they might also get into a lot of trouble.

What kind of consumer do you prefer to deal with? Tankers are needed to transport liquids. A reefer is required for shipping crops.

Consider the wood transporter as an example of how to describe the business you desire. They work for one client and delivers timber to a different port on schedule. Ensure you can carry products both ways if you're traveling long-distance.

Consider things from your customer's perspective; they will have expectations that you must satisfy. Consider what they want and whether you can satisfy their needs easily.

When you put it all together, can you earn money in the niche you've created? Because you're essentially writing a business strategy, research is crucial. Is it possible to make what you would like in that niche, or will you have to develop or add another?

Get on the street with the niche — if you've already identified one shipper, you're probably in good condition. It doesn't matter how well you prepare if you don't attempt to pump up business in your sector. If you've already identified folks who are interested, that's fantastic! However, don't be scared to promote yourself.

- Factors to Examine Trucking Niche

It is critical to have port access to nearby ports. Every port has its own set of restrictions, but if you can ship & load at the dock, you'll have more options. Remember that they need you just as much as you do — if not more. Having the option to cross into Canada brings up new potential for special creation. Your broker, as well as you if you're working under your authority, will be able to source you more cargoes in both directions. Add certifications to your commercial driver's license.

Hazardous material, tankers, and double combinations are all certificates that enhance your versatility and, as a result, your specialty options. You can achieve success by locating major rail stations and the shippers that work with those terminals. Many are supplied by many trucks, but they can give a lot of business if you satisfy them with your dedication and effort.

- Examples of Niches in Trucking

When creating your company strategy, don't be scared to go outside the box. Consider the following suggestions.

Agricultural equipment needs shipping all year, and it's a lucrative long-haul specialty.

Tanker shipping that is dedicated or specialized is a lucrative and powerful specialty. While the cleaning procedure is more time-consuming, it is a necessary part of the specialty and may be worthwhile. Lignin is a by-product of paper mills. They require the lignin to be transported to a processing facility. This specialty may allow you to stay at home late at night and on weekends. Year-round, oil, gas, & diesel haulage are all in great demand.

A large agriculture or food products business may exist in your area. Set up long-distance deliveries and pick-ups in the target region, and you'll have a steady stream of customers.

- Successful Drivers Are Trucking Professionals

You can't be everything to everyone. We are sure you'll be hauling for anybody, anyplace in your early years. But, if you'd rather be the owner-operator or even not, you must keep your eyes open throughout this period and look for suitable niches.

Your CDL training should assist you. Even if you don't need to be an owner-operator, specialty hunting might be beneficial. Some businesses may operate in a niche that suits you, and you'll reap most of the similar benefits that a niche market provides. Your specialization can lead to a long and happy career in trucking.

Finding a specialty is critical for owner-operators, so consider what niche you may carve out for yourself as you construct your strategy to become one.

3. Owner-Operators' Best Niche Industry

As an owner-operator, the essential choice you will make is choosing the proper market niche. Your chances as a company owner might be numbered if you choose the incorrect market.

- Dry Van – Worst Strategy

We have no objections to a dry van. The machinery is adaptable and may be utilized in a variety of sectors. It also has a lower entry barrier because of the inexpensive cost of the equipment. Dry van, on the other hand, has stiff competition. It appeals to large corporations (think Schneider) with a lot of resources. It also appeals to new owner-operators because of the low entrance hurdle. It can only mean one thing: fierce rivalry. It's difficult to acquire good-paying loads with so much competition. More significantly, securing direct shippers who might become regular customers is difficult. You'll be forced to work via brokers and load boards, which take 15% to 20% of the revenue for themselves.

- Specialized Loads - Smart Strategy

Working in a market that your rivals shun is a better approach. Because of their complexity, large carriers seek to avoid specialty cargoes. Owner-operators and small companies now have access to the specialized load market. This scenario presents you with an opportunity.

Naturally, the kind of specialty loads you can transport is determined by your permissions, driving abilities, and expertise. The location is also crucial (e.g., cattle, frac fluids, etc.).

These sorts of cargoes, on the other hand, are available in every market. Take into account loads that have been chilled recently (Reefer)

Advantages of Specialized Loads

Consider the following if you are a new owner-operator. The meat and vegetable sectors are the quickest and easiest to help. These loads offer several advantages.

Consistency

One aspect of this sector that we like is its constancy. Fresh meat and fruit are delivered regularly from major metropolitan regions around the country. It's normal to receive recurring shipments from the same shippers.

Easy to Find Shipper

Shippers are often easy to locate. Get your goods available to shippers at the local produce market. Hunts Point Produce Market (NY), Chicago International Produce Market (IL), and others are examples of produce marketplaces. Another option is to go straight to the wholesalers. Simply call them and inform them that you can offer them safe and dependable transportation.

Works in Recession

It is our personal favourite. Recessions aren't a problem for reefer shipments.

For owner-operators looking for revenue consistency, this characteristic makes them highly appealing. You're delivering food, and regardless of the economy, people need to eat.

Smart Pay

The bottom line is, after all, the essential factor. Hauling these sorts of cargoes pays handsomely, especially if you work directly for shippers.

Other specialized load options

- Examples of Specialized Loads

Other sorts of specialized cargoes are beneficial to novice owner-operators. However, some of them will necessitate the addition of additional permissions to your driver's license.

Tankers

An owner-operator can specialize in liquid & dry bulk tanker cargoes, both of which are extremely profitable sectors. Food-grade liquids are transported by one type of liquid tanker, whereas another transport hazardous products. Moving these weights, on the other hand, is difficult and needs prior knowledge. Then there's the equipment expense. These trailers, particularly for dry bulk, may be rather costly.

Flatbeds

Because large carriers avoid flatbed cargo, you may concentrate on them.

The issue is finding lucrative cargoes for both the outbound and return trips.

When there is a difficulty, however, there is also an opportunity.

Livestock and cattle

Pulling animals and livestock may also pay well for truckers. These charges, however, are dependent on your location. For an owner-operator that lives in the cattle-producing area, this option might be a fantastic fit.

CHAPTER 4. WAYS TO FIND TRUCK CONTRACTS

We observe that the world we are living in today has completely changed from the past 20 years. All the rules and regulations of how we lead our lives and other things have drastically changed. One thing that has not changed is the trucking business. There have been changes in the trucking business because of the great transformation in technology, but we cannot deny that the transportation of items is still very much dependent on trucks. Like always, truck drivers are high in demand. With this pandemic and people shifting to online shopping, the need for trucks and the transportation and delivery system is rising. This business has been showing profits over the years, and many people are looking to invest in this business because, according to estimates, the trucking business is expected to flourish further. The trucking business has been through the pandemic stage and the recovery stage, freight recession, but one thing remains constant: the need for trucks and transportation.

1. Tips to Find Truck contracts

Once you have fulfilled all the requirements for the business, you will have to book a freight contract. In this chapter, we will discuss how we can get freight contracts. In this chapter, we will discuss a few ways how we can get orders.

1. Hire A Freight, Brokers

It is one of the best options to get orders if you are starting. Trucking start-ups of independent drivers do not necessarily know many people, so this will benefit them.

If you talk to a broker, they will have a prior relationship with the shippers; they will already know the business rates and will be able to advise you in the best way and help you get contracts. With their expertise, they can also advise you regarding the rates and fuel costs of several orders. The only downside, in this case, is that the broker will charge you a sum of money for their services.

2. Hire Dispatch Service

It is also easy and simple, but it also costs money if you hire a direct dispatcher. It is necessary for someone who has no networking and does not know where to start. An experienced dispatcher will connect you to either shipper directly, or they will introduce you to the brokers. The advantage of hiring a dispatcher is that they will be able to provide other administrative tasks. They will help you with the accounting aspect of the business and can also ensure that the billing invoices are generated in time. Apart from that, they can better guide the drivers and solve problems the business faces because of their experience and expertise.

3. Sign up with Load Boards

It is by far the easiest way to find loads. The only problem is that load boards are online applications that you join for free or with a fee and see all the available projects online. Due to this nature, you will have to either trust the shipper or do your background check for the client to avoid fraud. The good part is that you will find loads and clients from all the states and customize them according to your requirements. You will be able to see the latest listings, and you can easily book projects online.

Before joining a load board, you should research what load board you should be a part of. With a good load board, you can see and track what you want and get customers and orders according to yourself.

4. Try to Get Contracts from the Government

The government is always looking for contractors to outsource their contracts. Getting government contracts is a smart move, and if you can create a good impression on the government officials, they tend to repeat the service provider. The government at all levels has trucking and transportation's needs, whether it is the federal government or the state government. To become a contractor for the government, you will have to get registered with the government as a service provider. It may seem difficult, but you will get a constant workflow if you enter into such a scenario. The main way to get such contracts is to call the related government offices and ask for details and requirements.

5. Go the Conventional Way

It will be going by the Book. Be your broker. Try to look for the kind of business in your neighborhood and get in touch with people in the business. You might have to go door to door to advertise your business. Introduce yourself to people, tell them about your services, and then you can get orders. You can look for different companies and call them to get orders. Even if you do not get orders, you can inquire about the shipping needs of different companies, and then you can prepare accordingly so that whenever such an opportunity arises, you are prepared beforehand.

6. Networking

It cannot be stressed more on this point that networking is essential. In general, it is always a good idea for small businesses to start making some links with people around and related to the field. The rules are the same for the freight business. You might ask where and how to start; a simple answer to this question can be seen at events. Look upon the internet what is going on in the industry; associations and groups are related to each industry.

Try to enter groups and attend events that might be beneficial for getting work and orders. Do not expect that you will be getting work right away, but your face will become more visible. Share your contact information; maybe you will get a referral at some point.

All associations are not easy to get into and are membership-based, look for the ones you can enter easily into and then move forward from that point. In these events, you will find competitor companies and their representatives. Try to learn from them, listen carefully, share some information that can be useful, and learn something new.

The basic reason to network is to make yourself visible; there is a lot of work-related to transportation, and businesses have to employ trucking companies; they are on the lookout for good services at a decent price.

Maybe you see that a company does not require your services at a given time but might require services in the future; you should always be prepared for such a situation.

7. Become A Broker

Now, this is another route that not many people take. If you try all the above strategies and you are still not convinced with the type of work and jobs you are getting, you might want to take control of yourself and become a broker yourself. It is a long shot and not always successful. You will have to take classes and work with an experienced broker to learn how to become a broker. It is a good idea for your business if you can complete orders and meet deadlines with projects. But in most cases, it is still much better to leave the brokerage tasks to the professionals and stick to your job.

2. Ways to Find High-Paying Freight Loads

Discovering the best paying freight loads to transport is essential for any operator, small fleet, or broker. It is the most challenging aspect of running a trucking firm for many owners. Tragically, most truckers & owner-operators fail due to a lack of knowledge of obtaining suitable loads.

Tools to Find High Paying Freight Loads

Every independent owner operator's objective is always to locate higher-earning cargoes. However, it appears that 95% of independents can obtain enough load board goods to maintain their business afloat, find a comfortable zone, and stay there. That's one of the reasons the usual owner-operator earns only $40,000 per year. OOIDA provided that number. Because the report states "after taxes and fees," it's reasonable to estimate their annual taxable income is around $55,000.

- Don't Be Average

Without the hassles of owning a vehicle, a corporate driver may comfortably earn $70,000 or even more nowadays. Is it worth it to purchase your truck for $55,000 a year? Only if you set out to be ordinary. Usually, new owner-operators fall into a comfort bubble, fat and happy, as soon as the paychecks cover the costs. They didn't set out to be typical. They just didn't set any goals for themselves.

The initial set of tools will concentrate on selling abilities and a positive business mentality. Knowing what the higher-paid loads are and how to get them is one thing. It's another thing entirely to be able to complete the transaction and book them. And it's not just about the cheaper freight. You want to reserve it personally with the consumer at some point. Who needs a cut-throat middleman? Brokers are important to your success, but their objective is to take as much profit as possible.

- Read Books That Have the Biggest Impact First

Hundreds of fantastic books are available to buy on the internet. That's fantastic, but the vast majority of them have nothing to do with you or the distinctiveness of independent trucking.

- Your Website Functions as a Sales Brochure

Even a one-man performance counts as a business. You'll need somewhere to share your tale. We've been in the twenty-first century for over two decades. What happened to your website? It may appear to be a difficult chore, but it isn't. For your tale, all you need is a basic website with some striking images. Even if you're not sure yet, get your web domain as a ".com" as soon as possible. Get it off the marketplace and lock it up.

It can be accomplished in one of two ways. You may construct it yourself or pay someone to do it. If you decide to contract it out, there are a couple of things to keep in mind. Who are the owner of your website and domain name? If it isn't going to be you, get out of there.

Who will create, update, and publish the website? It's your narrative, but it has to appear professional.

How much will this set you back? You're not attempting to compete for online traffic with the biggest names. You're making an online pamphlet to promote your company. You ought to be able to get this for $1,000 to $1,500 if you hire it out. A thousand words are worth a thousand pictures. You want beautiful photos of your gear as well as yourself. Make sure the photos are taken by someone who understands what they're doing.

- Trucker's Edge Pro, a Fantastic Load Board Service

DAT® has existed for a longer period than the internet. They get the most loads, brokers, and data required to manage any size business. Trucker's Edge Pro and two lighter variants are available for small businesses with a few trucks or simply one truck.

It's not only about locating the next load at Trucker's Edge. It can get brokers to contact you, discover better lanes, even foretell your future if you're using it to its maximum potential. You may examine the lane statistics, brokers credit scores and time to pay even on the following load. You could even be able to discover a tri-haul that will get you anywhere you need to go for a significantly lower cost per mile.

- Use Google Earth to Locate Shippers

There's a good possibility you'll be encircled by other shippers & receivers wherever you're picking up or delivering. Call them in by putting on your big boy trousers. Place a business card in each person's hand, and make sure it includes your credentials and website information. Take thorough notes and follow up. If it were simple, everyone would do it.

- Identify Your Unique Selling Proposition

Every company has something valuable to offer. There's no incentive for someone to do business with you if you don't have any value. What is the USP (Unique Selling Proposition) of your business? Are you simply another self-employed business owner? Is there anything exceptional, unique, or unusual about how you've to offer? Write down the specifics and explain your narrative. Heavy loads, LTL, high-value cargo, safe parking, and paid parking are all examples of USPs. "The rich are in the niches," as those of us who run online companies like The Trucking Podcast like to say. It is also true in the transportation industry. Especially from the load boards, you can earn a decent living carrying chicken egg freight, but there's always a greater haul for the owner-operator who's ready to work for it.

3. Ways to Make More Money

It seems like making money as a truck driver is simple and clear: grab freight here, transport it there, and bill the client. To the untrained eye, owning a trucking fleet or being an owner-operator appears to be a dream job.

Long, arduous hours, a never-ending search for cargo or truckers (or both!) and a never-ending struggle to keep ahead of expenses are all too familiar to those of us in the sector. There is, however, no greater way to make a career for individuals who do this in their blood. The key to generating excellent money in cargo transportation is to maximize equipment utilization and control expenses to transport as many loaded miles as feasible.

It's a difficult playing field, and even the most seasoned road warrior may struggle to prevail if they don't take a systematic approach. If not properly handled, the logistical & financial requirements of running a trucking company may be daunting. Striking competition, growing prices, volatile markets, and stringent laws are just a few of the obstacles that thwart business owners' ability to enjoy steady profits. However, trucking is a vital industry that has weathered economic downturns, worldwide pandemics, technological advancements, and environmental restrictions. It will continue to be a vital operation for decades to come, with plenty of room for expansion. Trucking is a vast sector with great benefits for those prepared to work hard, working efficiently, and devotes themselves to function at high productivity.

There are just three things you can do to boost the earnings of your trucking company:

- Find the Cost Per Mile

You will not be capable of determining a rate-per-mile to charge clients that will generate profit until you know precisely how much it needs to run your trucking firm.

You must include variable (running expenses) and fixed costs to determine the real cost of delivering a load (overhead). It is where meticulous recordkeeping and financial reporting are required. Make sure you keep track of every dollar you spend on big-ticket goods, out-of-pocket costs, and even modest office supplies. Every money, no matter how tiny, contributes to the larger picture.

Chaotic books, inability to grasp some critical business indicators, and not inputting the correct measures into accounting systems are all issues that most trucking firms face. All trucking businesses should prepare monthly financial summaries that correctly capture all transactional information and review these reports regularly to maintain the greatest financial management. Using an online cost-per-mile converter to calculate your cost-per-mile is a simple exercise with this level of data. Fill in the data boxes of the calculator with the data recorded into your journals for taxation purposes, and your company's unique cost-per-mile figure will be shown.

- Set a Competitive Rate in Your Trucking Business

Setting a competitive rate-per-mile that lures clients while supporting your company's bottom line is crucial to your trucking company's success. It's a tricky balance to strike: the rate must be sufficient to cover all of your expenditures, make a profit, and remain competitive.

3 Steps to Finding a Competitive Rate-per-Mile and Balancing Profit

Step 1: Find out what your company's cost per mile is.

Step 2: Calculate the Profit Margin: After you've determined your firm's cost-per-mile.

You'll need to add a profit margin to get the rate-per-mile that the company will charge consumers. Be conscious that competition is fierce, and profit margins in the trucking industry are quite low when matched to most other sectors. Make sure you don't overprice yourself out of the market by padding this cost with an exorbitant profit margin.

Step 3: Compare Rates to Competitors

The trucking business is extremely competitive and cyclical, resulting in dramatic rate and profit margin swings. The trucking sector had a particularly difficult time from 2012 to 2016, with profit rates ranging from 2.5 percent to 3.8 percent. Profits soared to an average of 6% in

2017 and continued to rise in 2018 before margins dropped again in 2019. By the end of 2020, margins had risen beyond 6% once more. Keep profit margins low and compare your per-mile charge to the competition frequently to stay competitive.

How to compare rates to those of competitors:

1. Decide which freight lane you want to use.

2. Make your way to a loading dock.

3. Choose ten similar loads that are moving in the same direction.

4. Calculate the optimal price by contacting the brokers and asking them how much they pay.

5. Add 10% to 15% to the price brokers charge shippers to arrive at the final pricing.

6. Repeat the same on the return trip.

After comparing rates, you may need to focus on lowering costs or committing to carrying additional loaded miles to increase profit margins and stay competitive.

- Increase the Number of Loaded Miles Driven

Truckers like driving long distances laden with cargo and, more significantly, it brings in the cash. Along with driver difficulties, it's the most pressing worry for most trucking business owners, fleet managers, and dispatchers. When capacity is limited, obtaining extra freight to continue trucks moving and optimize equipment usage might be simple, but it's more typically a difficult task. The same load is competed for by established fleets, rising enterprises, and new start-ups. The ideal technique is to be persistent and use every possible tactic to book freight.

- Strike the Right Balance

Changing any of the three main activities described above will have repercussions throughout your organization, which may or may not culminate in the intended result.

— Raising your per-mile pricing may boost income, but would it make you less competitive & cost your business?

- Cutting expenditures to save money may save you money, but will it impede operations and your ability to provide excellent customer service?

– Driving more loaded kilometers might put a strain on your personnel and reduce the life of your equipment.

Trucking businesses are always seeking to enhance their profits and stay competitive. Knowing what to do and when to do it is a guessing game without a clear method. Let's assume you decide to replace your 5-year-old tractor with a newer, more fuel-efficient one. Will the lower fuel prices outweigh the new equipment's higher monthly operating expenses? What if you take on that additional customer? Will deploying more trucks & drivers to complete the contract result in a profit, or will it result in a loss?

The best way to position your firm to earn the maximum investment return is to balance the three essential acts carefully. According to industry analyst David Boyd, the study of relevant monthly financial reports provides a broad picture of the firm, showing strengths and shortcomings.

Bottom Line

To generate a great deal of income in trucking, each vehicle and driver must work as efficiently as possible. Costs must be kept under control, and income must be maximized whenever feasible through higher loaded miles & accessorial fees. Working hard, driving safely, providing excellent customer service, controlling costs, and keeping an eye on your competitors for comparable rates are the keys to generating good money. There is no greater way to live for people who have it in their blood.

4. Highest Paying Companies

Beginning your transportation career with a reputable trucking business might be advantageous in the long term.

You must not only profit from working in a professional setting, but you can also make some quick cash. Reputable trucking businesses provide high-paying jobs to keep their personnel motivated to provide high-quality service. As a result, such opportunities must be grabbed to have a successful hauling career.

We've created a list of the highest-paying trucking firms that you may apply for in this post.

Job Prospects and Pay for Truck Drivers

There has been a growth in the need for truck driver employment as the market for shipping services has increased. For efficient operations, many different firms rely on the timely delivery of products and services. At the same moment, people all across the country may be looking for various transportation services.

Trucking firms must be more proactive, alert, and responsive to meet all of these customer demands. The great news is that trucking businesses are continuously on the hunt for skilled truck drivers to fulfill current expectations. In the next years, demand for these services and job possibilities is projected to skyrocket. Furthermore, truck drivers would get a better wage than they did previously.

Average Income of Truck Drivers

With 2 - 3 years of driving expertise and a Bachelor's degree, a truck motorist's average yearly pay is $60,911. It may differ depending on the state in which you live.

- Entry-Level

A trucker with less than a year of experience may expect to earn about $57,193 per year.

- Mid-Level

If you have five years or more of driving experience, you can expect to earn around $65,034 per year on average.

- Master-Level

You may make around $68,777 per year if you have more than 10 years of driving experience.

Examining the Highest-Paying Trucking Firms

It might be tough to find the proper firm to work for if you want to pursue a career in trucking. You may simply discover your desired job with a little information and good advice.

Such possibilities not only assure a great future for you, but they also provide you an advantage. It is why we've compiled a list of well-known trucking firms that are both dependable and profitable.

1. Walmart

Walmart is among the most well-known and quickly expanding worldwide internet businesses, serving customers all over the world. It is one of the most well-known and reputable companies globally, with over 11,500 locations worldwide. Walmart was founded in 1962 with the primary purpose of assisting people in saving money for a decent life.

Walmart was founded by Sam Walton, who launched only with one store in Rogers, Arkansas. Walmart has continued to develop since then, becoming one of the leading retail companies in the world. Every year,

Walmart truckers drive millions of miles to deliver numerous items to Walmart and Sam's Club stores around the country.

- Job Opportunities

Walmart relies significantly on its distribution and supply services being delivered on time. Its big fleet and competent drivers are dedicated to efficiently completing all duties. The good news is that for professional truck drivers, Walmart is virtually always open. Professional drivers with spotless records & experience are invited to join the team.

Walmart wants qualified personnel since it does not sacrifice the quality or efficiency of its services. Drivers are clearly among the most important roles at Walmart, but there are many other employment vacancies.

- Salary and Benefits

Walmart workers are one of the company's most important assets, having been named one of the finest trucking businesses in the world. It is because it values its workers, who work diligently to ensure that operations run smoothly. Employees receive not only a competitive salary but also a variety of other privileges and advantages.

Walmart offers its employees a slew of benefits in addition to competitive pay. PTOs, 401(k), medical, dental, health insurance, short-term disabilities, and paid safety days are just a few of Walmart's benefits. In addition, there are incentives for safe driving, compensated training and activity, flexible work hours, and weekly home time.

2. Sysco

Sysco is a globally recognized company that specializes in selling, advertising, and distributing food items. The majority of food goods are delivered to restaurants, healthcare facilities, and educational institutions. Sysco also offers the necessary equipment and materials for dependable food service and other sectors.

Sysco, a global leader in food services, now serves customers in 90 countries. It employs over 69,000 people and has 320 distribution centers in these nations, serving approximately 650,000 distinct client locations. Sysco created a significant turnover of $60 billion during 2019 due to its extensive network of services.

- Job Opportunities

Professionalism and a committed mindset are required while providing distribution services throughout the world. It is because Sysco values people with these characteristics. Delivering food supplies from one site to another necessitates experienced drivers who can deliver the goods on time. As a result, Sysco actively recruits and hires skilled truck drivers capable of doing the job quickly and successfully.

Because the firm has such a wide infrastructure, truckers are not the only people it is searching for. Individuals with diverse skill sets must operate such a wide array of food services for flawless operations. Consequently, positions in many areas, such as maintenance, warehousing, sales, merchandising, & information technology, are open.

- Benefits and Salary

A prominent company like Sysco consistently rewards its workers for their dedication and hard work. They achieve this by providing competitive pay packages and a variety of perks to their employees. It's not only aids employees to become more motivated but also enhances the company's overall performance.

Working as a truck driver for Sysco may pay up to $90,000 per year. An Administrative Assistant, on the other hand, may expect to make approximately $30,405 per year. On the other hand, pay scales and perks vary depending on the role and your level of expertise. A Development Operations Engineer, for example, may make up to $150,105 per year! Paid time off, a retirement plan, health insurance, and other perks are also available.

3. Brady Trucking

Brady Transportation is one of America's most dependable and secure trucking companies. Larry Brady founded the firm in 1980, and it has since become a hallmark of excellence and quality. The firm has been offering exceptional transportation services for over three decades, having been founded in 1996. It now has a vast fleet of trailers capable of completing any assignment.

The firm specializes in providing a diverse range of trustworthy trucking services. Customers may get regional, local, and long-haul transportation services from them. Brady Trucking also excels in delivering customized equipment solutions on schedule.

- Job Opportunities

Truck drivers, we can all agree, are the lifeblood of any trucking firm. They are among the company's most important assets since they can ensure that services are delivered on time. A positive mentality and professionalism are essential to succeed in this endeavor. As a result, Brady Trucking adheres to the hiring of competent truck drivers.

While drivers are an important component of any trucking firm, we must not overlook the value of other employees. Other than driving, several divisions house individuals with the various skill set to guarantee smooth operations and communication. Driver operators, operators, and non-drivers who can provide the necessary assistance are welcome to apply.

- Benefits and Salary

The majority of successful businesses consider their workers to be their most valuable asset. As a result, employers place a premium on employee happiness. Providing monetary advantages is one method to do this. Brady Trucking, for example, pays its hardworking employees far more than other companies.

A truck driver may get $37,541 per year on average in this city. An Over-the-Road Truck Driver, on the other hand, may earn an astounding $76,796 each year. Aside from that, there are additional perks like healthcare, retirement plans, mentorship, family time, and so forth.

4. Epes Transport

Epes Transport is among North Carolina's largest privately-owned trucking firms. Epes, formerly known as "The Transport Company," commenced services in Blackstone, Virginia, during 1931. For even more than 55 years, the company has been run by a family. Epes Carriers Inc., based in Greensboro, North Carolina, bought the firm in 1987. Penske Logistics later purchased it in 2018.

Epes Transport is committed to delivering cost-effective, dependable, and safe transportation services. Its goal is to provide exceptional shipping services and be the first choice of its clients. Epes Transport now provides short-haul regional transportation services within a 250-mile range of its terminals.

- Job Opportunities

Epes Transport is a dependable trucking company that believes in giving its employees the best transportation solution possible. It's only feasible if employees' objectives are in line with the company's. Epes Transport oversees several divisions to guarantee excellence and quality in all areas of service. The whole crew, not just the drivers, ensures that services are delivered on time.

The firm has a variety of employment vacancies for people with a variety of skill sets. Management, customer support, strategy, operation, finance, human resource management, marketing, administration, driver recruiting, & safety departments all have vacancies.

- Benefits and Salary

Almost every company that has had a successful journey credit its success to its personnel. The professional and devoted teamwork of an organization's personnel is essential to its success. One of these companies is Epes Transport. The firm has a good incentive system in place to keep its staff happy. Depending on their services, high-performing employees are awarded greater wages and perks. Epes Transport provides incentives and benefits such as 401k, medical coverage, retirement benefits, and a training program. For comparison, a driver's income ranges from $36,896 to $163,100 per year for owner-operators.

5. Acme Truck Line Inc.

Acme was founded in 1960 and started as an oilfield transporter. The firm had just six vehicles, three workers, and two garages at the time. The firm evolved, becoming one of the most reputable trucking firms in the country. Acme is now regarded as a market leader in transportation services, with a fleet of over 1500 vehicles.

It has over 80 offices and 40 service stations around the country, providing high-quality services. Based in Gretna, Louisiana, Acme provides dependable interstate trucking services for equipment, goods, and other supplies.

- Job Opportunities

Drivers are without a doubt the foundation of any trucking firm. Acme has always emphasized the quality of its services provided by its drivers and owner-operators. However, this does not imply that the drivers solely govern the firm.

Acme has a staff of devoted employees that are committed to providing excellent service at all times.

Even if you don't have driving experience, you can join the marketing, administration, security, or other departments. If you're a skilled driver with a track record, don't miss out on the chance to work for Acme as a driver or owner-operator.

- Benefits and Salary

At Acme, a truck driver may earn around $74,236 per year, whereas an owner-operator may earn up to $121,144. These figures indicate that Acme employees are highly compensated for their efforts. All respectable and dependable trucking companies make certain that their personnel are adequately cared for. However, it's worth noting that Acme offers more than simply financial advantages.

The firm guarantees a variety of advantages to its workers depending on their productivity and skills. Like any other reputable trucking company, Acme offers a variety of short- and long-term incentives to its employees. Different insurance and retirement schemes may be among them.

6. Mercer Transportation

Mercer Transportation was established in 1977 to provide safety and service. The firm has grown to become one of the largest freight companies in the USA during the previous four decades. The business claims to provide dependable transportation services that are supplied on time and in a safe manner. Mercer Transportation provides unparalleled transportation services with a fleet of approximately 2300 vehicles and 11,000 carriers.

The firm delivers diverse equipment to the military and commercial sectors via transportation services. You may anticipate dependable services from a system of more than 90 representatives around the country and a professional customer support service.

* Job Opportunities

Mercer Transportation, for example, is constantly looking for experienced truckers who can execute the job well. Truck drivers are the lifeblood of any trucking firm, which is why most companies look for dependable and competent drivers to transport a variety of shipments across the country. Mercer Transportation is a trucking company that places a high value on its drivers. They not just actively search for qualified persons, but they hire them. It is not only the drivers who make timely services feasible, as in any other business. It takes a whole team effort from many departments. As a result, other than truck-driving employment, there is always the chance of joining Mercer Transportation. Permit assistant, truck inspection trainer, coordinator/ customer service, ELD camera technician, and available positions.

* Benefits and Salary

A skilled and devoted group of expert's employees is at the heart of any successful business. Such businesses make certain that their employees' requirements are met and that they are happy. As a result, businesses provide monetary incentives and various other perks in exchange for employee services.

A popular method of paying for employee services is to provide competitive wage packages and additional incentives.

Medical, insurance plans, retirement benefits, and work/life compatibility are among the various perks available. Mercer Transportation provides all of these benefits, as well as a competitive pay package. An owner-operator with Mercer Transportation may make up to $157,359 per year on average.

7. Anderson Trucking Service

Anderson Trucking Service is a kinship and operated business that has been in operation since 1955. The firm is committed to providing dependable transportation solutions to various industries within the United States and even internationally. Its main goal is to be the best trucking company globally and exceed client expectations at all times. Anderson Trucking Service specializes in the transportation of a wide range of interstate products and equipment. Their most popular services are dry van, emergency, specialty pad-wrapped, heavy-haul, flatbed, international, LTL, & temperature-controlled shipment. All of these services come with the assurance that items and equipment will arrive on time and in good condition.

- Job Opportunities

Becoming a well-known trucking firm requires a significant amount of effort. Obtaining a professional workforce with a positive mentality is the secret to success among the many. As a result, Anderson Trucking Service invites qualified individuals with the necessary abilities to join an industry leader. Individuals with various skill sets are necessary to guarantee that day-to-day activities run smoothly.

Anderson Trucking Service is looking for people who want to work in a business environment and professional truck drivers. The firm for various employment vacancies constantly seeks professional applicants. Technicians, salespeople, and others are among them.

- Benefits and Salary

Almost all companies with a success story as Anderson Trucking Service have capable workers on their team. These are people who are committed to the cause and are extremely competent and driven. As a result, businesses make every effort to keep them. They do it by offering a variety of monetary incentives. Medical insurance, accident insurance, dental and medical insurance, FSA, disabilities insurance, 401K, Employee Assistance, and other benefits. Anderson Trucking Service additionally offers a variety of incentives based on employee success. The benefits given will be better if the performance is better.

8. Trimac Transportation

Trimac Transportation, which was founded in 1945, is a prominent bulk carrier in the United States. It is one of the most dependable transportation businesses because of its quick and dependable trucking solutions. Trimac Transportation is next to none when it comes to providing safe and dependable service to its customers. For decades, it has consistently been able to satisfy the requirements of bulk shipping, logistics, and other associated services.

Trimac is qualified to fulfill the most current standards, with over 100 branches across the United States. Their prompt and efficient transportation services guarantee complete client pleasure and dependability anytime it is needed.

- Job Opportunities

For efficient service delivery, reputable trucking firms like Trimac rely on their skilled personnel. Their experienced drivers are prepared to do any work that is assigned to them. Trimac, like most trucking firms, hires professional drivers and is continuously looking for bright and experienced truckers throughout the United States.

There are several job opportunities right now. Trimac is an excellent place to start if you want to pursue a career in trucking. Even if you don't know how to drive, you can still work in the business world. Experienced drivers, owner-operators, service, plus industrial and office jobs are just a few of the key employment openings available.

- Benefits and Salary

Employees at Trimac Transportation are highly rewarded for the high level of service they deliver. They are paid industry-leading wages, as well as a variety of bonuses and other benefits. All of these monetary incentives are contingent on employee productivity and records.

A 401(k) plan, dental coverage, employee discounts, and medical, life, and eyesight insurance are all included in the benefits package. Furthermore, a truck driver's average annual pay in this city is $70,677.

9. Western Express

Wayne and Donna Wise, who founded Western Express in 1991, established the groundwork for the company.

The firm has been serving consumers with dependable transportation services throughout the country for more than twenty years. Their vast fleet of approximately 3000 power units or over 7500 trailers is sufficient to fulfill the needs of today's customers. Customers benefit from the company's usage of cutting-edge technologies.

Western Express is based in Nashville, Tennessee, and operates a fully GPS-tracking fleet. Long-haul, short-haul, flatbed, & different logistical services are available to the commercial and public sectors.

- Job Opportunities

A trucking company's most valuable asset is its drivers. They will not be able to supply trucking services without them. Many trucking firms, such as Western Express, place a premium on employing the finest truck drivers. To guarantee prompt delivery of services, they look for candidates with a professional attitude, expertise, and spotless background.

Western Express has the advantage of offering a broad selection of career opportunities for drivers alone. Depending on your preferences, they contain flatbed, dry van, regional, OTR, leasing, or owner-operators. You can also apply for corporate positions if you have talents other than driving.

- Benefits and Salary

A long-term approach for achieving success is to provide market-competitive compensation packages with additional perks. Western Express, for example, is dedicated to providing clients with dependable trucking services.

Simultaneously, it takes steps to guarantee that its staff is well-fed. As a result, Western Express follows the industry standard of paying its employees greater compensation. Employees might also benefit from a variety of other perks depending on their employment contracts. Paid holidays, a 401K program, flexible routes, and various work possibilities are among them. All of these advantages add up to a bright and prosperous future at Western Express.

10. DOT Transportation Inc.

The trucking company DOT Transportation Inc. is among the most well-known in the business. The company began providing services in 1960, with its owner Robert Tracy making the first delivery. The firm has since expanded to become one of the leading transportation providers in the country.

DOT Transportation is much more than competent in fulfilling its clients' current expectations, with a fleet of over 1300 vehicles, 12 distribution locations, and over 2000 workers. The firm has yet to have its first layoff in almost 29 years. It's because the Department of Transportation considers all of its employees to be important assets.

- Job Opportunities

As a trucking firm, you must hire skilled truck drivers. This is why the Department of Transportation prefers to hire the finest of the best. Because trucking businesses rely on their drivers, they make certain that these employees can provide acceptable services.

Individuals interested in starting a profession with a spotless trucking service may apply for various roles at the firm.

Experienced truck drivers are among the most sought-after jobs. The Department of Transportation needs both regional and local truck drivers. You may join the squad at DOT Transportation if you have some strong truck-driving abilities.

- Benefits and Salary

Every trucking firm recognizes that driving a truck isn't an easy profession. Rather, maintaining a consistent level of service over your career is quite tough. With this in consideration, DOT Transportation has devised a dependable method of compensating its personnel for their efforts, including high wages and various bonuses.

A DOT Transportation transport driver may make up to $78,000 annually, which is very amazing. This organization also offers a variety of other advantages. Medical plans, 401(k) plans, revenue sharing, paid vacation time, tuition reimbursement schemes, and incentive-based compensation are examples of these benefits.

CHAPTER 5. REEFER LOADS

We'll look at reefer trucks in this chapter. We'll explore where they originated from, what they are, what they do, and why they are so important to the logistics sector. What's the problem with refrigerated freight, anyway? Anyone in the transportation industry will tell you that reefer transportation is a peculiar beast. Hauling reefer freight differs significantly from operating dry freight. It's a good idea to have a basic grasp of reefer freight, regardless of your position in the logistics sector.

1. Explanation of Reefers Loads

The term "reefer" refers to something refrigerated. The vehicle is a typical semi-cab. The reefer, on the other hand, is only a trailer. A "reefer truck" is a semi that tows a refrigerated trailer to transport fragile products. These trailers are not the same as chiller vans, which are insulated and ventilated. What distinguishes a reefer trailer from other trailers? Reefers have a built-in cooling system.

As a rcsult, you may carry both frozen and refrigerated freight. A reefer might also be temperature controlled to transport hot products. It is, however, a rare occurrence. Reefers can be found utilizing a variety of cooling methods. Both diesel-powered generators & cryogenic cooling equipment may be seen. Any cargo that requires temperature control, monitoring and maintenance within defined limitations is considered reefer freight. LTL, FTL, intermodal, ocean, & air freight are all examples of reefer freight. Food, chemicals, and medicines are the most typical items that require reefer freight.

Temperature control in reefer freight is divided into three categories:

* Frozen: The freight should be maintained at a temperature of -10 degrees Fahrenheit.

- Refrigerated: This shipment is usually maintained between 32 to 36 degrees Fahrenheit.

- Maintained/ Heated: When it's 16 degrees outside and the shipment needs to be kept at 32 degrees, the reefer technically works as a heater.

A closed system is used in reefer units. A refrigerated trailer technology is all about removing heat and keeping a consistent temperature. They work by collecting heat and distributing it throughout the system. The majority of reefer trucks are usually 53 feet long, although they are also available in different dimensions. Only reefer trucks can transport necessary products. There are numerous branches to the logistics tree. One of the most significant types of freight is reefer freight.

Dry goods can also be transported using reefer trailers. As a result, you have a lot of options as a carrier. Dry freight trips, especially during peak growing seasons, can be crucial in receiving your workers to the higher-paying reefer freight. With reefer freight, there is a greater level of risk and obligation. Drivers must be particularly cautious when making sure the reefer unit gets adjusted to the proper temperature. You must also ensure if the reefer unit system is in good working order. You may have to bear the expense of the entire cargo if there is a failure that damages the product. You must identify and recruit dedicated and trustworthy workers as a fleet manager. If you want to maintain those workers while maintaining expenses minimal, a fleet management program can assist keep things operating smoothly and guarantee drivers are paid on schedule.

2. Brief History

People and businesses were scrambling to discover the most effective way to carry fragile commodities as early as the mid-1800s. For many years, railroads were the only viable option for transporting this type of cargo. On the other hand, companies sought a more portable, quicker, and less expensive alternative to the vehicle.

Frederick McKinley Jones was born in Cincinnati, Ohio, in 1893 and served in the United States Army during World War I. He was self-educated in a variety of mechanical and electrical disciplines after the war. He created one of the essential technologies in the cinema industry soon after training to make a transmitter for their hometown's radio network. His invention allowed sound to be included in motion pictures for the first time.

Jones developed the first portable air-cooling devices for vehicles in 1938. He was granted a patent in 1940. By 1949, he had taken on a business partner and had established a multimillion-dollar corporation. It includes the debut of the world's first completely refrigerated truck.

During World War II, Jones' development of the compact cooling unit proved critical. It allowed non - durable items to be transported across battlefields to military clinics and tents. As you may notice, the reefer trailer has been a monumental discovery in the history of the globe.

3.   Reasons to Use Reefers Loads

Long-distance transportation of short shelf life and temperature-sensitive commodities necessitates the use of reefer trucks. The best common examples are frozen meats & fresh fruit. To keep goods chilled, companies employ reefer units. That is, you may adjust a reefer unit to a certain temperature level to maintain the temperature of a product but not to modify the temperature of the goods. The necessary degree in the case of frozen meat may differ. Let's pretend that a container of ground beef needs to be transported and preserved at 33 degrees Fahrenheit for ease. If the product is already frozen when placed into the reefer trailer, the temperature may be maintained. Under no circumstances can you expect the trailer to carry unfrozen meat and lower the temperature below freezing to freeze the food. The cycle of the reefer unit isn't capable of this. The meat is going to go bad.

4. Ways to Find Reefers Loads

Truckers, like any other company owner, must market their services and acquire clients. Truckers, unlike other businesses, require customers who carry freight to the appropriate place at the right time.

It's tough to build a shipper chain that delivers freight to the correct location at the right time. Many truckers lack the time and money required to establish this system of clients and channels.

It is why drivers must find cargoes from several sources. Truckers most commonly use the few strategies outlined below to find cargoes. Drivers can place themselves in the possible position to negotiate the best rates by employing a mix of the following strategies.

1. Direct from Shippers

The ideal and easy scenario is to obtain cargoes directly from shippers and personally inform them of your services. You will create a customer list if you have the time to complete this stage. These customers will become the lifeblood of your trucking company, providing you with cargoes regularly. If you treat them properly, they will seek your services frequently and pay you handsomely.

Truckers that can build connections with shippers place themselves in the best position to make huge profits. They earn their direct sales commissions by searching for, negotiating with, and selling to the client. However, this approach is tough and time-consuming.

It might be tough to locate and contact shippers who have frequent routes and regular volumes. Contract carriers are generally used to transport consistent lanes. Contracts are given through a competitive bidding procedure that is generally reserved for larger airlines. Without a partnership, most truckers are blocked out and incapable of competing on these channels. The time and money it takes shippers to execute the scrutiny & selection procedure for smaller carriers is why. Building ties with numerous clients in each freight market that the driver has cargo waiting at the destination. Truckers might need a staff of salesmen to make this work. Big customers are likely to demand that carriers accept tenders via electronic integration such as EDI or APIs. It allows the shipper to send load offers to its carriers electronically. You will require a TMS system to participate in EDI or APIs.

2. Visit Produce Markets

Almost every major city in the United States has a product marketplace that transports goods. Many are well-publicized and easy to locate. Start building contacts in the marketplace that is ideally accessible for you.

Approach the proprietors of the businesses and strike up a discussion with them. Inquire about their shipping requirements. Inform them that you have equipment accessible and can lift loads for them. Start a discussion with other drivers while you're there. Inquire as to how they obtain their cargoes. If they're using a broker, acquire the broker's contact information and phone them. You'll have a profile of potential clients in no time. Follow up with clients regularly until you have a few.

The following is a list of prominent metropolitan produce marketplaces around the United States. It will assist you in getting started:

- Agricultural Marketing Service, United States Department of Agriculture (All states)
- Farmers Market in Atlanta (GA)
- Agricultural Marketing Service, United States Department of Agriculture (USA wide)
- Produce Market of Maryland (MD)
- Produce Center of New England (MA)
- Hunts Point Produce Market New York (NY)
- East Side Produce Market in Detroit (MI)
- Farmers' Markets in Your State (FL)
- Produce in Houston (TX)
- Philadelphia Wholesale Produce Market (PA)
- Fruit is grown in Indianapolis (IN)
- Produce Market in St. Louis (MO)
- International Produce Market in Chicago (IL)
- San Francisco Produce Market (CA)
- San Antonio Wholesale Produce Market (TX)

It's worth noting that according to some load boards, the two markets with the largest reefer cargoes are Atlanta (Georgia) &Miami (Florida).

3. Contact Wholesalers

A second alternative is to go to a wholesaler in your area.

Using the internet, you may compile a list. Speak with the official in charge of the shipping department. Let them know you have the equipment and are willing to transport goods for their business every week.

Don't tell a potential customer what you want when you chat with them. They know you're looking for a load. They receive such calls daily. You must discover a method to stand out from the crowd. Instead, explain how you can assist the shipping manager and how you are unique. You can inform them about the following:

- You are always on time.
- (This is an important one!) You are dutiful.
- Your equipment performs admirably.
- You are happy to come every week.
- You may work throughout the holidays.

Please inform the shipping manager whether you can work vacations (Item #5). Only a small percentage of truckers are ready to work on festivals. This offering will stand you besides the competition. It will, at the very least, put your foot in the gate. It's upon you to establish a reputation after that.

4. Freight Broker

Truckers should think of freight brokers as outsourced sales crew. Truckers should demand a fair charge from the cargo in exchange for this service. Freight brokers may also be paid a reasonable commission. Truckers who form partnerships with reputable freight brokers can use the brokers' shipper networks to build a dense network of dependable cargoes.

Owner-operators & small carriers may not be invited to bid on contracted routes, although freight brokers are frequently invited to bid. It is due to freight brokers' daily approach to numbers of drivers and their ability to match cargoes with vehicles.

It allows shippers to work with smaller carriers without vetting and executing contracts with each owner-operator and small carrier individually.

5. Load Boards

Truckers can locate loads listed by freight brokers on public load boards. Although there are numerous free choices, the most prominent load boards require a monthly registration fee for the service. Truckers may search through tens of thousands of loads that have been uploaded in real-time. The majority of the loads are spot market loads. These are transactional and infrequent loads. Truckers contact freight brokers personally to obtain further information regarding the load and to negotiate to price. If a deal is struck, the two parties will exchange authority & insurance information before signing a rate confirmation.

It might take time to be set up with various freight brokers, but it is a fantastic method for truckers to develop connections with specific freight brokers. With the help of a freight broker, a transactional load may often convert into a consistent routine channel.

One of the additional benefits of load boards is that truckers may verify evaluations of freight brokers and creditworthiness before taking a cargo. Working with unknown freight brokers becomes less risky as a result of this.

6. Apps that Match Loads

Load matching applications work in a similar way to load boards in terms of concept. Truckers may look for loads using these Smartphone apps. This approach was created through a new digital freight broker who began automating the load search process for shippers and drivers.

Most of the bigger freight brokers now provide load matching applications. To link truckers and shippers, freight matching markets and load boards use the same principles. Truckers accepting advertised loads at the advertised rate and then transferring the cargo with minimal to no human involvement are known as load matching. It eliminates the headache of negotiating pricing and the back-and-forth communication required to get a load set up. Because all procedures run through the trucker's phone app, it also improves document submission and payment.

Convoy, J.B. Hunt 360, & Uber Freight are the three largest in the industry. Freight Waves SONAR has more than 150,000 indexes, most of which are modified frequently. Suppose you want to follow the freight industry, both contract and spot pricing. Hauling spot rate, tender, and marketplace balance indexes are among the world's quickest and most reliable freight statistics.

The SONAR freight tender indices are based on genuine electronic cargo needs from customers to carriers, so you can be confident that the indicator is tracking a real load operation.

SONAR provides unique data from real load tender, electronic sorting devices, haulage management systems, and data from hundreds of third-party worldwide cargo and logistics index providers such as the ACT, Freights, DTN, Drewry, TCA and Benchmarking.

SONAR provides the most up-to-date freight industry statistics in the globe, including all main forms of transportation. The SONAR podium is the first freight forecasting & analytics stage that uses authentic freight agreement tenders to give real-time freight market knowledge.

6. Boost Your Success Rate

It's possible that you won't obtain a customer on your first visit. Don't be disheartened. It occurs. Leave them a souvenir as a simple way to stay in front of them even when you aren't there. Purchase some "promotional pens" on the internet. Ascertain that they are familiar with your company's name and contact details. If there is room, have them write something like, "We haul on holidays!" These are available in bulk quantities of 100 for around $70. If they say they don't have any business for you, ask if you may leave a couple of pens. The majority of people will cheerfully accept the pen. They'll always have your details beside them now. They could call you the next time they're in a shipping bind.

7. Maintain the Flow of Funds

Working straight with shippers has the advantage of paying you more money. You may cost them the same amount as brokers (know your rates per mile) and keep 100% profit. It is an additional 15% to 20% that goes straight to your profit margin.

Remember that most shippers pay their bills over a 30- to 60-day period. This payment schedule indicates that you will be paid weeks after you have completed the task. If you can't manage to wait for payment, this delay might be an issue. Factoring your freight bills is the solution.

Factoring is a viable alternative to rapid payments. Within a day, the factor pays up to 95% of the freight charge. Once your shipper settles the invoice in full, the remaining 5% is refunded, minus a modest charge (30 to 60 days later). Several factors can also give fuel advancements, which can be helpful in a pinch.

CHAPTER 6. HOTSHOT TRUCKING

The concept of the hotshot trucking business began as a "good idea." Nowadays, they are among the most demanded modes of transportation. Even though such operations are a component of the transportation sector, they differ in numerous ways from conventional trucking. The market for such services continues to rise across the country, owing to their numerous advantages. Hotshot solutions are yet another possible alternative if you need loads transported.

1. Hotshot Trucking

Hotshot truckers are used by shippers and brokers that have tiny cargoes that ought to be delivered urgently.

These truckers are experts in delivering time-sensitive, project-critical goods such as agricultural machinery, developmental equipment and supplies, heavy machinery, and more.

Instead of heavy-duty, Class 8 semis, hotshot drivers usually use super-duty pickups with trailers. Hotshot trucking may be a profitable venture if done correctly. You have the option of becoming an owner-operator — that is, owning and operating a hotshot business by your MC number — or leasing with another firm. This chapter will go through the business's advantages and disadvantages, where to get established, and a few secret suggestions for success.

2. Benefits and Drawbacks of Hotshot Trucking

Many drivers begin their careers in hot shot trucking. The Federal Motor Carrier Safety Administration (FMCSA) attempts to discourage prospective drivers from getting their commercial driver's license (CDL) and immediately purchasing a semi-truck, a career move that frequently fails. Instead, it's a better strategy to get driving expertise on a hotshot truck until your CDL grows so that when you're ready to switch to a semi, you'll have an easier time qualifying for insurance. Furthermore, because the laws and criteria for running a hotshot & semi business are virtually the same, getting your feet wet in the hotshot sector is a great way to prepare for the transition to hauling bigger freight (if that's the road you want to take). Another major benefit of hotshot hauling is that it has a reduced entrance barrier and cheaper operating expenses. For example, costs for Class 8 semis may be as high as $2,500-3,000 per month, while pickup payments are typically closer to $1,000 per month. In addition, smaller vehicles often have greater gas mileage.

Hotshot truckers may often earn as much as — if not higher than — Class 8 truckers. These cost savings frequently benefit customers. Because the payments for heavy-duty vehicles, such as semis, are greater, those drivers and carriers must naturally ask higher for less than truckload (LTL) or partial freight to make the loads worthwhile.

On the other hand, Hotshot trucking is much simpler to enter into, so you'll be up against a few strong and constant competitions. To avoid rivals underbidding, owner-operators must place a strong emphasis on service quality.

3. Best Way to Start Hotshot Trucking Company

In the trucking industry, there are two major deal breakers: health and insurance. So, before you even start your LLC, be sure unexpectedly expensive premiums or delays won't catch you off guard.

Anyone who operates a commercial motor vehicle, including hotshot drivers, must get a Department of Transportation (DOT) health card. Therefore, the first step is to arrange a physical examination with a medical examiner from the FMCSA-approved national registry. These exams generally cost approximately $120 and include basic elements such as your medical history, eyesight, hearing, and urine tests. If you're in good health, you'll be issued a DOT medical certificate that will allow you to drive commercial vehicles for the next 24 months. You will need to take another physical test to extend your certificate after 24 months.

We suggest getting a free business insurance quotation from Progressive, which takes your VIN (VIN).

High insurance rates may quickly cut into your profitability, so getting a preliminary quotation will help you figure out if it's better to start your own LLC (i.e., become an owner-operator) or lease with another firm. Insurance estimates are dependent on your driving history and experience, so if you recently got your CDL and have a terrible driving record, your insurance costs are likely to be sky-high, making leasing the most practical option. Leasing is an excellent option for rookie drivers since it allows you to get your feet wet at a lower cost. However, if you have considerable expertise and your insurance prices appear reasonable, you may wish to proceed with the formation of your LLC.

The next phase is to go to your state's website and register a business. They'll provide you with the Employer Identification Number (EIN), which you'll need to create a company bank account and accept payments from clients. Then you apply for a motor carrier or MC number with the FMCSA (operating authority). It allows you to operate across state boundaries and appoint legal BOC-3 agents to represent you in the states where you do business.

Commercial insurance is, nevertheless, one of the most important criteria for generating your MC number. Most brokers demand $1 million liabilities and $100,000 cargo insurance coverage, which may cost anywhere from $1,000 to $2,500 per month depending on your expertise, age, and state of residency. Because the procedure will take weeks, your registrations must be completed correctly and without mistakes the first time. DAT Authority can assist with this because they specialize in managing authority paperwork, state and federal permits, and state DOT requirements for hotshot trucks.

Overall, hot shot trucking startup expenses might easily range from $15,000 to $30,000, depending on personal circumstances. For instance, if you already possess a vehicle, all you need is a trailer and the associated legal costs. However, suppose you don't already possess a truck or trailer. In that case, you'll have to spend $5,000 for your vehicle, $10,000-15,000 for a trailer, & $3,000 as insurance down payments, on top of the estimated $1,000 for your LLC and the other expenses stated above — all of which may rapidly add up to a lot of money.

4. Pieces of Equipment Need for Hotshot Trucking

Hotshot truck drivers, first and foremost, require a pickup truck and a flatbed trailer for carrying cargo. Having a dual-pickup truck is something we advocate, but it is a matter of personal choice. Bumper pull trailers, gooseneck trailers, tilt deck trailers, and dovetail trailers all have benefits and drawbacks, depending on what you're carrying. Straps, shackles, and tarps are just a few of the minimal necessities. When driving a hotshot, you don't need especially heavy-duty chains because your weight will never be high enough to necessitate something so thick. Tarping is a technique that requires some practice (imagine wrapping a huge Christmas present), but it is highly effective for keeping freight dry.

We typically suggest that hotshot truckers keep 20 ratchet straps, four 20' 3/8" chains, four binders, and a winch bar in their truck, plus two 6' drop tarps. These are some of the fundamentals.

5. Ways to Find Business for Hotshot Trucking

Ways to Find Business for Hotshot Trucking

Load boards are the most efficient way for truckers to discover hot shot freight since it is time-sensitive, and firms will be seeking trucks in their region that can pick up goods and get on the road as soon as possible.

While utilizing a smaller load board to acquire hotshots may sound appealing, especially for companies that deal regionally or locally, these tools are generally not worth it because they are considerably more constrained in terms of choices. DAT's load boards are among the most extensive freight networks available, and they make finding hot shot freight straightforward. You may bookmark your preferred routes & areas for quick searching later, so you can set up alerts to be informed when a match appears in a specified geographic region.

The bulk of ads on DAT's load boards are placed by hotshot freight brokers engaging on shippers' accounts, and the system also gives you information like broker credit scores & average time to pay, which may help you make sure you're working with the appropriate people.

6. Tips to Run Successful Hotshot Trucking Business

Running loads on weekends (which pay more) and sticking it out for approx. Three years are two general pieces of advice. We make it upfront. It may seem like a long time when you're just starting, but we have a few more recommendations that will help you find your bearings as fast as possible.

"½ the weight, ½ the rate" is a good rule to follow. That means that if a cargo takes up roughly half of what we can handle (either half of the weight limit or half of the actual space), it should pay around half of the charges per mile we are looking for. So, if we are aiming for $2 per mile with a 40' trailer & 9,000 pounds of load, a cargo weighing 4,500 pounds in 20' or less has to cost at least $1 per mile. Operating a hotshot costs about $0.75-0.80 per mile (though this varies depending on individual payments); thus, the benefit of "half the weight, half the rate" is that the first half of the load covers the expenditures. At that point, whatever cost per mile we can get for the other halves of the trailer is profit in the pocket.

People make the error of not utilizing their time. The more driving you do, the greater you get out – as long as you stick to the Hours of

Operation rules. Trucking already has long hours (leaving little to no time for stuff like the side hustle and bustle or pursuing a degree), and it will take some time to figure out how to work your shift successfully, organize your week, and skip regions to avoid heading home empty (deadhead). That kind of on-the-ground expertise, which can help you make better business decisions, can only be gained by putting in the time and miles. It's also crucial to remember that hotshot hauling is all about statistics.

You won't be able to make a single phone call and immediately obtain a good load. The quicker you make 25 phone calls, the better your chances of landing a high-paying job. The same is true for your driving experience: the more miles you log, the more you'll learn which regions are ideal for locating loads.

If you're just getting started in the truckload industry, DAT gives a complimentary weekly report called Trend lines that will provide you with a sense of what's going on. As you gain more expertise, you'll have a better idea of what you need to charge, which will help you quote better pricing to brokers and clients, so you don't lose money.

7. Best Tools for Success

Although it may not be for everyone, we usually recommend that you join the Owner-Operator Independent Drivers Association (OOIDA), a nonprofit that advocates for independent truckers. OOIDA not only assists the DOT with new rules, but they can also assist with audits, inspections, and other logistical challenges, which might be useful if you operate a single-vehicle. The DAT One network is an amazing all-in-one resource for independent truckers. Their membership costs are cheap, and it's usually a wonderful organization to be a part of. You'll discover factoring services, cargo tracking systems, operating authority facilities, fleet compliance tools, and more, as well as a free Smartphone app that takes a lot of the effort out of the process. DAT also provides up-to-date truckload pricing information, allowing you to barter the lowest costs for hotshot loads.

To top it off, OOIDA representatives receive a discount on DAT's tools. A spreadsheet system called Airtable is another tool that may help you operate and maintain your business more efficiently. Rather than having one interface for registering loads, another for managing costs, and a third for producing bills, the Air table lets you handle all of your business's elements from one place.

That way, you may immediately input information feeds into your bills while simultaneously keeping track of your costs. Air table is free for the most basic functions, but subscription options for extra data and services cost $10 or $20 per month. Air table is one of those extremely adaptable technologies that can truly empower small companies in several ways if you understand how to utilize it. We've been utilizing the Air table to create a job application form, for example. Anyone interested in working with me only has to provide photos of their driver's license and medical card. I've gathered all of the documents needed for a legitimate job application at that time, and they don't have to submit out any further paperwork. It saves incoming candidates time by eliminating the need to fill out several redundant forms, and it also ensures that if they are hired, we already have all of their documentation on file.

CHAPTER 7. COST & MANAGEMENT FOR TRUCKING

BUSINESS

There are several advantages to owning and operating a trucking company. You may pick and choose which firms to cooperate with, as well as what loads to transport and how frequently you'll run. You may be paid more because you own the firm and receive a larger portion of the earnings.

Operational Cost Of Trucking

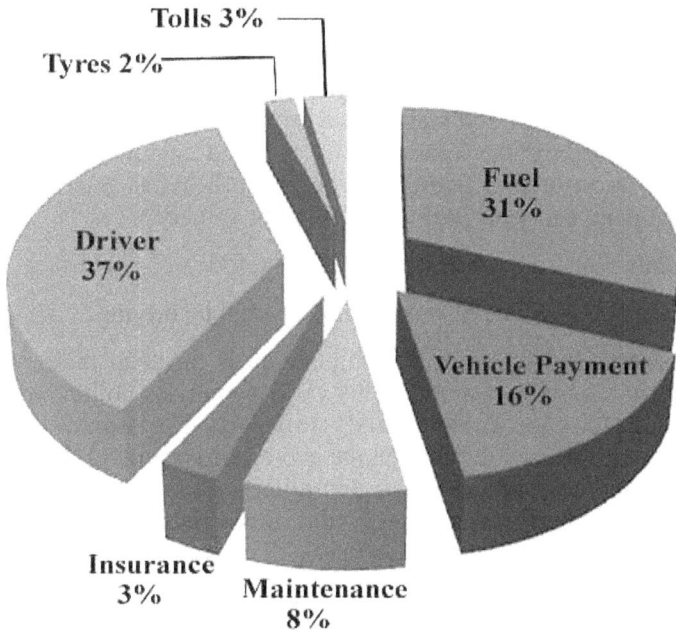

Tolls 3%
Tyres 2%
Fuel 31%
Driver 37%
Vehicle Payment 16%
Insurance 3%
Maintenance 8%

Despite all of the advantages listed, it's worth noting that beginning a trucking company might be a daunting task. It comes with its own set of obstacles and problems. That is why, despite the potential rewards, few people consider establishing a trucking firm. This chapter is for beginner owner-operators.

1. Estimate the Cost per Mile

It's like running with your eyes blindfolded if you run a trucking firm without understanding your costs.

You can't charge your shippers the greatest per-mile fee if you don't know how much each mile costs your vehicles. It is tough to turn a profit as a result of this.

Carriers that do not manage and control their operational expenditures may be forced to close their doors shortly. In 2015, 310 transporters with six different or more trucks were pressured to shut across the country. Trucking is a competitive industry, and bad bookkeeping may jeopardize a company's prospects of survival.

You must calculate your company's expenses to compute your expenses per mile accurately. Fixed costs, variable costs, and wages are the three types of expenses. You won't get a comprehensive view of your company's bottom line if you leave out just one expense of conducting business from your calculations.

Compute Your Costs per Mile

Estimating your "all-in" cost per mile is one of the essential measures you can do when you commence your trucking firm. You may estimate your projected profit by knowing this cost and calculating what you'll make. The most crucial figure for you is profit. After all, expenditures have been paid, and your profit is the amount you keep.

To calculate your cost per mile, complete the four steps below:

- Step 1: Calculate how many miles you'll be driving

The most crucial figure in this computation is the total miles you will commute in a particular month. This value comprises both compensated and deadhead (non-compensated) mileage. The spreadsheet and examples that follow consider that the average driver travels around 8400 miles each month. Mileage varies depending on the owner-operator. The majority of owner-operators, on the other hand, report traveling approximately 100,000 miles each year.

- Step 2: Determine your fixed costs.

Fixed expenditures don't change from month to month, no matter how many miles you travel. Truck payments, for example, are called fixed expenditures. Irrespective of how many km you drive, they remain the same. Fixed expenditures include insurance, license plates (IRP), and a variety of permits.

This table depicts an example of a startup owner-fixed operator's expenditures

Fixed costs (monthly)	
Truck payments	$1,400
Trailer payments	
Insurance - Collision	$480
Insurance - Deadhead	$60
Insurance - Cargo	
Insurance - Health	$400
Insurance - Workmen's comp	
License plates	$125
Permits	$50
Parking expenses	
Estimated total	**$2,515**

As you may notice from the list, the majority of fixed expenditures are simple to compute.

Some expenses are paid in one lump sum rather than regularly. License plates, for example, are generally paid yearly. We anticipate an annual cost of $1,500, or $125 each month ($1,500 / 12 = $125). This approach makes it easier to calculate the "all-in" cost per mile.

- Step 3: Determine variable costs.

The direct expenditures of driving every mile area are known as variable expenses. They rise and fall in proportion to the volume of miles you travel in a particular month. Fuel, for example, is a variable cost. For every mile you drive, you must purchase diesel. Fuel prices will rise correspondingly if you go more kilometers in a week than normal. You also won't have to pay for petrol if you don't go any miles in a particular week. Fuel, food, the phone, tires, and maintenance are all examples of variable expenditures. Variable expenditures for an owner-operator are shown in the table below.

Variable costs (monthly)	
Fuel	$2,000
Meals/lodging	$600
Telephone	$160
Satellite	
Tolls	$160
Loading/unloading fees	
Tires	$300
Maintenance	$450
Repairs	$600
Factoring fees	
Broker fees	$1,125
Miscellaneous expenses	$450
Estimated total	**$5,845**

The two most variable expenditures are petrol and broker fees, as you can see. Lower variable expenses (per mile) and better profitability can be achieved by lowering fuel prices and supplant brokers with your direct clientele.

• Step 4: Determine the cost per mile.

The final stage is to bring it all together. We can determine your expenses per mile based on the number of miles, monthly fixed charges, and monthly variable costs. Divide the amount by the number of miles you traveled that month to get the "cost per mile." For example, to compute "fixed expenses per mile," divide $2515 (fixed expenses) by 8,400 (miles), yielding $0.30 per mile. We compute variable expenses to be $0.70 using the same technique. When both values are added together, the "total cost per mile" is $1.00. One thing to keep in mind is that, while your fixed costs remain constant, your "fixed costs per mile" decreases as the frequency of miles you travel grows. Regardless matter how many kilometers you travel, your "variable expenses per mile" usually stay the same. The tables that follow give a summary of all that has been said thus far.

Financial Summary	
Monthly miles	8,400
Fixed costs per mile	$0.30
Variable costs per mile	$0.70
Estimated cost per mile	$1.00

Variable costs (monthly)	
Fuel	$2,000
Meals/lodging	$600
Telephone	$160
Satellite	
Tolls	$160
Loading/unloading fees	
Tires	$300
Maintenance	$450
Repairs	$600
Factoring fees	
Broker fees	$1,125
Miscellaneous expenses	$450
Estimated total	$5,845

Fixed costs (monthly)	
Truck payments	$1,400
Trailer payments	
Insurance - Collision	$480
Insurance - Deadhead	$60
Insurance - Cargo	
Insurance - Health	$400
Insurance - Workmen's comp	
License plates	$125
Permits	$50
Parking expenses	
Estimated total	$2,515

Using this data, we can calculate that if you travel 8,400 miles each month, $1.00 per kilometer will cover all expenditures. Every nickel above $1.00 is profit for you. As a result, if you bill $2.00 per mile, you will profit $1.00 per mile.

Important Success Advice

Reducing your greatest variable costs is the most efficient approach to enhance your profit. Fuel & broker fees are the two most variable expenditures in the scenario above. You have some influence over such expenses, which may have a significant impact on your profits.

* Keep an eye on the fuel

One of the most common blunders made by novice (and seasoned) truckers believes that the lowest pump rate (fuel + tax) is the best method to acquire fuel. It isn't always the case, however. Prices at the pump may be deceptive.

Truckers are required to make payments in every state they pass through. The tax is calculated depending on the number of gallons used (and kilometers traveled in some regions) in a given jurisdiction. As a result, you should purchase petrol at the lowest base price possible.

* Reduce the number of brokers you utilize

You give away a percentage of your profits every time you acquire a load from a load board or a broker. If you charge enough per mile, pulling a load for a lower price is preferable to doing nothing at all. So, if utilized appropriately, load boards & brokers may be beneficial. Develop partnerships with direct shippers to reduce your reliance on brokers' load boards and improve your independence.

Only by using this strategy will you be able to make a respectable living in the trucking profession.

2. Strategy to Buy Fuel

Fuel management methods have never been more important than now, with the sector confronting record-high diesel costs – over $3 a gallon in several parts of the country. However, it's important to remember that good fuel management isn't just the duty of the fuel controller. Rather, all major participants in the trucking business, including drivers, accountants, and top-level management, should be involved.

Many fleets, particularly smaller ones, wouldn't have the flexibility of making this a full-time job for one person; it's typically juggled alongside various other tasks.

Without top-down and bottom-up assistance for fuel management techniques, potential savings from better fuel purchase plans might fade away, lowering a fleet's profit margins.

1. Learn the Basics

An effective fuel buys management strategy should have two goals: to reduce a fleet's gross fuel purchase expenses while also providing drivers with filling stations that satisfy the carrier's requirements for facilities and quality. Fleets risk losing drivers if refueling choices are based purely on pricing without taking driver requirements into account. What's essential is to understand that efficient fuel purchase management is a long-term program, not a one-time effort.

It's also exhausting labor because it necessitates the person or persons in authority of fuel purchase administration calling various truck stops & chains regularly to bargain discounts or rebates, all while staying on top of regulatory changes that affect them. It's also crucial to determine whether truckers are having any issues with the gasoline purchase programmed and, if required, make improvements. In terms of which truck stops are allowed, drivers are also the finest source of knowledge.

A fuel purchase scheme can only succeed if drivers cooperate and follow the rules. What is the significance of all of this? A tractor that travels 110,000 miles annually gets 5.5 mpg needs 20,000 gallons of fuel per year. Each one-cent reduction in a gallon of petrol price equates to a $200 annual savings per tractor. According to our findings, fleets that do not have active fuel buy management programmers might save five cents per gallon annually or $1,000 each tractor. That's $100,000 per year for a fleet of 100 vehicles.

2. Select A Fuel Management Company

Someone must be assigned to the task of designing and managing a successful long-term fuel purchase plan. Someone should focus on fuel purchase to help create, access, and finally implement the program. That individual should be the point of contact for employees and drivers who require information on gasoline purchases and the interface with outside vendors & suppliers.

The individual in charge of designing and managing a gasoline purchase plan must at the very least have analytical abilities and a working knowledge of spreadsheets or online fuel converters.

Because the pump price does not accurately reflect the exact per-gallon price, fuel managers must be able to compute the original base price per gallon by understanding state fuel taxes & associated costs, as well as surcharges added on by truck stops. It will allow them to compare states with truck stops on an "apples to apples" basis. It is crucial since even little per-gallon savings may add up to big savings.

Good communication skills are also necessary since top management, administrative personnel, and drivers must understand the program's worth and what must be done. Good communication is especially crucial in gaining and sustaining driver support; the program's long-term viability depends on their approval.

Negotiation skills are also required. Fuel managers must negotiate fairly with numerous fuel suppliers while also looking out for the carrier's interests.

3. Establish A Limited Network

A limited purchasing network is essential to an efficient fuel management plan since you can't regulate gasoline prices if vehicles recharge anywhere.

It helps carriers concentrate buy volumes while ensuring that purchases are done at truck stations with the least pricing. It enables them to obtain larger discounts and rebates. A basic network consists of principal stops and emergency halting spots and refueling stations near important clients. Most carriers can easily operate within a network of truck stops spaced 400 miles apart, while others prefer to space them as close as 800 miles or as far apart as 200 miles.

With less than 200 sites, a fleet can likely offer comprehensive coverage across the United States.

One caveat: the method will not function unless drivers freely utilize the network. You can't just say, "Here it is, folks; these are your only options for refueling right now." The truth is that while drivers do not want to squander funds, they also do not want to refill at a cheap landfill. Sure, you'll save quite a half-cent per gallon, but you'll waste more time and energy attempting to persuade cars to use less desirable sites, and in the process, you'll enrage them.

The idea is to find a middle ground. You aim to boost the volume to receive better discounts while keeping drivers satisfied. Everyone benefits from giving drivers amenities such as free showers, excellent food, laundry facilities, and extra parking space, even if it means paying a penny or two more per gallon.

4. Apply Ex- Tax Rates

For efficient fuel management, you must understand the notion of "ex-tax" price. You can't fairly compare diesel costs between states without it.

Every truck passing through a region is obligated by law to "buy its way through," which means it must purchase as much fuel as it utilizes while passing through.

States utilize quarterly gasoline tax reporting to make the collecting process easier. The state estimates the number of gallons a fleet consumed based on the number of miles driven in the state during the quarter and the fleet's usual fuel economy.

If the number of gallons consumed exceeds the number of gallons bought, the carrier must pay the government tax on the differential. The state offers the carrier a tax credit if more gasoline is purchased than utilized.

Let's assume fleet travels 11,000 miles in one quarter, half in Ohio and half in Kentucky. The fleet will require 2,000 gallons of fuel to achieve 5.5 mpg, and the fuel purchasing manager must select where to acquire it. Using two-year-old diesel prices of $1.579/gal in Ohio & $1.499 in Kentucky, it appears that fuel in Ohio is $8/gal higher.

But, before you determine how much to purchase and where to buy it, keep in mind that no matter wherever your fill-up the tank, you'll have to pay each state's part of the gasoline tax. You'll also earn a tax credit if you purchase more fuel than you need for the miles you drive in a given state.

State-by-state differences in fuel taxation can be significant: It costs 26 cents per gallon in Ohio and 13 cents per gallon in Kentucky.

Because you'll have to pay the tax anyway, you should look at each state's "real" fuel pricing. That works out to $1.319 per gallon in Ohio ($1.579 - 0.26) and $1.369 per gallon in Kentucky ($1.369 - 0.13). So, it's $5 cheaper per gallon in Ohio.

5. Follow-ups

A gasoline purchase plan should not be a one-size-fits-all approach. To verify that it's producing the savings you want, evaluate it at least every 6 months, if not quarterly.

Fuel management is a difficult task. It requires close attention to market circumstances, pricing adjustments at truck stops, and tax rate changes. However, if correctly managed, the technique a fleet purchases gasoline may result in significant long-term savings.

3. Best Accounting Applications for Trucking Companies

There is a variety of software programs available that make bookkeeping easier. Many of the top accounting software brands are reviewed in this section.

Many small trucking firms still manage their finances with ledgers, spreadsheets, and file drawers. There are simple ways to handle accountancy without all the documentation if your firm falls into this group. For as low as $10 a month, you can update and manage your financials in real-time with online accounting software.

Today's market has a plethora of accounting software packages geared towards small enterprises. There are also software systems that are specifically designed for transportation firms. QuickBooks & Xero are cloud-based accounting software, which means you can manage your accounting data from anywhere using a Smartphone, laptop computer, or tablet. Many of these items come with phone applications that you can get from Play Store or the Apple App Store.

The accounting capabilities are more complex and user-friendly when utilizing standard accounting software such QuickBooks, Xero, or FreshBooks. The ability to conduct fleet-specific activities, including load tracking, settlements, and IFTA tax reporting, benefits from utilizing accounting software built for trucking firms.

The following is a list of industry-leading accounting software applications, as well as five of the most popular transportation software products:

- QuickBooks

Intuit-owned QuickBooks is the market leader in accounting software in the United States. In 2013, QuickBooks' cloud-based version was updated to make it simpler to use on a tablet or Smartphone. Your money and account information may be synced across all your gadgets, including the iPad, iPhone, and Android. The software tracks payables, receivables, and cash flow in real-time and prepares your data for tax season. The color-coded approach of the QuickBooks dashboard makes it simple to keep track of open invoices, past-due payments, and your overall cash position.

QuickBooks also allows you to create and send invoices from any location, and it automatically puts funds into your bank account once you are paid. QuickBooks integrates with other Intuit products and more than 90 third-party business apps, allowing you to increase your mobile reach.

Pricing

QuickBooks offers a free month-long trial period for users to test the program. Small company registrations start at $10 per month, while individual contractor subscriptions start at $5 per month. QuickBooks Essentials, the most popular subscription, costs $21 per month. The professional QuickBooks Plus program is available, costing $28 per month and includes inventory monitoring and tax preparation.

User Reviews

QuickBooks Accounting Invoice has over a million downloads on Google Play. The app has received over 16,000 reviews, with an average rating of 4.3 out of five stars. Google Play & iTunes both have QuickBooks accessible for download.

- Xero

Xero is New Zealand-based accounting software. Xero aims to dethrone QuickBooks as the most popular accounting software in the United States. Unlike QuickBooks, Xero was designed specifically for mobile devices. The Xero Touch app is compatible with iPhone, iPad, and Android devices. Xero provides real-time accounting transaction tracking as well as customized invoices that clients may pay online.

The account reconciliation function of the program is simple to use and enables you to complete what was formerly a time-consuming process in minutes. And over 300 third-party business apps are integrated with Xero. Because of this versatility, you may combine your company's bookkeeping with project management and customer relationship information.

Pricing

Xero, like QuickBooks, offers a one-month free trial. The software's Starter subscription costs $27.50 per month and includes limited invoicing, billing, and bank reconciliation. The basic bundle is $55 per month and allows for limitless transactions. The premium option, which costs $70 per month, includes payroll for up to 200 employees.

Xero Accounting has been downloaded over 100,000 times on Google Play. More than 1,700 users have given the app a 3.6-star rating on average. Xero is available on The Play Store and iTunes.

- FreshBooks

FreshBooks offers the ability to display one of its benefits when a client has checked your digital invoice. The usual consumer excuse of "not getting the invoice" is no longer valid. Like some other online accounting software, FreshBooks allows you to design invoices and accept digital payments from your clients. You may record billable hours on the tablet or Smartphone using the mobile app. You may also use your phone to take a snapshot of a receipt, which will be submitted to your company's expenditures. FreshBooks is a mobile app that works on both iOS and Android Smartphones.

Pricing

FreshBooks provides a 30-day free trial period. Starting at $15 per month, you may have up to five clients and unlimited invoices with a plan. FreshBooks Plus costs $25 per month and enables approximately 50 clients to be billed. The Premium plan costs $50 per month and allows you to bill up to 500 customers.

User Reviews

 More than 100,000 people have downloaded the FreshBooks Classic accounting app from Google Play. More than 1,700 people have given the app a positive review, giving it a 4.2-star rating. FreshBooks is available for download on Google Play and iTunes.

- Pro - Transport

ProTransport's software was created with over-the-road &fewer enterprises in mind. The program helps manage dispatch, tracks cars and equipment, and includes updates to the latest Department of Transportation regulatory standards, in addition to financial tasks.

Pricing

Pro-Transport does not provide pricing information on its website, although it does provide a free software demonstration.

- Trucking Office

This online trucking management software aids in the administration of a trucking company's commercial operations. Accounting and cash flow are covered by Trucking Office products and keeping track of IFTA taxes, maintenance costs, and more.

The software is cloud-based, allowing you to establish as numerous user accounts as your business need.

Pricing

Trucking Office's software is available for a free 30-day trial. For a firm with one to two vehicles, does the "Basic" plan, aimed at full truckload enterprises, charge as little as $20 per month? The "Pro" software, which provides a more comprehensive workflow for truckload & little businesses, starts at $30 per month.

- Rig-Books

Rig-Books are available in four distinct bundles, each aimed at enterprises with one to five trucks. Profits and expenditures are covered in the basic package, but there is no information on loads, customers, or vendors.

Rig Book's more advanced "Small Fleet" software lets businesses do invoices, load tracking, IFTA tax preparation, and manage numerous vehicles. Rig-Books are a web-based application that can be accessed from a computer, tablet, or Smartphone.

Pricing

Rig Books' website does not provide pricing information, although it does offer a free 30-day trial.

- Truck Bytes

The fact that Truck Bytes core platform is free sets it apart from competitors. Owner/operators or fleet managers may now execute accounting operations, manage clients, and check carrier settlements for free. The program may be accessed from any computer or mobile device with an internet connection.

The IFTA Fuel Tax service software from Truck Bytes is not free.

Pricing

The standard software from Truck Bytes is free to use. Upgrades to the plan that covers IFTA services and performance analysis for each truck start at $15 per month per truck.

- McLeod

McLeod Software is a software company based in Canada. The Load Master Dispatch solution from McLeod Software is a completely integrated dispatching system that integrates accounting and dispatch operations management. Customers may customize Load Master to meet their specific company needs, including freight invoicing, safety compliance, payroll, fuel tax reporting, and more.

Pricing

McLeod Software's website does not provide pricing information.

4. Trucking Company Own or Lease the Vehicles

Several factors influence whether a trucking firm chooses to buy or lease its trucks. Their decision may be influenced by their transportation demands, financial situation, ultimate growth approach, and other factors.

For example, a firm that needs highly specialized vehicles due to its business but has the financial capability to purchase them outright may choose a finance lease. They have the opportunity to buy the truck at the end of the leasing contract with this sort of lease.

A New Call to Action Has Been Created

Other businesses opt to acquire their fleets through full-service leasing, which includes vehicle servicing and maintenance. In this scenario, the trucking company pays a monthly fee that covers the lease fee and all other truck-related expenses. As one might anticipate, each option - buying, financing leasing, or full-service leasing - has its own set of advantages and disadvantages. Some businesses choose to purchase and rent at the same moment, whereas others prefer to lease.

Here's a quick summary of the three possibilities.

* Owning

Companies with a limited fleet and a long trading cycle are more likely to favor owning. It is due to the high capital expense of replacing the trucks.

They also benefit from the depreciation advantage of ownership, putting them in an improved financial condition. Because they have the trucks, they may sell them whenever they want, bringing in a significant amount of cash for the company. They may also use the truck as they like, whenever they need it because there is no usage restriction like there is with leasing.

* Leasing Finance

Finance leasing, as previously stated, is a convenient way to get a vehicle when you don't possess the funds to buy one. The truck can then be purchased at the termination of the tenancy. At this time, you may buy the truck for the residual value (the upfront cost minus the depreciated value), so keeping it is still a good deal. The finance leasing does not provide you with the same flexibility as buying.

Your mileage is usually limited to a certain amount, after which you will be penalized, which might pile up over time. Similarly, breaking a lease mid-term (which is also the scenario in full-service leasing) might be costly because the agreement compels you to pay specific fees.

* Leasing with a Full-Service Approach

Most trucking companies, especially those with a big fleet, prefer full-service leasing because of the numerous advantages it provides. Unlike owning or financial leasing, full-service leasing places the obligation for maintenance and servicing on the lessor. It is because full-service leasing businesses also offer fleet management services.

Although this option does not provide depreciation, the monthly rental fee is usually a tax-deductible cost.

Technology is changing at a rapid pace in the transportation business as well. Older truck models are being phased out in favor of newer ones. Companies that choose the leasing option benefit from upgrading to newer models when their lease periods end.

They don't require having an in-house professional team to aid run the technology in full-service leasing. It is handled by the fleet management business, which eliminates the lessee's staffing expenditures. Because drivers like new trucks, trucking businesses that continue to upgrade have higher staff retention rates. Despite the disadvantages of this choice, such as capped mileage and zero equity because the vehicles belong to the lease agreement, most trucking businesses prefer to lease their trucks rather than buy them, and some even buy & lease at the same moment.

Because the decision to lease versus buy a commercial truck is based on various considerations, it is not a simple one for businesses to make. Of course, there are financial reasons, but they aren't the only ones that influence decision-making. You should also think about your transportation routes, seasonality, organizational requirements, the nature of the business you run, and even the truck configurations.

Some fleet managers even combine lease and ownership since it makes the utmost sense to them. In this chapter, we'll look at the advantages and disadvantages of leasing vs. owning, and once you've considered all of the aspects, you'll be able to decide which is best for your business.

- The Benefits of Owning a Trucking Fleet

Around two of all fleet owners in the United States own their vehicles outright, and the reasons for their decision to buy instead of the lease could be due to a variety of factors. It could have been an issue of company culture, in which the corporation has always owned its automobiles and prefers to continue buying them.

You have full ownership and control over your vehicles when you buy them, and you have full authority over what happens to them during their entire service life. For certain businesses, having this level of control is critical, and they choose to exert it. For example, the vehicles in your truck fleets may accrue significant wear - and - tear in a short period, which will not be a concern if you buy those trucks.

If you're leasing them, though, the leasing company may need you to keep them in good working order so they can be resold or leased after your lease time. In most circumstances, you may also own the vehicle for significantly longer than you would if you were leasing it. Every 2 - 3 years, you'll most likely need to schedule a new commercial vehicle leasing deal with a leasing provider.

On the other hand, when you buy the vehicles, you can utilize them until they are no longer functional. The financial benefit of buying your vehicles is that you won't have any continuous monthly payments to worry about once they're paid off, allowing you to put your money to better use.

- The Drawbacks of Having a Truck Fleet

There are certain disadvantages to buying your vehicles, and the most significant of them is that you will be liable for all maintenance and routine maintenance. That means you'll need to set up a service shop in your business where they're being maintained and repaired regularly. You'd also have to keep a crew of capable repairmen on hand, which would add to your financial obligations.

When you consider how often you'll need to change tires and brakes, as well as everything else, to maintain your fleet of vehicles in good working order, this might be a significant expensive consideration. It will be particularly challenging to maintain your vehicles running in the later years of ownership when they have acquired considerable wear and tear.

Keeping them on the roads and running efficiently will cost you more. When your fleet of vehicles is old and becoming less reliable, it may be difficult to attract excellent drivers.

When acquiring a vehicle, you are also liable to high taxes, which can significantly increase the overall sticker cost of your truck.

- Advantages of Using a Truck Leasing Company to Lease Your Commercial Vehicles

When you pick heavy vehicle leasing for your truck, you won't have to deal with credit applications or any of the other upfront expenditures that come with the purchase. The main financial benefit of leasing is because you could pay for the vehicles in installments instead of having to stump up with a hefty deposit or a large sum of money upfront.

It will provide you with financial freedom, allowing you to employ your resources to keep your business running effectively. Your trucks will not depreciate over time if you lease them, and you will not have to hold them as debt on your accounting books. It will also help to maintain your fleet current, as you will be able to purchase a brand-new truck at the ending of the flexible lease period instead of owning it for the duration of its service life.

Commercial truck renting also eliminates the obligation for continuous repairs and maintenance, which means you won't need to hire a team of qualified mechanics to run your business.

- Commercial Truck Leasing Drawbacks for Your Business

Because you don't buy the truck, you won't be able to do everything you want with it. Leasing is very comparable to renting in terms of how it operates. Because you do not own it, you cannot make any changes or alter it in any way.

When you rent a truck, you must maintain it in excellent working order to be given to the truck renting firm in good working order and perhaps re-leased or resold to another client.

Some commercial vehicle leasing agreements stipulate annual mileage limits, which you must adhere to when leasing. It might be a deal-breaker or, at the very least, a significant impediment for some long-distance transportation companies.

If you go above your annual mileage limit, you may be liable to fines outlined in the lease agreement.

Ultimately, it becomes a legally binding agreement when you sign the contract, and you are obligated to follow the lease's conditions irrespective of your financial situation. Even if your business were to experience a big recession, you would still be required to make monthly payments to fulfill the conditions of your contract.

- Summary

When it comes right down to it, neither of these solutions is intrinsically superior to the other. It all comes down to whether the option is a good fit for your business's financial situation and general operations.

What is incredibly beneficial for one firm may be proven to be a significant strain for the other, so it all boils down to what is best for you right now.

5. Freight Factoring

When it comes to freight factoring services, there is a lot to learn.

It is a comprehensive section that will provide you with the inside information you need to make informed judgments about whether or not a factoring firm is suitable for your company and which one to choose.

If you work in the trucking industry, you've probably heard the term "freight factoring" a lot during the last several years. Although the freight factor has become a trendy solution for certain owner-operators and trucking firms to avoid revenue gaps, many drivers and company owners are still unsure what it is or how it works.

Admittedly, freight factoring can help many trucking businesses, particularly owner-operators who spend as much time on company accounts as they do on the road. First, we'll describe how the process works in plain English, and then we'll go through some frequently asked questions regarding it (while hopefully dispelling some of the rumors). Most truckers and freight business owners mistakenly believe factoring is a passing trend or a collection of predatory firms seeking fast cash. There's no reason to be concerned; this procedure (and several of the firms involved) have a long history. The major reason for its rise in popularity is global economic issues and the rising expense of transporting freight rather than anything else.

- Definition of Freight Factoring

Freight factoring is the process of selling a freight invoice of lading or unpaid bills to a factoring firm to convert your company's accounts receivable into cash. Rather than waiting for 30, 60, or maybe even 90 days for a consignment to be paid out, a factoring business will send you the money right now for a charge.

While transporting freight is not an easy profession, the basics of how one makes a livelihood doing it are rather straightforward: the client has goods to be hauled, you supply it, and your payments less your costs equals your profit.

Payments are usually never made promptly, with the industry typical being 40 days (or even more) to process reimbursements to drivers and transportation firms properly. These processing periods may make and break a freight company's budget, and many have been forced to look for work somewhere else to make ends meet.

When there are more "payouts" on the balance sheet than "pay-ins," many people have depended on borrowed funds or sometimes credit cards in the past to keep afloat. Not only is this difficult to manage, but it may also result in thousands of dollars in interest payments - especially for trucking businesses who work overtime.

When a firm or owner-operator uses freight factoring, they make their deliveries as usual; rather than waiting for payment, they pass or "sell" the job's invoice to a third-party entity. This firm will "purchase" the invoice for somewhat less than the entire amount required for the job, but they will make up for it by settling the invoice quickly. The freight firm goes about their business as usual now that they have money, while the freight factoring firm cashes the invoice and handles all of the waiting.

This sort of quick payment would appear to some freight firms – particularly smaller or privately held enterprises – as a lifeline for their monthly or weekly budget, letting them meet costs without accumulating debt. Some, on the other hand, are likely to be very suspicious about the transaction's expenses.

Fortunately, we've covered all you need to know about freight factoring in the following section.

Getting paid quickly in the transport industry might be critical to your success. Factoring works by submitting your bills on the same day to your factoring firm, which will process them and pay you on the invoice value immediately rather than weeks later. It provides you with the funds you require to keep your firm afloat. Freight factoring works since all parties involved have an incentive, just like any other commercial transaction.

As previously stated, the freight business or owner-operator benefits from quick payment rather than protracted delays. The incentive for the freight factoring firm is the proportion of the invoice they charge or "leave out" when procuring from the drivers, which converts to profit when they collect from the client later. On the other hand, the client benefits from dealing with a firm with the financial resources to wait for payment rather than a tiny freight company that is desperate to get paid.

- The function of a Freight Factoring Company

It's critical to understand the fundamental services a factoring firm provides to truckers and the distinctive services that set them apart from the competition. TAFS offers premium factoring services to buy your bills and pay you quickly, often in as low as one hour. In addition to factoring, TAFS offers premium solutions to consumers, which will assist you in staying ahead of the competitors in the market. Let's look into the invoice factoring process in more detail:

1. A firm (client) requires A to be delivered to B.

2. They engage you to transport it, and you check your factoring company's credit to determine whether the customer's load matches their services.

3. If it is the case, send an invoice and any related documents to your factoring firm as soon as the cargo is delivered. Paperwork is often filed online or via a mobile application.

4. They settle for the invoice, and you and your business are

reimbursed.

5. The payment is subsequently collected from the consumer by the factoring firm.

Now, based on various circumstances, there might be a few more phases to this procedure. For this discussion, consider applying for factoring as you would apply for health insurance or a credit card. That's because businesses and small business owners don't just employ factoring firms; they request them. And the conditions of the factoring contract will ultimately be determined by the content of this application.

Factoring firms, in general, base their plans on risk and volume. These are the questions the firm will ask to evaluate how qualified you are:

1. Monthly Invoice Amount - Like with Costco or Sam's Club, the more we factor, the lower the percentage we pay.

2. Customer Base – Do you work with several different broker offload boards or just one? Concentrating 100 percent of your attention on a single debtor might be dangerous.

3. Customer Days to Pay - Having $20K up for 25 days versus 75 days is a significant difference. In other words, the factoring business might have bought three times the number of invoices from the client who pays in 25 days.

4. How much of your bill do you need to run your business – When you deliver, factoring businesses can reduce their risk by merely advance 85 percent to 95 percent of the load. It may assist you in obtaining a reduced rate.

After that, the factoring business will make an offer. Examine the contract conditions for the following elements while evaluating the offer:

1. What is the maximum amount that may be borrowed? – It's also known as the maximum credit line or maximum factoring facility, and it restricts the amount of money you may borrow from a factoring firm. Many factoring firms obtain larger funds from other banks, and they will restrict a carrier's growth to increase their credit line with the debtors gradually.

2. Invoice percentage advanced on delivery day - Will you get all the money on delivery day, or will you maintain a "reserve" account with the finance company?

3. Invoice Aging - If a factor does not pay the whole amount, there is a significant chance the contract may include aging costs. The cost of factoring will rise as a result of this. You spend more on "age fees" the longer your consumer delays paying. You should

also keep track of check "clearing days." Your factoring business may have a 7-day clearance period, which means they apply the cheque to your account 7 days after receiving it. If your client pays the factor in 36 days and has seven days to clear the check, it will deposit to your account on day 45, thereby raising your aging cost.

4. Other costs - How much does it cost to transmit money to the carrier, and the processing fee? What is the cost if you have to be paid that day? Is there a charge for invoice preparation or submission? Is there an administration charge? Is there a charge for a default factor advance? Is there a registration charge or a price for a lien search? Is there a cost for terminating the contract or releasing the lien?

5. Number of days to get upfront payment after delivery - The majority of firms will set a cutoff time of noon and provide payments via ACH the following day. If the carrier violates the cut-off period, the deployed advance is postponed by 24 hours, often known as "qualifying time."

6. How would I get out of my contract? – There will be a contract duration with the factoring business. To get out of the agreement, you must send a termination notice at least 30 days before the contract's expiration date.

   The next step is to sell down your open account receivables, which are any invoices that the factoring firm has paid you for but has yet to collect from your client. You may be extending your arrangement with that element for another period if any of them are not satisfied.

As a result, freight factoring is not appropriate for every business, especially not for every operator.

- Application Process

While credit and invoicing checks, as well as the disclosure of other personal and company information, are not pleasant experiences, many freight factoring businesses' applications simply take a few minutes. Furthermore, while it takes to get the advance varies, the typical duration is about 24 hours.

Depending on the factoring business you choose, it might take as little as an hour. Some applications allow the factoring business to recover your receivables right away, so be cautious when filling up an application to ensure it is not a legally binding contract.

- Reason of Using Factoring Services

Every firm or owner-operator does not use factoring for the same reasons. While cash flow aid is important to practically everyone who participates, some larger firms are more interested in overall growth. Others just lack the capacity or manpower (permanent or temporary) to manage all of the communications and payments collection that multi-truck freighting entails. A factoring business can take away that back-office duty if you haven't done invoicing and collection in the past. It can save you hours in total that you could be spending delivering freight or looking for better-paying freight.

When you receive a cargo, a factoring business can assess the ability of the broker/shipper to pay. You are more vulnerable to danger if you do not have mechanisms to credit-check the customers.

Furthermore, a startling amount of new trucking firms are created each year, making it difficult for them to obtain funding the traditional method (i.e., from a bank). In many situations, factoring is the only method they can generate sufficient cash flow to last a few months.

The idea is that there is no good or bad method to employ freight factoring, as long as the risks and rewards are adequately assessed.

- Benefits and Drawbacks of Factoring Company

There are excellent, better, and poor companies in terms of some of those dangers, like with any business.

Before signing on the dotted line for a Freight Factoring company, it's a good idea to double-check the statistics and ask queries about any portions of the agreement that you're not sure about.

What's the Difference Between Non-Recourse and Recourse Factoring?

Some factoring firms claim to be non-recourse, but others are. So, what exactly is the distinction between recourse & non-recourse factoring? When they claim "non-recourse," they would like you to assume that if your consumer does not repay the factoring firm, they will not pursue you. It is only true if the client declares bankruptcy between the time you submit the invoice and the time they are responsible for making payment to the factoring firm. It is an uncommon occurrence. If your consumer just does not settle or pays late, all factoring firms will pursue you; it is only an issue once they will recover from you. Remember that factoring firms aren't in the industry of handing out free cash.

All factoring businesses have contract wording to ensure that they may recover from you if the clients do not pay on time.

Quality is important to customers as well.

The factoring firm has to accept the risk that a consumer may not pay up to generate money. However, you can't begrudge them for doing everything they can to reduce the danger. It is referred to as "reasonable assurance," and it simply indicates that the factoring business must have proof that your client can and should pay once the time arrives. Credit checks and other information collecting are generally part of the procedure (which, depending on the company, you may have to pay for).

Working with consumers that have been pre-approved by the financing firm helps to avoid this. If the consumer isn't in the credit verification process, you may often request that the factoring business investigate them to determine if they can be entrusted to pay.

Always check the small print.

Every factoring firm has its own set of procedures in place to reduce risk and increase revenue. What determines whether they are a good or terrible business is how their policies impact your capacity to generate money. Some firms, for example, may propose lower interest rates than others, which may appear to be too worth a try. Be wary of their charging you extra costs to cover the expense, such as aging charges, per invoice charges, swipe service charges, processing fees, and so on.

Some businesses may charge less because they cut corners on customer care or collections, whereas others cannot repay you when you need it.

When it relates to factoring, you typically get what you pay for, so always question what you receive for paying a higher fee. Small business loans, dispatching facilities, fuel vouchers, emergency roadside assistance, tire savings, insurance down payment help, and truck/trailer finance are some of the extra perks offered by certain firms.

Some even have weekend and holiday hours, while others are only open Monday through Friday from 8 a.m. to 5 p.m.

It all depends but failing to read the tiny print might lose you a great deal of freedom. Whether you're enthusiastic regarding freight factoring or certain it's not right for you or your firm after reading this piece, we hope it's no longer complicated or scary. If you decide to go through with it, make sure you assess all of the benefits and drawbacks beforehand and that it is a better match for the method you operate your firm.

CHAPTER 8. THE TRUCKERS

A truck driver makes a living by driving a truck and carrying products and materials over territory. They go to and from supply and distribution centers and production sites at various times of the day and night. They played an important role in industrialized civilizations. While trucking isn't the best job choice for everyone, it may be an excellent way to work and live for some. However, to truly appreciate the work, you must also like the 'lifestyle' of dwelling on the trip, as trucking is more of a way of life than a conventional occupation.

Truck drivers transport goods using tractor-trailers, either domestically or across the country. Almost all truckers start as over-the-road (OTR) drivers, which entails traveling vast miles and being away for three to four weeks at a time. The driver should connect and separate the cab from the trailer. However, suppose the driver is unable to drive to a repair shop or a truck stop safely. In that case, the business generally has heavy-vehicle roadside services that may be deployed quickly to the truck's location.

Driving a large truck is a completely different experience from driving a regular car. To avoid overheating the brakes, the driver must know what to do when traveling up or down a sharp gradient and the gearbox contains a lot of gears; the typical rig (18 ft) has 10 front drive gears & two reversing drive gears, but other rigs have 9, 13, 15, or 18 front drive gears. The truck is generally 70 to 80 feet long and weighs 20 to 30 times heavier than a vehicle (including the cab).

1. Turnover Rate in Trucking Business

The turnover rate in every sector is the proportion of employees that are not retained compared to the total number of employees in that industry.

If the percentage is more than 100%, it indicates that so many individuals quit/were fired that the total number of workers replaced is greater than the total of employees who remained.

Definition of turnover

The ratio of new drivers recruited to those who leave is known as turnover.

The trucking industry has traditionally had a higher turnover rate. It's a competitive industry. & Big businesses have a history of abusing their employees and making false promises.

Recruiters are compensated for bringing in new employees. They make incredible claims. Big bucks, plenty of free time, excellent equipment. After they loaded you onto a vehicle, those promises vanished. Didn't you make it to the weekend? It's too terrible.

We'll make every effort to bring you back home next weekend. Is your salary low? Sorry for the inconvenience. The delivery of goods was sluggish. Next week, we'll try to bring you some greater mileage. Or since the POS truck busted down, you lost miles? There was a problem with the driver!

But, ABC trucking offers 10 cents per mile more, newer trucks, and better lanes across the street? So, you leave your job and go there. As a result, the first business now needs a new driver. As needed, repeat the process.

When things don't appear to be moving their way, truck drivers are known for switching jobs. I've done it myself a few times when I'd had enough of the business I was operating for, often for no apparent reason. A greater benefit package or perhaps a higher quality truck may be available from another business.

The reality is that drivers are generally better off staying with one business for the duration of their careers, but the rivalry among firms for a small number of drivers to fill vacant jobs is so fierce that recruiters often make promises they can't fulfill.

Causes of High Turnover Rates

Because large major carriers are self-insured, they can recruit and train novice drivers. Unfortunately, many rookie truck drivers do not survive their initial year in the industry, which may be due to various factors. Some people are dismissed because they have too many accidents, some have family problems and realize they can't stay away from home, yet others may feel it's too much full responsibility for us to bear.

Because the big carriers recruit and train the majority of new drivers, they experience higher turnover rates. Does this mean they're terrible businesses? Not.

Because insurance prices are lower after a year of driving experience, many businesses demand a year of driving expertise. The individual who posted that remark on the forum failed to mention that the business, with a 20% turnover rate, exclusively recruits drivers with at least two years of experience. That implies the business only hires experienced people who know what to anticipate regularly and are equipped to make choices and manage the work. They have a greater probability of avoiding collisions as well.

- Loss of Employment Opportunities Due to Job-hopping

One thing is certain: future employers will consider the number of transportation firms for which you have worked, and job-hopping may lose you opportunities. For example, whereas Venezia permits "no upwards of 7 jobs in the past 5 years," Big Scott discovered one ad that stated, "no more than two workers within last three years." Keep in mind that the rainbow may vanish while pursuing that gold bar or a rainstorm could come in. Don't be the one to bring about your doom.

So, you can observe from the instances above, businesses are not always to blame for driver turnover. Most major carriers provide competitive compensation, trailers and late-model trucks, and contemporary amenities to make drivers' OTR lives easier. The new driver's reaction to the culture shift of their new profession and how they manage people, and tough circumstances will significantly affect whether or not they stay in trucking for the entire year.

Don't be misled into thinking that only the high turnover rate indicates a poor business. It's a difficult job to be a truck driver. In trucking, you can't fake it. Many drivers begin their careers at full speed, but many cannot keep up with the pace and ultimately fade. It will be obvious if you do not have a hard work ethic. It is frequently the case for individuals who drop out within their first year.

The drivers that understand availability and time management commit to on-time deliveries safely and show dependability and expertise will be given particular consideration. They would most likely be content and will not feel compelled to switch businesses. That individual can flourish anyplace, but they'll have it so nice that they will seldom consider moving to better pastures.

- Increasing Rate of Turnover with Large Carrier Companies

As per the American Trucking Associations, big truckload carriers' driver turnover rate has increased by 6%. Major truckload carriers have a driver turnover rate of 94 percent, up 20 percent from the very first quarter in 2017.

Large freight carriers are those with yearly revenue of more than $30 million.

An American Trucking Associations published the information in its quarterly earnings report on high driver turnover. The trucking industry is concerned about a driver shortage and rising driver turnover rates. The ATA's Chief Economist, Bob Costello, said:

"The increase in turnover is in line with the demand for drivers being tight. According to anecdotal evidence, carriers have difficulty hiring and keeping qualified drivers, resulting in pay increases.

The restricted driver market is expected to persist, causing carriers to worry in the coming months."

The scenario is only subtly different for smaller carriers. From the previous quarter, the percentage of driver turnover for small truckload carriers fell to 73 percent. However, as opposed to the initial quarter of 2017, the existing driver turnover rate for smaller carriers with even less to $30 million per annum sales has increased by 7 points.

Despite these findings, Costello believes there is an increase in the need for drivers due to increased freight activity. He said, "Turnover is a sign of demand for drivers, not a gauge of the driver shortage. We know that when freight demand rises, so will the need for drivers to transport those products, which typically leads to increased driver turnover or churn."

"Finding enough competent drivers is a huge problem for the trucking business, and if not addressed, the whole supply chain would be jeopardized," he said.

- Shortage of Drivers

In the trucking business, there is a severe driver shortage. Only the American Transportation Research Institute rated driver scarcity as the most pressing industry problem in the last year's study.

ATA American Trucking Associations estimates that the industry will need 900,000 additional commercial drivers over the next 10 years. Furthermore, about 440,000 drivers might be needed just to replace upcoming driver retirements. To keep up with the current rate of freight increase, 252,000 drivers would be required.

- Driver Retention

Trucking businesses confront a variety of challenges in recruiting competent drivers as a result of the driver shortage. However, carriers must be mindful of another major issue: driver retention.

Driver compensation has risen in recent years, which was previously thought to be a major cause of driver shortages and retention issues. The typical pay for a commercial driver has risen by 15% since 2013, as per the Driver Compensation Study.

However, boosting driver compensation isn't the only solution to the driver retention issue.

As in the 2018 Transportation Spotlight Report, 1,000 executives and managers were polled on how they plan to address driver retention. The survey's findings are as follows:

* 61% of those polled said they plan to invest in retention initiatives.
* Increased follow-up contact is favoured by 54% of respondents.
* 58% believe that launching training and development programs will be beneficial.
* Non-monetary strategies, like driver appreciation initiatives, are preferred by 53% of respondents.
* Performance incentives are something that 40% of people wish to try.
* 42% believe that raising compensation will help them retain drivers.

While these are all excellent concepts, one crucial element is overlooked: the usage of electronic logging instruments.

To remain compliant, most commercial drivers must now utilize electronic logging devices (ELDs). However, if the gadget isn't user-friendly or drivers don't receive help whenever they need it, their satisfaction and turnover rate will suffer.

According to a recent study done by KeepTruckin, just 21% of drivers are satisfied with the current ELD solution. Furthermore, every week, 73 percent of drivers encounter one or even more ELD problems.

Furthermore, they do not get the level of customer service that they deserve. Approximately 64% of drivers said they are dissatisfied with the level of customer support provided by their current ELD supplier.

2. Demand for Drivers

It's now or never. Maybe you need a diversity of scenery, and maybe you want to be your boss, maybe you need to drop everything and hit the road. Whatever your motivation, now is the best moment to obtain your CDL and join the ranks of those that keep America fed, moving, and happy. Now is the moment for becoming a truck driver and be a component of the backbone of our wonderful nation.

People are ecstatic to go to a website and get whatever they need or want and deliver it from their front door. Some businesses even advertise that they will deliver an item to your vehicle. It's occurring right now, in real-time, and it's how we operate as a society. And it's fantastic. It's good for the economy, good for our health, and particularly good for truck drivers.

On the other hand, Truck drivers view what most people regard as convenience as an opportunity. Who do you suppose transports all of the products that Americans consume throughout our vast country? Truck drivers are the solution.

Driving trucks is a dependable, stable, well-paying job that you can keep for as hard as you want it. In a time once jobs are being tried to push overseas or twelve-year-old kids are seated on tech jobs which, well, seem wonderful for the moment, until another wave of youngsters shows up and the brilliant job is gone, learning to drive trucks is a consistent, stable, well-paying job that you can keep for as long as you desire it. And there's never being a better moment to apply for this position than right now.

According to the American Trucking Associations, 51,000 additional truckers are needed to fulfill the needs of online, point-and-click businesses such as Amazon and Wal-Mart to transport products across the nation. And, according to the American Trucking Association, the need for truckers will only increase as more businesses begin to include an e-commerce component into their operations. Truck drivers are in high demand, which means that if they work for the proper business, they may write their tickets.

- Reasons for Shortage of Drivers

There are so many advantages to becoming a professional truck driver that it would be difficult to understand why there's such a high need for more. That has a lot to do with the fact that more products are being transported across the country than ever before and that it has to do with the reality that truck driving is a difficult profession.

Several trucking firms also employ dubious methods to recruit drivers, and they don't do a good job of keeping them satisfied or retaining them. When questioned about driving trucks, several experienced truck drivers remark, "Companies don't consider you as a person; you're a machine that earns income for them, not yourself, for them." Regrettably, this is a reality in the transportation business. Truckers don't feel valued, heard, cared for, or that they're a part of the business they work for. Despite the challenges of the job, truckers are often regarded as hired hands who do not need to be talked to with dignity or paid their due. Companies need excellent drivers, but they don't seem to care about making them feel valued and cared for. That is why there aren't enough individuals to fill the positions.

- Be Truth

We kept hearing that truckers are just not given the truth. Drivers are misled about salary, mileage, and time off, amongst other things, and this occurs because businesses do not value drivers as highly as they should. Truck drivers value honesty and openness, and many claims that if you're honest and open with me, I'll be as diligent and devoted as you can expect. When you demonstrate respect and care for the trucker's well-being by telling the truth, you will lose your drivers.

- Piece of Advice

The greatest piece of trucking advice I've received is respecting oneself and what you have to give a business. Years of expertise may be very valuable to a business. If you love yourself and respect yourself, you won't work for a business that lies and doesn't care about its drivers as individuals rather than money machines.

Respect for yourself will lead you to the finest trucking businesses and employment available. It's a no-brainer: if you're proud of yourself, your job, and your skills, that pride will shine through and render you a valuable investment.

- Pride Transportation Company

There are many trucking businesses in this wonderful country, though one name keeps coming up for exactly the correct reasons. Pride Transportation is a company that specializes in providing transportation services. If you create a list of all the things that make drivers unhappy, you won't find any of them at Pride Transport. "They treated me nicely and told me the truth" is among the first truckers who drive for Pride remark.

The folks at Pride place a high value on telling the truth. Why? Because it's a family-owned business, and the owners are truck drivers. That's a significant achievement. Because they are truckers, these people treat truckers. They have always been on the road, driven the miles, carried the freight, and some of those still do. It's about as nice as it gets when you work as a trucker for other drivers.

You'll find many of your concerns addressed, and a lot of your worries assuaged if you stop paying attention to all the screaming and check into a business-like Pride Transport. Nobody claims that driving a truck is an easy job, but if you work for a business that values you, shows you the truth, and goes out of its way to assist you, like Pride Transport does and does well, the advantages far exceed the drawbacks. So now is the moment to act. There are many possibilities.

If you believe you would like truck driving because of the independence, the wide road, and the opportunity to earn a lot of money, the present is the time to give it serious consideration. So now is the moment to act.

There are many possibilities. If you believe you would like truck driving because of the independence, the wide road, and the opportunity to earn a lot of money, here is the time to give it serious consideration.

However, as many drivers have said, recognize your value and take pleasure in what you take to the table; that way, you won't walk in blind and won't be taken advantage of. Be practical and search for an honest business, support its drivers, and understand what it takes to be a truck driver. Pride Transport is among such places, and it seems to be one of the few. A dynasty of truck drivers operates the company. You're in demand as a driver, so why not expect the best? With pride, you should drive.

3. Differences between Trucking and Other Occupations

Truck drivers use ground vehicles to carry products between places, most frequently in tractor-trailer combinations. Their job requires them to travel vast distances, often across several states. They are also responsible for ensuring that their goods are transported safely, involving securing them.

• Uniqueness

In the truck, the driver is seated behind the steering wheel. Certain professions should be discussed with family members before even contemplating applying for a career in the industry.

One of these jobs is truck driving. To be a CDL driver or an OTR (over-the-road) is more of a lifestyle than a profession in many respects. Its responsibilities, especially up to 300 days on the road each year, will undoubtedly restrict the number of hours spent at home, affecting your relationships with people around you. And, since it might take two years to move to a region driving job that enables you to come home weekly rather than every three weeks, your spouse or partner deserves a voice in your decision-making process before you determine whether truck driving for a career is right for you.

However, if you're drawn to adaptability, 20 hours alone each day, and a schedule that differs from the remainder of the population, this is a job worth considering. Consider the eight interesting facts regarding truck drivers in the United States below to help you have a conversation with loved ones and give you an idea of what to anticipate inside this line of work. What you discover may surprise you.

1. Days may start quite early. Most drivers like to drive in the light, while others like to drive at night. Unless they're phoning in to dispatch upon resuming from "time off," OTR truck drivers haven't any fixed beginning hours.

2. Throughout eight days, you may be asked to work upwards of 70 hours. You won't be able to drive again until you've taken a complete 34 hours off duty after working for 70 hours. Working 14-hour days may get you to the 70-hour maximum, but you can't drive for further than 11 hours per day. A 10-hour break must be taken at the end of your "Hours of Service."

3. While some drivers get paid hourly, most pay is based on the number of miles driven. When a delivery driver is not delivering, he or she is not compensated.

4. Employers that pay "practical miles" are compensated for each mile travelled on the work. On the other hand, Paid miles are more akin to drawing a straight line from point A to point B on a map, even though paths aren't always straight. Once you're a trainer, are ready to transport large freight or hazardous goods, or if an employer gives you a percentage of every load you run, your income may rise.

5. You won't usually know how much you'll be paid till the end of the year. A reasonable estimate for your first year would be $35,000, followed by $45,000 to $55,000.

6. You'll either perform "drop and hooks" or actual loading and unloading, both of which take two to three hours. Although an OTR driver virtually never has to unload freight, you are dependent on different shipping and receiving agencies adhering to your tight timetable.

7. The average motorist will travel 125,000 miles each year. It translates to approximately 2,500 miles each week or 500 miles per day. Consider that for a moment.

8. A truck driver's routine has numerous advantages, not the least of which is a unique perspective of the nation and friendship among your colleagues. To help you remain awake and focused, you'll mainly get to drive contemporary trucks with nice, ergonomically

built seats. It is fortunate since you spend most of the working days in an 8' by 8' area, but this should not limit your creativity or ambition.

Truck drivers have traditionally been regarded in high regard by the general population. The 'Knights of the Road,' half cowboy outlaws and part supply-chain sheriffs, have a long-standing cultural appeal. There is already a national week of gratitude! Just keep in mind that being a "professional tourist" is not simple, especially if you're young, unmarried, and eager to be on your own. Just for the loved ones and yourself, talk about the consequences of this lifestyle.

A good day is spent just on the road or on the way home for a truck driver.

4. Sample Questions about Truck Drivers Interview

Employers look for individuals who will fit in well with their work environment when recruiting truck drivers.

A job applicant must have a thorough understanding of the company's policies to succeed in the truck driver interview. What gets you an interview is giving the appropriate answers because of their expectations.

During the interview, a truck driver would be addressed a range of topics. \These may be linked to truck driving abilities, knowledge of traffic laws, interpersonal skills, and understanding of loading and unloading processes.

At least a single situational question appears in almost every interview, and it is used to assess the candidate's analytical and decision-making abilities. If you're confronted with a situational inquiry, whatever you say, don't take too long to reply since it may show your weak decision-making abilities. On the other side, a hasty response may jeopardize your candidacy.

To help you prepare for your next interview, here are 42 potential truck driver interview answers to questions.

1. Tell me about yourself in a few words.

I began my job as a driver's helper ten years ago as an enthusiastic truck driver. After two years in this position, I acquired a strong desire to work as a driver. After completing my training and obtaining my license, I was employed as a truck driver, and I have been doing deliveries for almost 8 years.

2. Why did you choose to serve as a trucker over other options?

I like working just on the road, so trucks have always piqued my interest.

It was the only logical option, given my passion for and skill in driving and repairing various cars.

3. Can you tell me about your experience as a truck driver?

For the last eight years, I've worked as a truck driver. During this period, I actively collected delivery orders, assisted with loading and unloading goods, and found routes to destinations. In addition, my job required me to plan routes and manage paperwork such as invoices and delivery papers.

4. What qualities do you possess that make you a strong candidate for the truck driver position?

To begin with, I am capable of driving a variety of vehicle kinds and sizes. In addition, I am skilled at conducting both routine and preventive maintenance on assigned cars. In addition, I have experience navigating quick and safe routes to locations using both conventional maps and GPS.

5. Do you believe that communication skills are necessary for a truck driver? Why do you think that is?

The ability to communicate is essential in the job of the truck driver. They must be aware of where products must be delivered and interact with dispatchers and consumers about delivery.

6. How crucial do you believe navigation is in the job?

The importance of navigation cannot be overstated. Truck drivers can fulfill their deadlines by completing deliveries on time and safely using maps and GPS.

7. Tell us about a moment at work when you shone brightly.

Many truck drivers declined to make deliveries due to one union strike. Only three of us were responsible for delivering goods to 17 truck drivers. But I was the unique one who delivered 20 things each day instead of the customary three.

8. Now, what do you believe the main responsibilities of the truck driver are?

A truck driver's major responsibilities include driving various types of trucks on various routes, assisting in loading or unloading, obtaining route clearance, maintaining delivery inventories, coordinating with management about route clearance, including vehicle safety and maintenance.

9. As a truck driver, what is your goal?

Deliver products on schedule, safely, effectively, and without damage and contribute to the employer's goal by delivering excellent customer service.

10. Have you ever had a client file a complaint against you?

I've never had a complaint filed against me since I'm a people person and a cautious driver.

11. What is the farthest distance you have travelled in your career?

I've driven 15,000 miles in three weeks, which is the greatest distance I've ever travelled.

12. In the trucking industry, it's really about meeting deadlines, particularly when it comes to deliveries. How do you ensure that deadlines are met?

When it comes to deadlines, I am extremely picky. I get up a bit earlier than my routine permits to account for any delays caused by unexpected events. I also make certain that the amount of time I take is appropriate.

13. What's your thought on road safety?

The most important element of truck driving is safety. It is necessary to ensure your seat belts are fastened and that the vehicle speed is followed. Inclement weather, such as rain and snow, necessitates driving at a very slow speed.

14. Do you have any experience with the documentation associated with the trucking industry?

I'm acquainted with bills that a truck driver is responsible for while delivering products. I always double-check that loaded goods match my given inventory paperwork and that delivery receipts are signed.

15. What is the best way to characterize your driving record?

Clean. In the last 10 years, I have not broken the law once.

16. Do you believe that cooperation is important in this profession?

I think the job requires even more cooperation on lengthy trips since assistants frequently accompany the drivers. Furthermore, if my schedule permits, I would always assist a fellow driver experiencing mechanical difficulties.

17. What would you do if any of your co-workers used the company vehicle for personal gain?

I shall discreetly notify the corporate management of the unauthorized/ unusual behaviour without engaging in any personal conversation with the colleague about the issue.

18. What do you do when a client asks you to help them with a delivery? What would you do if they asked you to deliver an item anywhere along your route?

I'd excuse the job and gently tell them that parcel delivery is not part of the company's policies. As a result, I am not permitted to do so. I'll also inform the management about the issue.

19. How would you feel about spending most of your day on the road?

I don't mind working outside since I like being in nature. One of the major reasons I love my job is because I got to work outside.

20. What method do you use to map out your route?

My job or delivery dictates the majority of my route planning. I prioritize routes mainly based on delivery timings.

21. Did you ever missed a delivery deadline?

I have a perfect track record of delivering on schedule. I've never missed a delivery before.

22. What would you do if you were involved in a car accident that wasn't your fault?

My first concern would be to make sure everyone engaged in the collision is okay. Once that's confirmed, I'll speak with another party and attempt to explain why they're to blame. If there is a question of remuneration, I will discuss it with them as well.

23. What would you do if you were running late due to unforeseen circumstances?

I would contact the client or my boss to inform them that I was running late. I wouldn't rush because I wouldn't want to risk my safety.

24. Do you have a good understanding of basic vehicle maintenance?

Basic and advanced vehicle maintenance and repair are second nature to me.

25. How do you remain awake on lengthy flights?

I take numerous pauses to sleep and drink coffee to keep myself awake.

26. Explain to me about a moment when you were driving, and you missed or almost lost focus. What exactly did you do?

I didn't lose focus when driving on the highway since I was weary. Because my kid was sick, but I had to leave the family for work, I was experiencing a lot of stress. I realized I was buried in contemplation after just a fraction of a second. Fortunately, I travelled at a moderate pace and avoided any accidents since the road was also clean.

27. How do you interact with your frequent customers?

My frequent customers and I have a friendly connection. They put their confidence in me to deliver their packages, and I ensure I don't let them down

28. Have you previously driven a vehicle for a reason other than delivering goods?

I've driven dump trucks, delivery trucks, and moving vehicles throughout my career.

29. When you're on the road, how do you remain motivated?

I maintain a constant level of motivation since I am always looking for the light to the head of the tunnel - the pleasure of knowing that I had done a great job.

30. What do you consider to be your best strength?

My ability to operate and maintain a variety of heavy-duty vehicles is one of my strongest assets. Aside from that, I am customer service-focused and can work long hours without difficulty.

31. What is your biggest flaw?

Because I am a quick learner, I believe I sometimes take on as I can handle.

Even though I have never skipped a deadline, I want to put in a lot of effort to fulfill them.

32. Have you previously had a dispatcher give you erroneous information? What steps did you take to address the problem?

Only once have I gotten erroneous information from a dispatcher. And, because it was an honest error, I didn't think it was fair to report it. Thankfully, I had plenty of time to do the job, and I met the deadline without difficulty. I did talk with the dispatcher and asked him to be more cautious from now on.

33. What do you do if a customer becomes angry or irritated with you?

I rarely lose my composure. I carefully listen to the customer to figure out why he's behaving the way he is. If possible, I attempt to fix the problem as soon as feasible because I have a path to follow, and timing is important.

34. Can you tell me about a moment when you committed a big mistake? What steps did you take to fix it?

I recently made the error of failing to prioritize my delivery as it should've been. That made meeting my deadline tough — or so it appeared. I didn't lose anything since the two locations that were switched by mistake were close to one other. I've learned to be more cautious in the future.

35. What would you do if you really were not at fault for a driving infraction but were nonetheless pulled over?

Dash cams are standard equipment in all contemporary vehicles. It would be my only hope. If I were accused of breaking traffic laws when I hadn't, I'd just display them the video to establish my innocence.

36. What methods do you use to keep in touch with dispatchers?

I make effective use of the communication tools that have been given to me. I make it a point to contact them regularly so that any consumer questions may be promptly addressed. I also inform them about goods that have been delivered and any problems that may affect delivery schedules.

37. When driving a truck, what is your primary concern?

My first worry is for my safety. Then there's the issue of timing.

38. Do you prefer to work in a group or on your own?

The truck driver is often self-employed. However, I like meeting new people and socializing, so I wouldn't mind helping in a group setting.

39. Do you have the ability to do physical labour?

Yes, I can do various physical activities, including heavy lifting, unloading and loading freight.

40. In five years, where can you see yourself?

I'd want to be in charge of a truck fleet in a managerial position in an ideal world.

41. Can you tell me when you'll be available for this position?

I am ready to get started right now.

42. Do you possess any queries that you'd want to ask me?

I've been considering joining your company for many years and have always wondered how you keep your workers. In addition, I'd want to learn more about the company's culture.

CHAPTER 9. TRUCK ACCIDENTS

Most truck transporters on the road must travel long distances to drop off the goods they are transporting. That means they'll be driving on roads they've never been on before and through locations they're unfamiliar with. Now, because certain highways do not allow huge trucks to function, a trucker must utilize the suitable GPS to guide them in the appropriate path so that they do not take these roads. They should also pay attention to the warning signs that indicate the presence of a low-lying bridge ahead since a large truck may not be able to pass beneath it.

1. Predictable Causes of Trucking Accidents

Accidents relating to heavy vehicles & trailer trucks are more or less critical.

They can occur for an array of reasons as well as in any weather. When a big truck is hit with a traveler vehicle, the public in the small car is mainly exposed to serious injury, if not deceased. Driving an 18-wheeler, either at highway speeds or through Metropolitan Street, is a hard attempt; consequently, truck drivers must commence significant training and attain a particular license. According to thorough investigations, truck accidents are usually the consequence of a driver's carelessness, for instance, speeding up or driving too narrowly beside another vehicle. Distracted driving is the main source of all motor car incidents in the United States. The Nebraska Department of Transportation (NDOT) has confirmed that the state's accident counts have reached a decade high.

2. The Different Types of Trucks

Trucking accidents can involve various huge trucks, including:

- Garbage trucks and dump trucks, in addition to large trucks.

Both of those trucks are common on our roads and have significant blind areas and restricted visibility. Because these trucks generally operate within city limits and in densely populated areas, collisions involving them frequently result in considerable property damage and pedestrian & bicycle accidents.

- Trucks with flatbeds have open containers, and spills into a major highway from an incorrectly loaded flatbed can lead to a multi-car incident with significant damage to all involved.

- Trucks that transport fuel. Tankers transport either liquids or gases, which may be explosive or poisonous. Even a minor incident involving tanker trucks might have disastrous results.

Other large trucks you may come across regularly include:

- Box trucks
- Cement trucks
- Delivery trucks
- Tow trucks

Truck driver errors cause a substantial percentage of truck accidents. The Robert Pahlke Law Group may assist you in seeking reimbursement for your medical costs, lost earnings, and other losses, regardless of the type of truck that caused your accident. Our legal staff has over 80+ years of collective expertise, and we'd love to talk to you about your compensation options. Contact us for assistance in finding the reason for your accident, determining who should be held accountable, and selecting what sorts of compensation to pursue.

3. Trucking Accidents and Their Causes

The following are examples of common trucker's faults that result in accidents:

- Driving while distracted
- Tiredness
- Impaired driving
- Excessive speed

- Inexperience
- Failure to follow traffic laws
- Poor judgment

It is well known that the faster you drive, the longer it will take you to come to a complete stop. When the truck is approximate Eighty feet long & weighs about 80,000 pounds, this reality is amplified. The longer it requires an 18-wheeler to arrive at a complete stop, the higher the potential for danger and disaster. Even a minor lapse in concentration on the side of a trucker can lead to significant injury or death.

Errors in Passenger Cars

Truckers are not primarily to blame for traffic collisions. Passenger car drivers can also play a role in accidents in the following manner:

- Driving in the blind spot of a truck driver
- Performing illegal maneuvers
- Texting while driving
- Following too closely
- Cutting off a truck
- Driving when drunk

Cargo or Loading Errors

Accidents are defined as unintentional and unplanned events that are neither foreseeable nor prevented. The logistics of transporting hundreds of pounds of freight can be complex, necessitating precision. Improper loading, like unsecured boxes, crates, or barrels, can result in a large shift in weight, causing a trucker to lose control of their vehicle.

Negligence by the employer

Commercial trucking businesses are required by federal rules to examine, maintain, and repair trucks on a routine basis and retain repair and maintenance reports for the previous 30 days on file. Suppose trucking businesses fail to train drivers thoroughly, impose unreasonable time constraints on drivers, promote or allow drivers to break hours of service limitations, fail to check or maintain their trucks, or screen new hires adequately. In that case, they may be held liable for a crash.

Regulations for Truck Maintenance

Manufacturer faults and design flaws can also cause trucking accidents.

When trucks travel on open roadways with damaged automobile parts, major accidents can occur. If parts of a vehicle are determined to be defectively developed or constructed and fail during transit, the parts maker may be held accountable. • Defective tires are the most common form of vehicle problem seen in accidents.

*   Failures of the power train
*   Suspension issues
*   Faulty brakes
*   Steering difficulties

4. Bridge Collisions

Truckers and others on the road may suffer severe or fatal injuries as a result of bridge collisions. Unfortunately, they are frequently caused by a truck driver's or a trucking company's irresponsibility. It means that if you are unfortunate enough to be engaged in a bridge hit accident, you may find yourself paying for someone else's mistake. On the other hand, bridge strikes are regarded by the Federal Motor Carrier Safety Administration (FMCSA) as a major hazard that could be avoided if truckers operated their trucks safely.

5. What Is a Bridge Strike

A bridge strike occurs when a heavy commercial vehicle or its cargo does not have adequate space to drive safely beneath an overpass or bridge. When a truck or its cargo collides with an overhead structure, a serious crash, jackknife, or cargo spill can occur. When a careless truck driver causes a bridge strike, other drivers on the road may be killed or injured.

When a tractor-trailer hits an overpass structure, the bridge may collapse, or debris may fall, causing damage to the truck and other cars close or under the bridge. Innocent persons may suffer severe or fatal injuries as a result of the effect on the bridge framework. Drivers atop the bridge, ignorant of what is going on below, can easily fall several feet and collide with the road below. Furthermore, bridge impacts might result in secondary collisions when drivers attempt to evade falling debris and collide with other vehicles. In summary, a bridge collision is likely to result in serious injuries.

6. How Can Truckers Prevent Bridge Strikes?

Truck drivers can avert bridge collisions by being more aware of route limits, remaining attentive to road signs, and utilizing only navigation systems suited for trucks and buses, according to the FMCSA. The following are the most important steps a driver can take to prevent a bridge strike:

- Route planning: The route should be thoroughly analyzed in advance by using a satellite navigation system with data on vehicle height constraints. Maps with clearly stated bridge heights should also be available to truck drivers.

- Checking vehicle heights: Before embarking on a trip, drivers should double-check the truck's and load's maximum heights. This figure must be double-checked against the headboard's recorded height. Height inspections for best practices can be recorded using a checklist.

- Load security training: Load security training is required for truck drivers. Bridge strikes are frequently caused by insecure loading.

- En route communication systems: If a truck driver is forced to take an unanticipated route due to a road closure, the driver should pull over to a safe location and call for assistance in locating alternate routes that avoid low bridges.

7. Bridge Strikes: Who Is Responsible?

A party that causes a bridge impact accident may be held accountable for any injuries that ensue.

The trucker and the transportation business could both be held accountable. It's possible that the driver and trucking firm was irresponsible in loading the vehicle above the height limit, resulting in a vertical clearing collision. Truckers may be irresponsible if they do not adequately plan their routes or use navigation systems not intended for heavy commercial trucks. Distracted drivers or those who fail to heed written safety warnings may collide with an overpass, resulting in a tragic bridge strike catastrophe.

If the negligence of a truck driver or a trucking firm is proven, the parties involved may be held legally liable for any losses that ensue. Other motorists who have been wounded in a bridge hit truck accident may seek compensation from the responsible parties.

8. Scenario When Company Is Liable for Driver Negligence

The fundamental theory of liability that might hold a firm accountable for a traffic collision caused by a trucker employee is "respondeat superior" (a Latin term meaning "let the executive answer"). An employer may be held accountable for wrongful conduct performed by the employee or agents if the acts were unintended and occurred while the employee was on the job.

- Is the motorist an employee or a self-employed individual?

The injured person must first establish that the trucker is a company employee instead of an independent contractor. It is because independent contractors are often not held accountable for their actions.

Although the regulations in each state may differ, the focus is often on whether the employer has the authority to govern the precise manner and means by which the task must be completed. An independent contractor's relationship is likely if the employer oversees the result of the work but not how it is achieved. For instance, if a trucker used his truck, provided his gas, bought his liability insurance, presumed the repair costs, was paid on a "per route" grounds, & received no employment benefits, the business did not withhold taxes from the motorist's paychecks or teach the driver on how to make deliveries or drive the truck—the truck driver is most likely an independent contractor.

- What Is "Within the Scope of Employment" Legislation?
- It might be difficult to determine what defines an act committed "while on the job." Courts typically consider the following factors:
- The employee's intent at the time of the accident;
- The nature, time, and location of the employee's conduct;
- The sort of work the employee was recruited to do;
- Incidental acts the employer must feasibly expect the employee to do;
- The employee's amount of freedom in conducting his or her duties and the amount of time spent in the personal activity.

For instance, if a truck driver rear-ends a vehicle while performing a delivery, the employer is likely liable for any injuries sustained since the truck driver was acting "in the course of work." Let's say a truck driver quits work early to attend a basketball game & collides with another vehicle outside the stadium.

It could be argued that the corporation should not be held accountable for the truck driver's negligence because he was not working "to the extent of employment."

9. Impact of Truck Collision on Multiple Defendants

When a physical injury lawsuit is brought against several defendants, they may all be held equally liable for the plaintiff's losses, or they may only be liable for the damage caused. A weary driver, for example, may share blame for an accident with the producer of bad tires. The plaintiff has the option of using both the vehicle (or the driver's company) and the manufacturer.

If it's unclear how much blame each side bears, the manufacturer may be forced to pay its portion, plus whatever the driver cannot pay because he or she does not have enough insurance to compensate the plaintiff's losses. A disadvantage of having several defendants with ambiguous percentages of fault is that reaching a settlement and avoiding a trial may be more difficult.

10. What If the Acts of the Driver Were Intentional?

In general, an employer is not accountable for an employee's deliberate torts (such as assault, battery, or kidnapping). The rationale is that when an employee's actions are unrelated to the business enterprise, the "respondent" concept is not being fulfilled. For instance, if a truck driver collides with another vehicle since the other vehicle's driver was napping with the truck driver's wife, the company is unlikely to be held accountable.

11. Regulations at the State and Federal Level

Operators, owners, and manufacturers of semi-trucks must follow a slew of federal and state rules. The amount of weight a rig may haul, the amount of time a driver can drive without stopping, and quality assurance in production and maintenance are just a few of the types of behavior controlled in the trucking industry. If a trucker is at fault in an accident, there is a good probability that a law, rule, or ordinance was broken, and any infraction raises a plaintiff's chances of prevailing at trial. The better a defendant's chances of prevailing at court, the more inclined he or she is to settle before trial. The higher insurance standards imposed on semi-truck owners and operators are another major part of federal and state regulation. A defendant in any lawsuit can only compromise for an amount he or she could afford—or the maximum amount authorized by his or her insurance provider (i.e., the policy limit). Because of the higher minimum coverage limits for semi-truck insurance mandated by law, the plaintiff will not be stuck with a modest payout despite the driver or company only insured the minimum amount. In "typical" vehicle accident instances, this is frequently not with the minimum required insurance.

CHAPTER 10. INDUSTRY RECESSIONS AND THE BUSINESS CYCLE

For trucking firms, 2019 will indeed be known as a particularly difficult year. The industry as a whole did not turn a profit. It was mostly due to excess capacity being introduced to the marketplace in 2017 & 2018, after which the freight industry slowed (2019).

Spot prices were capped in 2019 due to low spot rates & demand from customers to transfer freight to cheaper carriers, causing spot rates to float near the market floor. All of this, along with the reality that carrier's rates in most categories have increased by double digits since the previous freight recession in 2016. In only two years, driver pay, equipment, and insurance prices have all risen dramatically.

Some asset-based carriers discussed driver compensation hikes of up to 30% while still failing to attract and retain drivers.

Carriers face challenges in recruiting and retaining drivers, but some experts claim that a good social media strategy may help with both.

1. Definition of Recession

A recession does not have a common definition. The National Bureau of Economic Research (NBER), a non-profit largely regarded as the most authoritative judge of the business cycle in the United States, makes the decision based on somewhat subjective thresholds applied to various economic indicators.

Expansions occur once the economy is booming, while recessions occur once the economy is collapsing. In practice, recessions are usually a brief period of falling economic activity that begins with two consecutive quarters of dropping real Gross Domestic Product (GDP).

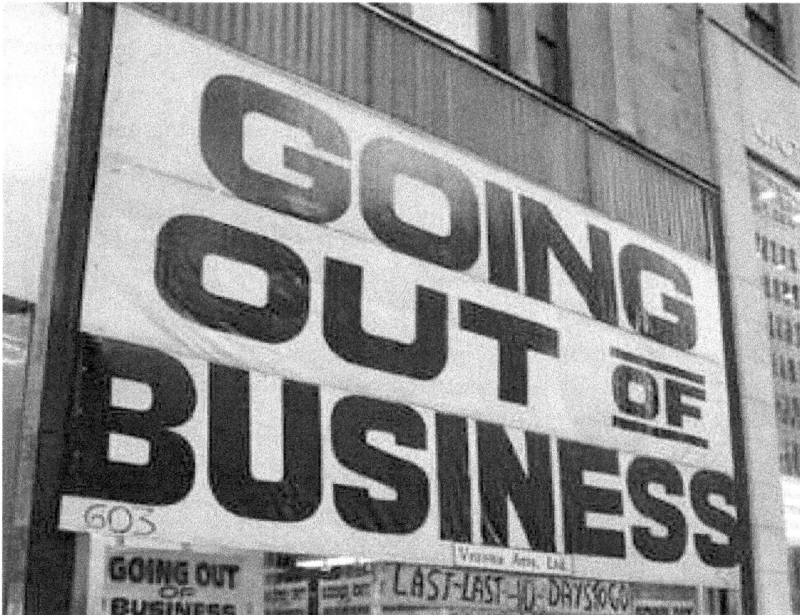

This bird's-eye view ignores more complicated economic situations that nonetheless cause genuine havoc for businesses and individuals, such as local or sector-specific collapses, short-term contractions, and activity slowdowns that do not convert into outright contractions. An example of an industry-specific shape of contraction and expansion is the freight sector business cycle.

To the untrained eye, trucking appears to be a harsh and relentless business where only the powerful thrive. The scenario, according to an insider, is hopeful.

According to Amit Mehrotra, a transport expert at Deutsche Bank, Trucking is "the most cyclical business on the globe." I tend to agree, and I'm hard-pressed to think of a business where the ups and downs are as severe as the downs.

The trucking industry's cyclical nature makes it more of a spinning wheel, with the market continually moving up and down. Earlier this year, large-scale transportation executives expressed their optimism for the next year. The majority of them fell short of their targets. Knight-Swift, the leading operator, said that it will miss its quarterly profit in recent weeks and called the forecast for 2020 "murky."

The corporate media has also taken notice. The never-ending stream of negative news and bankruptcies has convinced most Americans that the sector is suffering and has poor financial health. Trucks manufacturers have laid off workers and warned of difficult conditions as a result of order cancellations. As a result, truck manufacturers will be less likely to produce too many vehicles, and dealers & lenders will be less likely to provide liberal terms to get vehicles out of stock.

- The freight sector is in the midst of a downturn that took place In October 2018.

- The freight sector goes through a full industry-specific market cycle roughly every four years, with the average freight recession lasting around ten months.

While freight sector downturns frequently precede macroeconomic recessions by several months, only approximately half of freight industry downturns in the last four decades have spilled over into the larger economy or coincided with a macro recession.

When freight downturns do not correspond with larger economic downturns, they are much briefer, lasting only seven months on average.

Anyone who has spent enough time in the freight sector has seen its ups and downs. The most well-known headline measures in the sector — truck prices, deliveries, and truck orders — indicate a clear cyclicality.

It is unsurprising in some respects. The larger economy also follows a cycle, with periodic boom (expansions) and busts (recessions), which economists refer to as the business cycle. The freight sector is subject to macroeconomic ebbs & flows since it offers a service to firms and customers.

However, the freight sector has its own rhythm that is separate from the larger business cycle, which we refer to as the freight sector business cycle.

2. The Freight Industry's Business Cycle

We utilise the same methodologies used to predict the wider economic business cycle to identify the freight industry business cycle.

We construct a Freight-Weighted Manufacturing Output index relying on seasonally-adjusted industrial manufacturing and retail sales that accounts for variations in the sorts of products that emerge out of U.S. industries and the types of commodities that flow on the country's freight network, rather than using the aggregate output indicator (real GDP) to identify the cyclical business cycle.

The Freight-Weighted Manufacturing Output index may then be used to detect turning points: When the index rises, the shipping economy is booming; when the index falls for six months or longer, the shipping economy is in decline.

The Freight-Weighted Manufacturing Output index is shaded in the chart below for months when the general economy is in a recession, the freight sector is in a downturn, or both are in a recession.

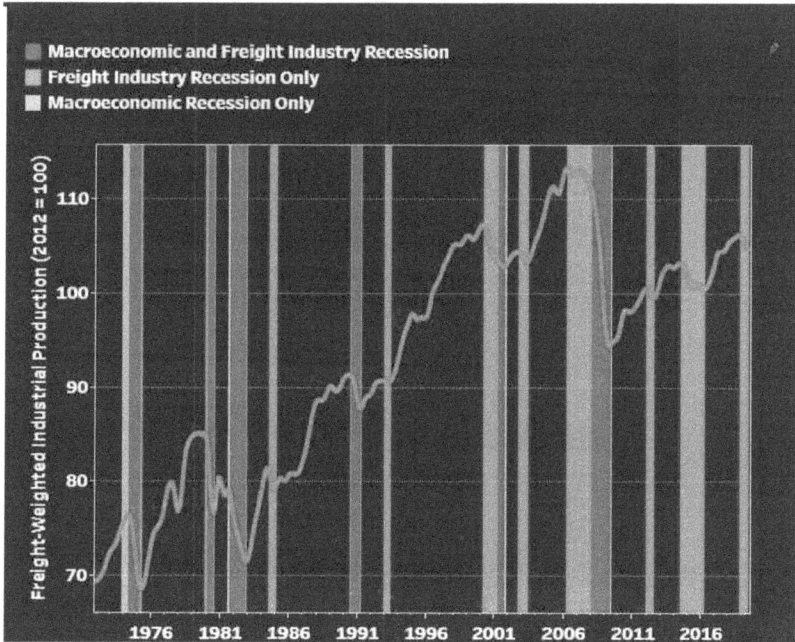

When the US economy as a whole is in a slump, the freight sector is nearly always in a slump (85 % since 1972). However, the inverse is not true: When the freight sector has been in a slump for the bulk of the year (62 percent), the larger US economy has managed to grow.

According to this study, the freight sector has faced twice as many recessions as the broader economy since 1972.

- During this time period, the normal freight business recession lasted 10 months, which was somewhat less than the regular economic downturn (12 months).

- When a freight sector downturn does not coincide with a larger economic downturn, these periods of declining freight activity are considerably shorter, spanning only seven months on average.

- During this time span, the average freight sector boom lasted 31 months, almost half as long as the average economic boom (66 months).

- The freight industry's normal entire business cycle, from peak to peak, has been 42 months, compared to 78 months for the total economic cycle.

Another approach to see the intersection of macroeconomic with freight sector recessions is to look at the graph below.

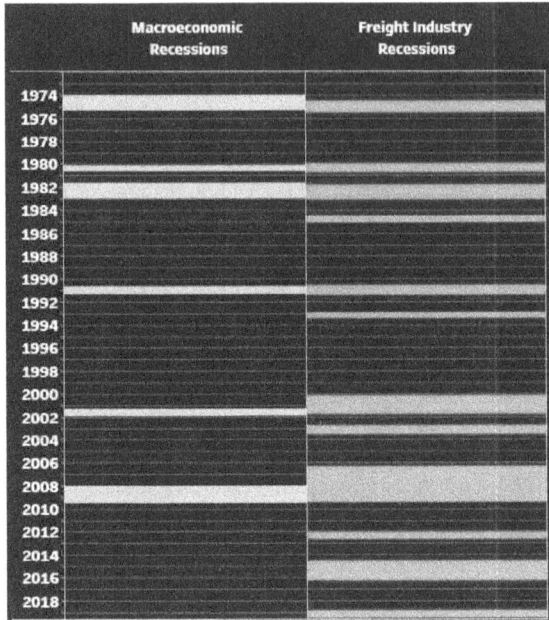

3. Demand and Supply

The need for trucking operations is a big element of the transportation economy, but it's far from the only moving portion. The speed with which supply adheres to changes in demand has a significant impact on price fluctuations — and prices are what truly important to participants in any freight industry (e.g., shippers and carriers). When industry experts discuss the ups and downs of freight, they usually refer to pricing fluctuations.

We used a similar method to identify pivotal moments in freight market to gain a sense of how rapidly supply reacts in the freight sector — and, in turn, flows over to prices. We searched for similar underlying patterns in heavy truck and trailer manufacturing, as well as long-distance full-truckload freight pricing, and then pinpointed turning moments. The findings closely match the Freight Weighted Manufacturing Output index's cyclical peaks and troughs, implying 11 freight sector cycles since 1972. The proximal roots, intensity, and resolution of each cycle are all different. Considering on freight downturns over the last twenty years, the supply trend softens around 5 months beyond demand, and prices generally cease falling and turn the corner three to ten months after demand. A major uncertainty for the time being is how soon demand will start to improve. It does not appear to be imminent given the current economic situation.

Of course, increasing the number of trucks and trailers isn't the only technique supply responds to demand. During a downturn, drivers can reduce the number of hours they work (though they still have to cover the expenses of their equipment.

So, they may be more likely to keep working even if rates drop), the market can entice new motorists (or drivers can leave to work in other job positions), and motorists can become more (or less) productive and efficient.

4. Is Freight at the Top of the Business Cycle?

The haulage economy has entered downturn prior to the rest of the economy in 4 of the 6 macroeconomic downturns since 1972, and in the most recent 3 downturns (the economic downturns that started in July 1990, March 2001, and December 2007), resulting those periods by anywhere around one and 21 months.

Whereas freight can lead the larger economic cycle, it can also be an imprecise leading indicator, comparable to other early warning signs of a business cycle pivotal moment. Over the last four decades, the freight industry has gone into recession half of the time, while the whole of the economy has kept growing. Since the 1980s, as the service sector — which has a more indirect relationship to the country's freight network — has become a greater and larger portion of the US economy, this dissociation of the transportation economy and the broader economy cycle has grown even more evident.

5. Bottom Line

In a competitive market, price instabilities — either a surplus (or shortage) of demand driving up prices or a surplus (or shortfall) of supply driving down prices — seldom endure long. Prices are driven up and down by a continual cat-and-mouse dance between demand and supply.

It is especially true in the freight business, as both shippers & carriers are used to ups & downs and can react fast (though not painlessly). Anyone who has had their finger on the pulse of the business for more than a few years has seen a movement in the market, both for the good and for the worst.

These cyclical freight sector recessions, like any other, generate genuine hardship for those who work in the industry: businesses fail, individuals lose their jobs, even families are affected. When they don't coincide with larger economic downturns, however, they tend to be brief. In this regard, the freight industry's relatively fast response to rising (or dropping) costs is a significant asset, allowing it to adapt in timely manner to an ever-changing economy.

CHAPTER 11. HAIR FOLLICLE TESTING

Transportation professions are quite delicate. Driving a truck is a dangerous job, and it's critical that our roadways remain secure at all times. The safety of the drivers, their passengers, and other drivers on the road is critical. Trucking firms have measures in place to guarantee that this is accomplished.

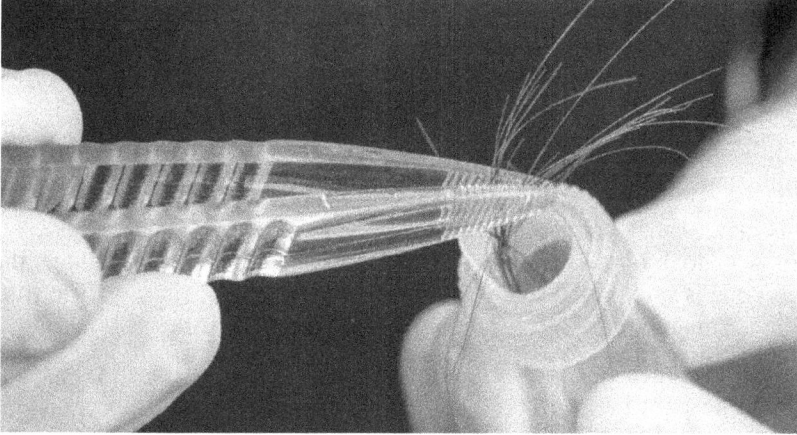

Hair drug testing is one of them. In this section, we'll look at trucking firms that do hair drug testing.

1. Explanation of Hair Drug Screening

This section will give further information for people who are unfamiliar with the notion and concept of hair drug testing. A urinalysis can be likened to hair drug testing. This is due to the fact that the carrier business you wish to deal with schedules a visit to a hair follicle screening facility.

A little section of hair will be shipped out at the testing centre by an expert. This is a sample of hair that will be utilised in the testing. A hair drug test is designed to determine two things. The first is the existence of a controlled substance. The second is a by-product of a previously taken medication.

Every medication consumed is broken down further in the body into various metabolites, which can be detected in the bloodstream. The goal of hair drug screening is to determine if the drug or some of its residues are present. A by-product can provide a lot of information about the initial medication.

That is why hair cells are so important in drug testing for hair. The blood supply comes from the follicles. When a person takes a drug, the drug's metabolites enter the bloodstream. These soak into the hair strands through the hair follicles. That is because the strands of hair are the ones that are tested in the lab.

2. Validity Period of Test

This is still a contentious issue. According to standard practise, hair drug screening can identify substances 3 month previous to the test. This is the industry standard for many trucking businesses.

3. Importance of Hair Drug Testing

In the United States, this examination is not required by law. Hair drug testing, on the other hand, is crucial. Hair drug testing has been implemented into the systems of a number of carriers.

It is critical that you are familiar of this practise as a CDL trucker. The primary goal of these tests is to avoid casualties and guarantee that everyone is safe on the roadways. It has a fantastic aspect to it. The truck drivers safeguard the safety and security of their co-workers.

Driving a truck is a difficult undertaking; only responsible persons should be permitted to do so. Allowing drug addicts to gain control of these enormous machinery is extremely risky. As a result, it is critical to show a fact. To put it another way, any motorist who is hired must be drug-free.

Trucking businesses must be certain that their large vehicles are being handled safely and responsibly. When these vehicles are not turned over to competent and sober individuals, the consequences are sometimes catastrophic and terrible.

4. Facts about Hair Screening

Below are the interesting facts about hair screening test.

1. Involvement of the government

In the year 2015, the concept of hair drug screening became widespread. United States President Barrack Obama approved the FAST Act transportation measure into law on December 5th of that year. The bill included hair follicle drug screening as a procedure that had been approved by the Transportation department.

Since then, the technique has expanded in popularity and use. Testing is insufficient to fulfil all of the criteria. The Department of Transportation has laid forth these criteria.

However, it is still widely used. Many trucking businesses, in fact, have made hair drug screening a standard procedure. This is done before they interview any candidate for a position.

2. Marijuana in the Environment

There are also individuals who do not consume cannabis but are exposed to those who do for various reasons. This group of drivers is concerned about the effects of marijuana smoking in the environment. It's not that bad that you're in the company of marijuana smokers. It does not guarantee that your test will be positive for marijuana. This is due to the type of the test.

The content of drugs or their metabolites is checked during hair drug testing. In order for the medicine to work, it must first reach your circulation. After that, it might proceed through metabolism and emit by-products into your body. There is no way for ambient smoke to reach your bloodstream if it settles on your hair. That way, it won't show up in the search results.

3. Baldness

There are certain situations where the individual being examined is bald, and no hair strand can be extracted from the head. However, all optimism is not gone in such a situation. It is due to the fact that body hair can also be utilized. It may be utilised as long as the skin hair is around one and a half inches long.

Hair samples can be taken from the thigh, armpit, or maybe the chest in certain other institutions. However, it should be noted that there may be a downside.

A 'refusal' is a motorist who does not have enough hair for the sample. A company's job offer to such a driver is frequently rescinded.

4. The nature of the outcomes

The results of a hair drug screening are kept strictly private. Even negative results, in fact, cannot be transmitted to the Transportation department. It is also prohibited for one firm to share its results with other businesses.

5. Hair Product Effects

Some drivers are concerned that using hair products would affect the findings of hair drug tests. Trucking businesses frequently make hiring and firing decisions. All of this is based on the results of the hair drug testing procedures. The good news is that it isn't all that bad, even if a motorist is a hair product aficionado. Gels and lotions have no impact on the nature of hair strands. They stay on the surface & that's all there is to it. There is no need to be concerned about people who use shampoos, since there is no evidence that shampoos influence the results of hair drug tests.

Some drivers have even dyed their hair a different colour. The hair drug tests, as well as the findings, stay intact for them. You might be a driver who uses various hair treatments and preparations. If it is the situation, you should be able to get your hair tested for drugs without difficulty.

6. Additional Testing

Hair drug testing is now used by trucking businesses. However, this is insufficient.

This is true if the aim is to fulfil all of the drug testing criteria set out by the Transportation department at the federal level.

There is a requirement to do more testing in this situation. The procedure entails adding a urine test, often known as a urinalysis in some circumstances. But only if the aim is to fulfil all of the Dept of Transportation's standards and conditions. That does not exclude trucking businesses from using hair drug screening as a primary consideration in hiring decisions.

5. Companies Who Follows Hair Drug Testing

A growing number of companies are opting for hair follicle drug testing because of its capacity to dig deeper into a person's drug usage history. The legal profession and employers are increasingly relying on them since they are more difficult to defraud than traditional testing methods. On the other hand, Trucking firms might make clearing the hair follicle screening a prerequisite for employment. So far, we've been able to collect a list of firms that prefer hair follicle testing, and we've included it below.

* ABF Freight System
* Crete Carrier
* Acme Truck Line
* Boyd Bros. Transportation Inc.
* C.R. England
* Cassens Transport Company
* Central Freight Lines
* AAA Cooper
* Central Transport International, Inc.
* Covenant Transport
* CRST Expedited
* Estenson Logistics
* Decker Truck Line Inc.
* Marten Transport
* Eagle Express Lines
* A & R Logistics
* Estes
* First Fleet, Inc.
* CTL Transportation, LLC
* Martin Transportation

Systems

- G & P Trucking Company, Inc.
- CT Transportation, LLC
- Hunt Transportation
- Falcon Transport Co.
- K & B Transportation
- Groendyke Transport
- Knight Transportation
- Mesilla Valley Transportation
- Swift Transportation Co., Inc.
- Millis Transfer, Inc.
- TMC Transportation
- Stevens Transport
- Tango Transport, LLC
- Ward Transport & Logistics Corp.
- The Waggoners Trucking

- Martin Transport
- Shaffer Trucking
- Old Dominion Freight Line
- P & S Transportation
- MCT Transportation, LLC
- Prime Inc.
- Schneider
- Roehl Transport, Inc.
- Rush Trucking
- Melton Truck Lines, Inc.
- Salmon Companies
- Hub Group
- Western Express
- Super Service
- TransAm Trucking
- Venture Express, Inc.
- Southern Refrigerated Transport
- USA Truck

CONCLUSION

Many individuals assume that running a trucking company is simple and straightforward. They frequently believe that anyone can establish and operate a trucking company. Owner operators, on the other hand, require both technical and commercial competence to succeed. The trucking business is a multibillion business with limitless opportunities for anyone prepared to take a chance. Today's trucking companies come in a variety of shapes and sizes. Each kind offers a distinct set of services. A trucking company may be as little as single vehicle with single operator, or as huge as hundreds of trucks managed by one company although operated by a variety of drivers. According to the United States Labor Department, a truck hauls approximately 70% of everything you put on, eat, use, or have around your house, at school, or at work. It's also generally a vehicle that ships the parts or raw material use to produce such items from vendors to a maker and after that to a shop where we can procure them. We sometimes wish to have someone with more expertise than ourselves to assist us through a procedure, but we don't always have the opportunity. We all become lost and require instructions at times in our lives. We hope that this book has provided you with a thorough understanding of the trucking business.

www.ingramcontent.com/pod-product-compliance
Lightning Source LLC
Chambersburg PA
CBHW070303200326
41518CB00010B/1872